Curry, Callaloo & Calypso

Curry, Callaloo & Calypso

The real taste of Trinidad & Tobago

Wendy Rahamut

MACMILLAN

For ADARA

Macmillan Education
Between Towns Road, Oxford, OX4 3PP
A division of Macmillan Publishers Limited
Companies and representatives throughout the world

www.macmillan-caribbean.com

ISBN: 978-0-230-03857-8

Design by John Barker
Typeset by CjB Editorial Plus
Photographs by Michael Bonaparte except pp 12–13 by Alex Smailes
Cover design by John Barker
Cover photographs by Michael Bonaparte

Printed and bound in Malaysia
2015 2014 2013 2012 2011
10 9 8 7 6 5 4 3 2 1

Contents

Introduction

We are a nation in love with our foods and never is the time not right to enjoy a good pot of pelau, hot doubles, a spicy roti and curry, or a hot shark and bake. The idea for a 'T & T' cookbook came to me a few years ago when I realized that globalization and foreign influences might dilute our local cuisine – or that was my opinion at the time. I envisaged a book that would showcase all our indigenous foods, by way of old and new recipes, for present and future generations! When I actually started to collect the recipes I realized that much is still cooking in our home kitchens, and as a result of globalization we have in fact embraced many more recipes into our lives. There is even a renewed interest in cooking local sparked by the Internet and cooking programmes on both cable and local TV.

Growing up in the sixties in the town of San Fernando (it's now a city), local food was not celebrated as it is today. Indian and Creole foods were mainly cooked in people's homes, by either hired cooks or the head of the household. The only Indian food for sale was found in a wrap roti from roti shops and doubles at the street corner doubles vendor. Creole foods were hardly ever served up outside. School lunches brought from home were rarely shared between friends! Snacks then included pepper mango and chilli bibbi, and the occasional aloo pie from the school snackette. Eating out was only for special occasions and the choices were slim: Chinese food at Marsang's restaurant in San Fernando, where they wokked up some of the tastiest Cantonese dishes I have ever tasted, and, when we were in Port of Spain, Ling Nam restaurant on Charlotte Street. Steak dinners were enjoyed at Chaconia Inn or Bel Air Restaurant, Piarco, and these were just for the grown-ups. Usually, for any celebration, the entertaining was done at home.

Fast forward to the twenty-first century: industrialization, education, travel, migration to urban areas, inter-racial marriages and technological advancement have all worked in favour of knocking down racial divides and bringing together our ethnicities. This unity of our races is no more apparent than in our cuisine. Today, the foods reflecting the rich culinary heritage of our forefathers are enjoyed by everyone, so much so that our cuisine has transcended itself, marking out a permanent place on our cultural landscape and on the world culinary map. Our 50:40:10 per cent ethnic make-up of African:Indian:European and Chinese respectively is shown in a cuisine that is bold, explosive in flavour, eclectic and addictive.

Opposite: Nariva Swamp meets the sea. *Above:* Port of Spain

Our annual Carnival unites our people further; calypsonians even pay homage to both cuisine and country with calypsos such as Denyse Plummer's 'Nah Leaving' and David Rudder's 'Trini to d Bone'. What began as the land of calypso, steel band and limbo, has evolved into the land of calypso, soca (a more upbeat calypso music), chutney (a fiery Indian *baggan* or song), most recently chutney soca (a fusion of Indian and African music), limbo and of course, still, the ever-engaging always-mesmerizing steel-band music. Carnival is a festival which pulls many foreign visitors to our shores and gives us a chance to display our warm hospitality. In so doing we are able to 'show off' the many foods we as Trinidadians and Tobagonians hold dear to our hearts – bake and shark, crab and dumpling, corn soup, pelau, roti, rum punch, stew, accras, callaloo and coo coo, mauby, sugar cakes and bene balls, to name but a few!

Curry, Callaloo & Calypso celebrates this unity by embracing all our cuisines; no more are ethnic-specific foods prepared only at home by the relevant ethnic group. Good cooks abound on our islands, some with modern techniques and some who still hold on to traditional methods. Ours is cooking from the soul, always good, always tasty, gutsy and comforting.

Breakfast is offered in sada rotis, sandwiched with a variety of cooked vegetables, and bakes, also with a variety of fillings, fish salads and accras (fritters). Lunch, which used to be the main meal of the day, is now mostly enjoyed while on the job, purchased at many small eateries across our islands and comprising a hot local lunch of a hearty soup or stewed meat or fish, provision, peas, rice and a salad. Dinner is home-cooked: a stew, grilled or curried meat or fish, with a provision or rice, and a vegetable. Dessert is usually cake and ice cream, but not just any ice cream – local flavours here range from coconut to sour sop, passion fruit, guava, and even Guinness. Fresh fruits are enjoyed round the clock. Nothing beats peeling down a starch mango with your teeth and biting into the sweet flesh, while juice runs down to your elbows! Or savouring a sugary ripe sapodilla, rich with aromatics, tender and juicy, or being amazed at the beauty of a Pink Lady paw paw just sliced open.

Carnival characters

Steel bands

Lunch menu board

Lunch
* Macaroni Pie
* Veg. Rice
* Dasheen & Saltfish
* Stewed Chicken
* Red Beans
* Lentil Peas
* Green Salad

Mangrove roots

Goats

We are an agriculturally rich nation. The foundation of our cuisine is found in the heart of the Paramin Hills, from where we reap the bounty of fresh herbs. These herbs are ground together to form a herb paste which we use to marinate our seafood and meats prior to cooking. Our provisions, vegetables and fruits are grown locally and offered at our outdoor markets and vegetable stands.

Coconut is a big ingredient with a seductive flavour. We use the milk in soups and rice dishes, we make candies from grated coconut, and it's an important ingredient in coconut bake, sweet bread and drops. Stewed with sugar and spices it is used to fill turnovers and fancy sweet bread rolls.

The now defunct sugar-cane industry once gave us our sweet cane sugar, which in turn was processed into world-class local rums. Our first-grade granulated and brown sugars, thickest and blackest molasses, were used to prepare local candies and jams. We still enjoy cane sugar but sadly it's now imported from Guyana and other Caribbean countries. Today it has melted to a small cottage industry with a sprinkling of farmers selling fresh cut cane and sweet cane juice.

From our oceans we get our fish and seafood fresh on a daily basis. We fish our rivers for cascadura and other river fish and we catch mud crabs in our mangrove swamps. Meat plays an important part in our cuisine; beef, goat, lamb, chicken and pork are consumed regularly and are either home-grown or imported. Our forests provide the perfect environment for seasonal wild-meat hunting, during which time (October to December) agouti, lappe, iguana and manicou are hunted and cooked.

When we start a Trini pot cooking, we first fry a mixture of garlic, onions, herbs and peppers in some oil before adding our meats. This resembles the *sofrito* of the Spanish Caribbean islands, and it's a method that was left by our Spanish forefathers. Other times we caramelize sugar to a rich brown colour then add the meat. This effective browning method comes from our African ancestors and results in a perfectly coloured stew. Bright red roucou (annatto) was also used to give a rich-coloured stew. The chonkeying of our dhals and chokas (burning of garlic and pepper and/or cumin in hot oil) is a culinary gift from our Indian brothers and sisters – split pea soup magically turns into dhal when it is chonkeyed; even the sautéing of our curries in hot oil with garlic is indigenous and essential to a true Trini curry. All these techniques are important to a Trinidadian cook and it's what makes our cuisine so special.

Guava

Bundles of chive at market

Between the covers of *Curry, Callaloo & Calypso* you will find traditional recipes like saltfish buljol, breadfruit oiled down, rotis, curries, stews and dumplings, bakes and accras, callaloo and coo coo. Foods that I grew up enjoying as a girl, and foods I still prepare and look forward to eating today with my family. You will also find some personal favourites that make me nostalgic for my old Trinidad, like my mother's coconut cake, old-fashioned guava cheese, aloo poori roti, juicy sugar cakes.

I am a true lover of the foods of my islands. I hope the spirit of my recipes will bring you back to your kitchen and that you too will fall in love with a cuisine that is stunningly diverse and exceptionally delicious.

Coconut vendor, Queen's Park Savannah

A brief culinary history

When Christopher Columbus sailed to the shores of Trinidad and Tobago in 1498, the only visible inhabitants were the Carib and Arawak tribes. Their diet included root vegetables, such as cassava from which they made bread and cakes. They also used cassava as a main ingredient in a dish called 'matete', made with crab, lobster or cascadura, and ate it frequently with wild meat like manicou.

Yams and plantains were other popular staples, as was corn which was roasted or boiled. Today roast and boiled corn vendors are still found in the country with their open-fire coal-pot cooking. River fish, like cascadura, and oysters were eaten as well as shrimp, crab and chip chip. They also ate the fruits of palms such as peewah and the leaves of trees, more specifically the acoma, and susumba berries. Most were eaten raw or roasted.

Cutting cane

Cocoa on the tree

Peewah

Archbishop's House

Coconut and coconut milk were both eaten raw and used as an ingredient in their cooking. They made dumpling soup with roasted cocoa bean, coconut milk and cassava, and fish was especially enjoyed in soups, hence the birth or our own 'fish teas'.

When the Spanish came, with the arrival of Columbus, they brought with them a more sophisticated cuisine. They too used corn in abundance but they made pastelles and arepas, two very familiar dishes that we still enjoy today. The Spaniards also enjoyed wild meat and salted fish, or *bacalao*.

The years 1777 to 1787 saw the arrival of the French planters, who brought with them their slaves, amongst whom were a number of excellent cooks. The food was becoming more plentiful and exciting. The art of making coconut butter was a household one, and children were fed fresh cows' milk and tannia as a large part of their diet. The French enjoyed a diet rich in wild meat, roast suckling pig, vegetables and provisions.

Salted fish and salted meats were imported mainly for their slaves, who were fed on a mixture of vegetables and provisions, cooked with coconut and occasionally flavoured with salt meat. They called this sancocho, and nowadays we still enjoy this dish as a thick soup flavoured much the same way. The addition of salted meats is evident today in many local recipes such as callaloo, split pea based soups and stew peas.

The planters brought French bread with them, which we enjoy as hops, a dry and crusty roll. In those days there were a lot of pig farms around the East Dry River area, enabling the French settlers to make pudding and souse from the pigs' blood and trotters respectively after they were killed. These are still popular delicacies and a major part of our culinary heritage. 'Pudding and hops' is a popular evening meal for many today.

As settler immigration increased, each group brought their own slaves and in return each set of slaves brought with them varied ways in the kitchen. At this time the stage was set for African customs. We must remember that the slaves did not eat the same foods as their masters. They would make their own dishes from what was left over by the great house. While the masters feasted on wild meat their slaves used the dasheen bush to make callaloo and ate this with cassava foo-foo. They also made paime instead of pastelles with the corn and banana leaves.

The African slaves also had a great fancy for sweets, and those that worked on the sugar plantations sometimes received part of their wages in sugar and molasses. They used these products and turned them into delicious sweetmeats that we still enjoy today. Some have become quite rare, like 'nigger boy' – a caramel-type sweet, 'halay' – a sweet with a pulling quality much like bubble gum, made with sugar and water, and 'lavanee' – a hard square toffee-like sweet in various colours. Toolum, made with molasses, coconut and spices, is still very popular, as is chip chip – sugar cakes made with coconut pieces and sugar.

La Chapelle Old House

It would be remiss of me not to speak briefly about the cooking methods that were used in the early days. The slaves would cook for the plantation owners, much of the cooking taking place in a building away from the great house. In these buildings the slaves usually cooked on an open fire contained by large stones. The fire was made in the centre and the pots placed upon the frame of the stones. If baking was done on this fire the pot was placed over the fire, and the bread dough placed in the pot. The pot was then covered with a sheet of metal and some heat was placed on top of this metal sheet so as to give heat at both ends. This method was used to make what we know as 'pot bake'. Meats were spit-roasted on an open spit. Other baked items were cooked in a dirt oven, and many areas had a communal oven where anyone could go to bake their breads and cakes.

By 1797 the English had conquered the islands, also bringing their own slaves, and a distinctively different type of cooking began to surface. English expertise was shown in the making of jams and jellies, and beverages like mauby, sorrel and ginger beer.

In 1834 the slaves were emancipated, and from then they refused to work on the plantations. The skilled cooks amongst them set up shop on street corners, selling dishes they had learned to cook, such as souse and black pudding, and hence the parlour or shop-front refreshment stand was born. The land-owners then began to import workers from Barbados, who brought their own form of recipes such as float and accras and heavy coconut sweet bread. These were sold under rum shops and in some instances on the street corner. Workers also began to arrive from China, Portugal and Madeira, all leaving their mark on our culinary map. The largest group amongst these was the Chinese, whose cooking was changed considerably to suit the palates of the locals. Their cuisine is very popular as is evident by the number of Trinidad-Chinese restaurants that exist today.

East Indian immigrants began to arrive between 1845 and 1917, and were registered under the indenture-ship system to Trinidad. They brought with them spices like coriander, also called dhannia, cumin seed (geera), turmeric or saffron powder, fenugreek, dried legumes such as channa (chickpeas), rice, and two sorts of animal: the water buffalo for hard labour and a type of humped cattle that provided milk for their beloved yogurt and butter which was made into ghee. The spices were ground by hand on what was called a *sill* and made into curries, which have evolved through the years to the distinctively delicious curry that has become indigenous to our country.

The East Indians brought not only ingredients but their own specific methods of cooking. When they first arrived they began to cook on a *chulla*, or mud stove, made with a combination of river mud, leaves and sticks, and cow dung. Water was used to smooth the mud to get a finished look, a process called *leepay*. The fire burned from the base of the *chulla*. After the *chulla* came the coal pot, and then the oil stove followed by the gasoline stove and, of course, the electric stove.

Indentured labourer certificate

The Indians made their rotis on a tavah (tawah), or baking stone, over the *chulla*. They roasted vegetables to make chokas, ground peas for fritters, and preserved fruits such as mango for kutchela and amchar to ensure there was a constant supply of hot and sour condiments to accent their meals. They deep-fried small rotis known as 'pooris'; today we enjoy the same but we call them fried bakes. The rotis they cooked when they came were chapattis and parathas; the chapattis are now known as sada roti, the paratha has remained much the same. Through the years, they introduced the dhalpouri roti or split pea stuffed roti.

The immigrant Indians improvised in the kitchen to produce foods that were close to those of their motherland. This improvisation resulted in our local East Indian foods: Indian delicacies, flaky rotis, curries, condiments, vegetables and sweets, specific only to the Caribbean.

At the end of their indenture-ship period the Indians were given the choice of returning to India or remaining in Trinidad, where they were given the option to purchase land. Those that chose to stay purchased lands and either remained in the sugar industry or went into farming cocoa and coconuts on their own estates. Those that embraced cooking started to sell roti in the parlours. Those roti parlours have become a part of our 'fast food' empire here in Trinidad and are known as roti shops. Others chose to sell 'doubles' from bicycles with carts attached. These have become a national culinary institution, and today doubles vendors can be found all over the country at varying times of day.

After the Indians came many other settlers, such as the Syrians and more Europeans. They too have tried to preserve the foods of their homelands and these influences are noted in our cuisine as well.

Today many of our culinary customs are still observed and some of the methods that have been described here are still preserved in our rural areas. The foods that we now enjoy are a direct result of a fusion of those influences left to us by our forefathers. When we talk about the cuisine of Trinidad and Tobago, it is Indian and Creole foods which top the list of rich inherited dishes; both form the foundation of our national culinary landscape. These are the foods that have indeed etched a place for Trinidad and Tobago on the world culinary map.

Modern-day *chulla*

Maracas Bay

19

Snacks and Indian delicacies

Snacking is a popular pastime here in Trinidad and Tobago – that's because we love to 'lime', or get together, with friends and family for a good time. No lime is complete without food and drink. But our love of snacking goes beyond liming. We, as a nation, are in love with food. Who can blame us? There is always something delicious waiting to be consumed around the corner!

The number-one snack food item is our East Indian treat, doubles (a spicy curried channa filling coddled between two pieces of fried flavoured dough, bara). This has become so popular that, with other Indian delicacies, it is now a mainstay of our culinary culture. Although most of the Indian foods available in Trinidad and Tobago were inspired by our Indian ancestors, I'd say doubles is an invention all our own! It's Trinidadian street food as opposed to Trinidadian Indian food. Any and every Trini can be caught enjoying a doubles at some time. Any visit to Trinidad would be incomplete until you have tried doubles and some of the other Indian delicacies offered for sale by these vendors.

Pies are also a popular snack item. Also called turnovers, we enjoy them filled with fish, beef, chow mein vegetables and potato. Pie vendors sell from shops or on foot with their home-made goodies in their food baskets. Other delightful appetizers include crab backs, shrimp cocktail, curry crab stuffed dumplings, boiled and roast corn, wontons and arepas – to name just a few.

Country cricket match

We also love lip-puckering delights, such as our souses. Even our mango chow, a salsa made with green mangoes and seasonings of vinegar, pepper, salt and garlic, is so popular that vendors sell it at traffic intersections!

Other popular snack items are crispy fried channa and peanuts. Baked peanuts, skin on, are sold by roadside vendors, mostly in Port of Spain, and by vendors on foot at busy intersections. They are also sold at sporting events, especially cricket matches – where some vendors throw their packaged nuts up into the stands even before receiving payment!

Whether it's a beach lime, a cricket lime, or just a house gathering, Trinis snack from sunup to sundown, and you are sure to enjoy any of the addictive bites contained in this section.

Crispy fried channa

This was a popular home-made snack when I was growing up!

1 lb dried chickpeas (channa)
3 cups vegetable oil
1 tsp minced hot pepper
1 tsp salt
1 tsp chadon beni (cilantro)

The night before cooking, soak the chickpeas in a generous quantity of water.

Next morning, drain and dry on paper towels.

Heat the oil in a large deep pot or a wok. Add the chickpeas and fry on medium heat until golden and crisp and cooked.

Remove from the pot and drain on lots of brown paper or paper towels.

Mix the minced pepper, salt and chadon beni then sprinkle the mixture over the channa.

Makes about 3 cups

Baked peanuts

1 lb raw peanuts, shells on

Preheat the oven to 350°F.

Simply wash the peanuts and sprinkle lightly with salt. Spread in a single layer on a baking tray lined with parchment paper.

Bake for about 20–30 minutes, turning with a spoon every 10 minutes. When you can smell the nuts and the shell comes off easily they are cooked.

Butter-fried peanuts

1 lb peanuts, shelled
½ cup butter

Soak the peanuts in hot water and rub off the skin.

Melt the butter in a frying pan, add the peanuts and cook, turning frequently, until the nuts are golden and crisp. Sprinkle with salt.

Cool, and store in a glass bottle.

Note
If you prefer, fry the nuts in vegetable oil instead of butter.

Crispy fried channa (*top*) and butter-fried peanuts

shrimp wontons

1 lb shrimp, peeled and deveined

½ cup chopped water chestnuts

1 tbs chopped ginger

1 tbs chopped garlic

1 tsp sesame oil

2 tbs soy sauce

¼ cup chopped chives

24 wonton skins

vegetable oil for deep-frying

Chop the shrimp finely together with the water chestnuts, ginger and garlic. Add the sesame oil, soy sauce and chives.

Place 1 teaspoon of the filling onto the lower half of a wonton skin, with one point facing down. Dampen the edges, fold into a triangle shape and seal. Then bring the two points on each side up together to meet, and seal about ½ inch from the edge. Repeat with the remaining wonton skins.

Heat the oil and deep-fry the wontons until golden.

Makes 24

Garlic pepper wontons

12 prepared shrimp wontons (see above)

2 tbs vegetable oil

1 tbs chopped garlic

½ tbs chopped ginger

½ hot pepper, seeded and chopped

1 small onion, thinly sliced

½ cup chicken stock

1 tsp cornstarch

1 tbs soy sauce

⅓ cup chopped chives

Instead of deep-frying the wontons, steam them for 10 minutes in a bamboo steamer placed over a wok of simmering water.

Heat the oil in a wok and add the garlic, ginger, hot pepper and onion. Stir-fry for a few minutes until fragrant.

Combine the chicken stock with the cornstarch and soy sauce. Pour into the wok. Stir and add the wontons. Toss to cover with the sauce and cook until thick and bubbling.

Remove from the wok, sprinkle with chives and serve.

Makes 12

Beef pies

Filling

- **2 tbs vegetable oil**
- **1 cup chopped fresh herbs:
  chives, thyme, celery, parsley**
- **2 garlic cloves, chopped**
- **2 pimento peppers, seeded and
  chopped**
- **½ hot pepper, seeded and
  chopped**
- **1 onion, chopped**
- **1 lb ground beef**
- **stock, if necessary (see
  method)**
- **2 slices bread, crumbled**

Pastry

- **1 tsp salt**
- **2 cups flour**
- **⅔ cup shortening**
- **¼ cup iced water**
- **1 egg, beaten**

Heat the oil in a frying pan, add the herbs, garlic, peppers and onion and sauté until tender, about 4 minutes. Add the beef and cook until no longer pink, about 5 minutes. Add a little water or stock to moisten if necessary.

If the beef seems lumpy, put it into a food processor bowl and process for 30 seconds, just until fine.

Add the crumbled bread and combine. Season with salt and freshly ground black pepper to taste. Leave to cool.

Meanwhile, make the pastry. Place the salt and flour in a work bowl. Add the shortening and rub into the flour until the mixture resembles fine crumbs.

Add the water, a little at a time, to bring the dough together. (You may not need to add all the water.) Refrigerate for 30 minutes.

Preheat the oven to 375°F.

Divide the dough into two and roll each piece to about ¼ inch thickness. Cut out circles using a 3-inch cutter.

Place about 1 teaspoon of the filling onto half the rounds, cover with the other rounds and seal.

Brush with beaten egg and bake for 15 minutes until golden.

Makes about 24

Coconut-crusted fish fingers with hot orange dip

2 lb fish fillets, cut into 1 x 4-inch strips

2 garlic cloves, minced

1 tsp salt

2 cups all-purpose flour

1½ tsp baking powder

1 tbs coconut milk powder

1 tsp curry powder

1½ cups milk

2 cups finely shredded fresh coconut

vegetable oil for frying

Marinate the fish in the garlic and salt.

Make a smooth thick batter by combining 1½ cups flour, the baking powder, coconut milk powder, curry powder, milk and some salt. Whisk until smooth.

Put the remaining flour and the shredded coconut on two separate plates.

Dredge the fish in the flour, then dip into the batter. Now roll in the coconut. Repeat to use up all the fish strips.

Fry the fish fingers in hot oil until golden, drain, and serve with orange dip.

Makes about 16

Hot orange dip

1 cup orange marmalade

¼ tsp allspice powder

¼ tsp grated nutmeg

juice of 1 orange

½ Congo pepper, seeded and minced (optional)

1 tsp Chinese chilli sauce

1 tbs shredded ginger

Combine all the ingredients.
Serve with coconut-crusted fish fingers.

Fried arepas

vegetable oil for frying

Dough

1 cup cornmeal

¼ cup flour

1 tsp salt

1½ tsp baking powder

1 tbs softened butter

Filling

8 oz ground beef

1 garlic clove, minced

2 tbs fresh thyme

1 tbs vegetable oil

1 small onion, minced

½ hot pepper, seeded and chopped

⅓ cup raisins

2 tbs chopped olives

1 tbs capers

Combine the cornmeal, flour, salt and baking powder. Add the butter and rub into the flour until the mixture is like fine crumbs. Add enough water to make a soft but pliable dough.

Rest the dough, covered, for 30 minutes.

Form into 12 equal-sized balls. Oil the dough balls and cover with a damp cloth until ready for use.

To make the filling, season the meat with the garlic, thyme and salt and freshly ground black pepper.

Heat the oil in a sauté pan. Add the onion to the pan and sauté until soft. Add the hot pepper, then add the meat and fry until brown.

Stir in the raisins, olives and capers. Cover and finish cooking, adding a little water to prevent sticking, about 10 minutes.

Leave to cool then divide into 12 portions.

Press a piece of cornmeal dough into a circle about 5 inches in diameter. You may use a tortilla press here, but remember to place the dough between two pieces of waxed paper to prevent sticking.

Place one portion of filling onto the centre of the bottom half, fold over the top half to cover, and seal. Repeat with the remaining pieces of dough.

Fry the arepas in hot oil until light golden in colour, about 4 minutes per side.

Drain and serve with a spicy salsa.

Makes 12

' *The name arepa is Spanish. It is usually a type of fried cornmeal cake; however, our version is stuffed with meat.* '

Baked arepas

A lighter version of the traditional fried Trinidadian arepa.

Dough

2 cups cornmeal

1 cup flour

3 tsp baking powder

1 tsp brown sugar

½ tsp salt

½ cup butter

warm water to mix

vegetable oil for brushing

Filling

2 tbs vegetable oil

1 cup chopped fresh herbs: chives, thyme, celery, parsley

2 garlic cloves, chopped

2 pimento peppers, seeded and chopped

½ hot pepper, seeded and chopped

1 onion, chopped

1 lb ground beef

stock, if necessary (see method)

2 slices bread, crumbled

Combine all the dry ingredients. Add the butter and rub into the mixture. Add enough warm water to make a soft dough.

Divide into 16 pieces and cover with a damp tea towel.

To make the filling, heat the oil in a frying pan and add the herbs, garlic, peppers and onion. Sauté until tender, about 4 minutes. Add the beef and cook until no longer pink, about 5 minutes. Add a little water or stock to moisten if necessary.

If the beef seems lumpy put it into a food processor bowl and process for 30 seconds, just until fine.

Add the crumbled bread and combine. Season with salt and freshly ground black pepper to taste. Leave to cool.

Preheat the oven to 375°F. Place a little vegetable oil in a small bowl.

Form the pieces of dough into balls and rub with the oil.

Flatten each ball to about 4–5 inches width. Place a little filling on half the circle and fold to a half-moon shape. Seal with a fork and place on a lined baking sheet.

Brush the arepas with more oil and bake for 20 minutes.

Leave to cool on racks.

Makes 16

Peewah

Peewah, a small, roundish, orange-fleshed fruit comes into season for a few short weeks each year, usually around October. Available in abundance during this time, they resemble tiny green coconuts and grow in huge bunches from specific palm trees, being a member of the palm tree family (Palmacae). Each fruit is attached to the main branch by a tough fibrous stem. When ripe the skin turns a bright orange with hints of green and yellow.

Satisfying and delicious, peewah is traditionally eaten as a snack here in Trinidad and Tobago. But beware – you must first boil peewah before eating. It is usually prepared by boiling in well-salted water for about 40–50 minutes.

When cooked, the fruit, which should be full and roundish, will reveal a bright orange flesh under the inedible outer skin. Biting into a peewah one gets a mouthful of starchy, slightly fibrous textured flesh. The flavour is somewhat bland at first until the slight, distinctively bitter taste hits you at the back of your mouth.

Hot and spicy calypso seafood dip

This dip can be served hot or cold – the hot version is especially tasty as the flavours develop deliciously together. This is the perfect liming snack!

8 oz frozen crab meat, defrosted

6 oz cream cheese, softened

¼ cup sour cream

juice of 1 lime

1 jalapeno pepper, finely chopped, or ½ hot pepper, seeded and minced (more or less, to taste)

2 garlic cloves, minced

1 tbs finely chopped chives

½ tbs finely chopped chadon beni (cilantro)

2 large bags corn chips, to serve

Preheat the oven to 350°F.

Place the crab meat in a glass bowl and microwave for 2 minutes.

Put in a strainer and lightly squeeze to remove any excess water. Pick over to remove any cartilage and shell.

Place the softened cream cheese in a bowl and add the sour cream. Stir in the lime juice, pepper, garlic, chives and chadon beni. Add the crab meat and spoon into a small shallow, glass baking dish.

Bake for about 8–10 minutes just until bubbling.

Serve with corn chips.

Serves 10

Party cheese paste sandwiches

These cheese sandwiches are the most popular party sandwich on the island. Often the cheese paste is coloured with green or pink food colouring!

1 lb cheese, grated

1½ cups butter

1 tsp yellow mustard

1 tsp pepper sauce

Cream all the ingredients to a spreadable consistency. Use as a sandwich filling.

Enough for about 60 sandwiches

Party salmon spirals

1 large sandwich loaf, unsliced
butter
7½-oz tin pink salmon
½ cup mayonnaise
1 tsp Dijon mustard
1 tsp lime juice
1 tsp pepper sauce
⅓ cup finely chopped red bell
   pepper
⅓ cup thinly sliced chives

Remove the crust from the bread. Slice the loaf horizontally into ½-inch thick slices. You should get three long slices. Gently press each slice with the hands to flatten slightly and butter.

Drain and remove skin from the salmon.

In a small glass bowl combine the salmon, mayonnaise, mustard, lime juice and pepper sauce. Add the bell pepper and chives, stir, and add salt to taste.

Spread a third of the salmon mixture onto each piece of bread – do not spread too thickly.

Gently roll up tightly from the long side. Wrap firmly in plastic wrap and refrigerate for at least 1 hour.

To serve, remove the plastic and slice into ½-inch thick slices.

Makes about 24

Cassava fritters with chilli pineapple dip

1 lb uncooked cassava, peeled
   and cut into small pieces
3 garlic cloves
3 tbs chopped onion
¼ cup chopped chives
½ Congo pepper
1 tbs cornstarch
½ tsp baking powder
1 egg
oil for deep-frying
chilli pineapple dip (see page
   353)

Combine all the ingredients in a food processor and process to a fine paste.

Season with salt and freshly ground black pepper to taste.

Heat the oil and drop the mixture by teaspoonfuls into the hot oil. Fry until puffed and golden.

Serve with chilli pineapple dip.

Makes about 15

Profiteroles (puffs)

½ cup butter, cut into cubes

1 cup water

1 cup all-purpose flour

4 eggs

1 tsp salt

Preheat the oven to 425°F.

Place the butter and water in a saucepan on low heat until the butter melts. Bring to a boil.

Remove the pan from the heat and add the flour all at once. Stir quickly until the dough comes together and forms a lump or balls up in the pan.

Return to the heat and cook for about 5 minutes longer. There should be a film on th e inside surface of the pan.

Remove from the heat. Beat in the eggs, one at a time, beating well between each addition. The pastry should just hold its shape when lifted with a spoon. Stir in the salt.

Grease or line a baking sheet. Drop spoonfuls of the pastry onto the sheet or use a piping bag to pipe rounds, 1½–2 inches across.

Bake for 20 minutes then lower the temperature to 375°F and bake for 10–15 minutes longer. Remove from the oven, pierce each puff with a skewer, and return to the oven for 5 minutes to dry out.

Leave the puffs to cool then slice in half and fill with your chosen filling.

Makes 25

Cheese puffs

1 lb cheese, grated

½ cup butter

1 tsp yellow mustard

1 tsp pepper sauce

½ cup mayonnaise

½ cup finely chopped chives

Combine all the ingredients and fill into the puffs.

Chicken puffs

1 lb chicken breast, steamed and finely shredded

1 cup chopped chives

2 tbs chopped celery

1 tsp pepper sauce

1 tsp freshly ground black pepper

8 green olives, chopped

1 cup mayonnaise (more or less, to taste)

salt to taste

Combine all the ingredients and fill into the puffs.

Steamed chicken buns (pows)

Filling

2 tbs oyster sauce

1 tsp sesame oil

1 tsp cornstarch dissolved in 1 tbs water

6 dried black mushrooms, soaked in warm water for 2 hours

2 tbs vegetable oil

½ cup water chestnuts, finely chopped

1 tbs chopped ginger

8 oz minced chicken

4 blades chive, finely chopped

Dough

2½ cups all-purpose flour

3 tsp baking powder

¼ cup sugar

½ cup milk

⅓ cup water

¼ cup vegetable oil

Combine the oyster sauce, sesame oil, cornstarch and salt to taste to make a sauce.

Drain the mushrooms and chop finely.

Heat the oil in a wok, and add the mushrooms, chestnuts and ginger. Fry briefly then add the chicken, stir, and fry until no longer pink. Add the sauce and cook until thick. Add the chives, then remove from the heat and leave to cool.

To make the dough, place the dry ingredients in a mixing bowl. Combine the milk, water and oil and add to the flour mixture. Knead to a soft dough, cover and chill for 1 hour.

To assemble the buns, roll the dough into a log 16 inches long. Cut into 1-inch pieces and roll each into a ball.

Press one ball into a cup shape in your hands and fill with about 1 tablespoon of the chicken mixture. Gather the edges together, twist and seal. Repeat with the remaining pieces of dough.

Assemble a steamer. Put each pow onto a square of waxed paper. Place in the steamer and steam for 20 minutes.

Makes 16

salmon turnovers

Flaky pastry
- **2 cups all-purpose flour**
- **½ tsp salt**
- **¾ cup shortening**
- **¼ cup unsalted butter**
- **¼ cup iced water**
- **1 egg, lightly beaten with 1 tbs water**

Filling
- **14-oz tin salmon, drained and picked over**
- **1 cup chopped chives or spring onions, green and white parts**
- **1 tbs finely chopped chadon beni (cilantro)**
- **1 tbs fresh French thyme**
- **¼ cup chopped parsley**
- **2 pimento peppers, seeded and finely chopped**
- **juice of 1 lime**
- **1 tsp pepper sauce**
- **1 tsp Dijon mustard**
- **1 cup fresh breadcrumbs**
- **1 cup grated cheese**

Combine the flour with the salt. Cut the shortening and butter into the mixture until it resembles small peas.

Add enough iced water for the mixture to come together (you may not need it all). Bring the mixture together, divide into two, and pat each piece into a round.

Wrap and refrigerate for about 1 hour.

Preheat the oven to 400°F.

Place the salmon, chives, herbs and peppers in the bowl of a food processor and process just until the ingredients are very finely chopped. (If preparing by hand break the salmon into very tiny pieces and add the finely chopped herbs and peppers.)

Mix in the remaining filling ingredients. Season to taste with salt and freshly ground black pepper.

Roll out the pastry to about ¼ inch thickness. Stamp out rounds about 3 inches in diameter.

Place 1 tablespoon of filling onto the centre of the lower half of one pastry round. Fold the upper half over and seal by hand or crimp with a fork. Repeat until all the salmon and pastry is used up.

Place on a lined baking tray and brush with the beaten egg mixture.

Bake for 15 minutes until golden.

Makes 24

Cheese straws

- **8 oz cheese, grated**
- **1 cup butter**
- **2 cups flour**
- **dried herbs**

Preheat the oven to 375°F.

Mix the cheese, butter and flour together until well combined.

Roll out to ½ inch thickness and cut into straw lengths.

Place the cheese straws on a baking sheet, sprinkle with herbs and some salt and bake for 15 minutes.

Leave to cool.

Makes 50

sausage rolls

Popular at parties and in local bakeries.

1 tsp salt

2 cups flour

⅔ cup shortening

¼ cup iced water

24 x 3-inch hot dog lengths

1 egg, beaten

Place the salt and flour in a bowl. Add the shortening and rub into the flour until the mixture resembles fine crumbs.

Add the iced water a little at a time to bring the dough together (you may not need it all).

Refrigerate the dough for 30 minutes.

Preheat the oven to 400°F.

Divide the dough in two. Roll out each piece to about ½ inch thickness and cut into 3-inch wide strips.

Cut each strip into two 6-inch lengths. Place a hot dog onto each piece of pastry and roll up.

Seal at the bottom and place seam side down on a baking tray.

Bake for 15 minutes until golden.

Makes 24

Trinidad shrimp cocktail

24 medium shrimp, peeled and deveined

1 tsp ground Spanish thyme

½ tsp salt

2 cups shredded lettuce

lime slices to garnish

Sauce

½ cup ketchup

¼ cup fresh lime juice

1 tsp Worcestershire sauce

1 tsp pepper sauce (or more, to taste)

⅛ tsp allspice powder

1 tbs minced chadon beni (cilantro)

salt to taste

Marinate the shrimp in the Spanish thyme and salt.

Place the shrimp in a saucepan with about ½ cup water and steam. When they are pink and curled, drain and refrigerate.

Combine all the ingredients for the sauce.

Place the lettuce in four stemmed glasses.

Add the shrimp to the sauce and divide equally between the glasses. Garnish with lime slices.

Serve immediately or refrigerate until ready for use.

Serves 4

Curried crab and coconut dumplings

Dumplings

2 cups flour

1 tsp butter

2 tsp baking powder

½ tsp salt

Filling

6 oz crab meat

1 tsp lime juice

2 tbs vegetable oil

2 garlic cloves, chopped

1 small onion, chopped

1 pimento pepper, seeded and chopped

¼ tsp allspice powder

Curry sauce

2 tbs vegetable oil

2 garlic cloves, chopped

2 tbs chopped onion

1 hot pepper, seeded and chopped

2 tbs curry powder

½ cup water

1 cup coconut milk

¼ cup chopped chives

¼ cup chopped chadon beni (cilantro)

juice of 1 lime

To make the dumpling dough place all the ingredients in a mixing bowl. Rub the butter into the flour until the mixture is grainy. Slowly mix in enough water to form a stiff dough. Knead, then cover and let rest for about 30 minutes.

Season the crab with salt, freshly ground black pepper and the lime juice.

Heat the oil in a large sauté pan, add the garlic, onion and pimento pepper and cook for about 1 minute. Add the crab and allspice and toss to combine. Remove from the heat and leave to cool.

Cut the dumpling dough into 12 pieces. Make each piece into a ball then flatten each ball of dough into a 2½–3-inch circle. Place about 1 teaspoon of the crab mixture into the lower half of a circle. Fold the upper half over and seal. Repeat until all the dumplings have been filled.

To make the curry sauce, heat the oil in a sauté pan and add the garlic, onion and pepper.

Sauté until fragrant.

Combine the curry powder with the water. Add to the pan and cook until the mixture begins to dry.

Add the coconut milk and sprinkle with the chives and chadon beni. Cook until bubbling.

Drop the crab dumplings into the curry mixture, cover and steam for 10 minutes, turning the dumplings once. If the mixture seems too dry add a little more coconut milk.

Sprinkle on more chadon beni if wished. Stir in the lime juice, taste and adjust seasonings.

Serves 4–6

'Curry crab and dumplings is a traditional Trinidadian dish – a popular item at Carnival fetes! The recipe here is a snack version of the traditional dish. The dumplings are stuffed with crab and simmered in a curry and coconut broth.'

spinach accras

4 cups spinach leaves, washed

1 large onion, chopped

1 hot pepper, seeded and chopped

1 sweet red pepper, seeded and chopped

1 tsp salt

½ tsp grated nutmeg

4 garlic cloves, chopped

½ cup chopped chives

1 cup all-purpose flour

2 tsp baking powder

1 cup milk

vegetable oil for deep-frying

Steam the spinach, drain well and chop finely.

Place in a bowl and combine with the onion, peppers, salt, nutmeg, garlic and chives.

Mix the flour and baking powder then add to the spinach mixture.

Add the milk and stir to make a very thick batter.

Heat the oil and drop the mixture by teaspoonfuls into the hot oil. Fry until puffed and golden.

Makes 15

stuffed crab backs

This is a very traditional appetizer that remains popular because of its fantastic taste!

1 tbs fresh lime juice

1 lb fresh crab meat, picked over

2 tbs butter

2 onions, minced

2 garlic cloves, minced

½ cup finely chopped chives or spring onions, green and white parts

2 tbs fresh French thyme

1 tbs chopped celery

2 pimento peppers, seeded and chopped

1 hot pepper, seeded and chopped

1½ cups fresh breadcrumbs

6 crab shells

Gratin

1 cup toasted breadcrumbs

2 tbs chopped celery

2 tbs parmesan cheese

2 tbs softened butter

Mix the lime juice with the crab meat.

Melt the butter in a sauté pan, add the onion and garlic and cook until translucent, about 4 minutes.

Add the chives, thyme, celery, pimentos and hot pepper and cook for a further 4 minutes.

Remove from the heat, add the crab meat and turn into a large bowl. Stir to combine, and mix in the breadcrumbs. Season with salt.

Preheat the oven to 375°F.

Make the gratin by combining all the ingredients until the crumbs becomes coated with the butter.

Spoon the crab meat mixture into the shells and top with the gratin.

Bake for about 15 minutes, until the gratin is lightly browned.

Serves 6

Creamy stuffed eggs with capers and olives

These appetizers are making a comeback at parties for kids and grown-ups alike!

12 large eggs
1 tsp grated onion
4–6 tbs mayonnaise
1 tsp yellow mustard
1 tsp chopped capers
1 tsp chopped olives
½ tsp pepper sauce
1 tsp paprika
chopped parsley to garnish

Hard-boil the eggs. Cool and peel.

Slice the eggs in half. Gently scoop out the yolks and place in a bowl. Place the whites on a platter.

Combine the hard-boiled yolks with the onion, 4 tablespoons mayonnaise, the mustard, capers, olives and pepper sauce. Stir until creamy. Add more mayonnaise if needed.

Place into a piping bag fitted with a large star tube. Pipe into the egg whites, sprinkle with paprika and garnish with chopped parsley.

Refrigerate until ready to serve.

Makes 24

Hummos

Due to the recent popularity of Lebanese food, hummos is more available now than ever before.

14-oz tin chickpeas, drained and rinsed

4 garlic cloves, minced

juice of 1 large lime

1 tbs plain yogurt

½ tsp pepper sauce or any hot pepper, seeded and chopped

1 tbs sesame oil

1 tsp ground roasted geera (cumin)

1 tbs olive oil

2 tbs chopped chadon beni (cilantro) or parsley

1 tsp sumac (optional)

1 tbs olive oil

black olives to garnish

pitta bread or chips, to serve

Purée the chickpeas coarsely in either a food processor or a blender. If you are using a blender purée in two batches and add 1 tablespoon of water to each batch.

Add the garlic, lime juice, yogurt, pepper sauce or hot pepper, sesame oil and geera.

Continue to purée the mixture until smooth. Taste and add salt and freshly ground black pepper.

Transfer to a serving plate and sprinkle with chadon beni or parsley. Drizzle with olive oil and sprinkle with sumac, if using. Garnish with olives.

Serve with warm pitta bread or pitta chips.

Serves 6

Cassava chips with chadon beni mayo

This is another snack that is served a lot at Carnival fetes!

2 lb cassava

vegetable oil for deep-frying

chadon beni mayo (see page 352)

Peel the cassava and cut into 3-inch strips.

Heat the oil. Deep-fry the cassava strips until golden and crunchy.

Drain. Sprinkle with salt and serve with chadon beni mayo.

Carnival fish pies

1 lb fish fillets, steamed

1 tsp hot pepper sauce

1 tsp fresh lime juice

½ cup finely chopped mixed herbs (parsley, thyme, chadon beni/cilantro, chives)

2 large garlic cloves, minced

1 large potato, peeled, boiled and crushed

vegetable oil for frying

Dough

2 cups all-purpose flour

2 tsp baking powder

½ tsp salt

4 tbs shortening

Flake the fish and remove any bones. Add the pepper sauce, lime juice, herbs, garlic and crushed potato and mix well. Taste and add salt and freshly ground black pepper.

Make the dough by combining the flour with the baking powder, salt and shortening. Add enough water to make a soft but pliable and non-sticky dough. Knead into a ball, cover, and let rest for about 30 minutes.

Divide the dough into 10 pieces and roll each piece into a ball. Rest for 5 minutes.

Roll each ball of dough into a 5-inch circle. Place 1–2 tablespoons of the filling onto the lower half of the circle and fold the upper half over to cover in a half-moon shape. Seal and continue until all the dough and filling is used up.

Heat the oil in a frying pan and shallow-fry the pies until golden brown.

Drain and serve with chadon beni pesto (see page 132).

Makes 10

Cassava chips with chadon beni mayo

'When I was growing up, the only plantain chips I knew were home-made from green plantains fried in vegetable oil. My grandmother would fry up a batch to send to her loved ones overseas! Today they have become a popular packaged snack.'

Plantain chips

4 green plantains, peeled (see page 221)
vegetable oil for deep-frying

Cut the plantains in half and slice lengthways into about ¼-inch thick slices or across into ¼-inch thick rounds.

Deep-fry in hot oil on a medium heat until the plantains are light brown and crisp.

Drain on paper towels. Cool and sprinkle with salt.

Store in an airtight container.

Serves 4–6

'*Corn is a Trinidad fast food. We can buy both boiled and roasted from roadside vendors. During Carnival season boiled corn is a popular street food.*'

Boiled corn

10 ears corn, peeled

10 garlic cloves, minced

10 leaves chadon beni (cilantro)

2 tbs salt

1 tsp freshly ground black pepper

Place all the ingredients in a Dutch oven, cover with water, and boil for 40 minutes until the corn is tender.

To serve, cut each corn in half.

Makes 20

'A Trini Christmas would lose a lot of flavour without pastelles. I can remember spending many a sleepy night during my childhood helping my mother make them at Christmas time. My job then was to cut the string to length and tie the pastelles; my brother would be in charge of softening the leaves over the stove fire, and my sister would have the grand job of pressing out the cornmeal dough. Of course my mother filled and folded them. What a production line it was! And worth every minute of lost sleep!'

Chicken and beef pastelles

1 lb chopped beef and chicken (or chicken only)

1 tsp salt

1 tsp freshly ground black pepper

1 cup chopped chives

6 tbs chopped fresh thyme

2 tbs olive oil

2 onions, finely chopped

4 garlic cloves, chopped

2 pimento peppers, seeded and chopped

1 tbs chopped celery

½ Congo pepper, seeded and chopped (optional)

¼ cup good-quality tomato paste

¼ cup raisins

4 tbs capers

3 tbs stuffed olives, sliced

15–20 prepared fig leaves (see note)

Dough

2 cups yellow cornmeal

½ cup butter, at room temperature

1¼ tsp salt

2–3 cups warm water

Combine the beef with the chicken. Add the salt and black pepper. Add ¼ cup chopped chives and 1 tablespoon thyme.

Heat the olive oil in a large sauté pan. Add the onion and garlic and sauté until fragrant. Add the pimento peppers, celery, Congo pepper, if using, the remaining chives and 3 tablespoons thyme. Add the meat and cook until brown.

Stir in the tomato paste, cover and simmer for about 15 minutes. Add the raisins, capers and olives and stir to combine. Cook for about 5 minutes more. Taste and adjust seasoning.

Mix in the remaining thyme. Remove from the heat and leave to cool.

To make the dough, combine the cornmeal with the butter and salt by hand. Add the warm water and knead to make a soft, pliable dough. Divide into 12–15 balls and cover with a damp cloth to prevent drying.

Place one piece of dough on a greased fig leaf, and press to an 8-inch width. Spoon 2 tablespoons of filling onto the middle of the dough and fold and seal.

Wrap the fig leaf around and tie into a neat package.

Steam the pastelles for 45 minutes until cooked.

Makes 15–20

Note
To prepare fig leaves, steam them in a large pot of boiling water for 10 minutes until they become pliable and soft. Alternatively, they may be softened by waving them over an open flame.

Paime

This is a sweet cornmeal dumpling that is wrapped in banana leaves and steamed, a part of our Spanish influence.

2 cups grated fresh coconut

8 oz pumpkin, grated

1 cup granulated sugar

2 cups cornmeal

4 oz raisins

1 tsp cinnamon

½ tsp grated nutmeg

½ tsp white or black pepper

¼ cup melted butter

1 tsp vanilla extract

8 square banana leaves

In a large mixing bowl combine the coconut, pumpkin, sugar, cornmeal, raisins, spices and pepper.

Combine the butter with 1 cup water and the vanilla and add to the cornmeal mixture. The mixture should be of the consistency of wet dough. If too dry add a little more water.

Soften the banana leaves by steaming or passing over an open flame.

Place 2 tablespoons of the mixture onto a banana leaf and fold into a square package, pressing lightly to flatten.

Steam for 45–60 minutes.

Remove, drain, and serve warm or at room temperature as a snack.

Makes 8

' We consume a lot of avocados here, usually sliced with our meals. Sometimes they are mashed, mixed with salt, garlic and pepper and enjoyed with bake, hops or sada roti as a light meal. Recently we have begun to enjoy them in dips such as guacamole. '

Guacamole

2 ripe avocados

3 garlic cloves, crushed

1 tbs lime juice (more or less, to taste)

¼ cup sour cream or thick yogurt

½ hot pepper, seeded and finely chopped

¼ cup fresh chadon beni (cilantro) leaves

2 tbs chopped chives

Peel the avocados and chop finely.

In a mixing bowl combine the garlic, lime juice, sour cream, hot pepper, fresh chadon beni and salt and freshly ground black pepper to taste.

Stir in the avocado and mix gently.

Sprinkle with chives and serve.

Serves 8

Chinese vegetable dumplings

1 tsp sesame oil

2 tbs soy sauce

1 tbs Chinese chilli sauce

6 black Chinese mushrooms, soaked in warm water for 20 minutes

2 tbs vegetable oil

2 tbs minced ginger

4 garlic cloves, chopped

1 cup grated carrot

½ cup water chestnuts, chopped

½ cup bamboo shoots, chopped

½ cup chopped chives

1 pack wonton skins

In a small bowl combine the sesame oil, soy sauce and chilli sauce.

Drain the mushrooms, remove the stems and chop.

Heat the oil in a wok or sauté pan. Add the ginger and garlic and sauté until fragrant. Add carrot and sauté for 1 minute. Add the mushrooms, chopped water chestnuts, bamboo shoots and chives. Sauté for 1 minute.

Add the sauce ingredients and stir to combine. Remove from the heat, taste and adjust seasonings.

Leave the mixture to cool.

Place a wonton skin on the worktop. Spoon about 1 teaspoon of filling on the bottom part of the skin. Fold over into a triangle shape and seal the edges with water. Repeat until all the filling has been used up.

Steam for 15 minutes. Serve hot.

Makes about 36

'Pudding and souse were handed down to us from the African slaves – who in their turn had learned to prepare these delicacies from their French masters. Upon being given their freedom, the slaves sold these prepared foods on the roadside and hence the street-side refreshment stand was born. Souse is a pickling method of preparing meats and vegetables. Originally it was pigs' trotters that were soused: they were first cleaned and cooked and then soaked for many hours in a mixture of fresh lime juice, pepper and onion. Since then we have added chicken feet, cow skin, lambie, cucumber and green fig souse to our Trinidadian menu. We enjoy souse at any lime!'

Clockwise from top: cucumber souse, chicken foot souse, green fig souse

chicken foot souse

This recipe can also be used to souse other meats, such as pigs' trotters and cow skin.

2 lb chicken feet

2 small cucumbers, peeled and thinly sliced

2 large onions, thinly sliced

1 hot pepper, with seeds, thinly sliced

1 cup lime juice

1 cup finely chopped chadon beni (cilantro)

¼ cup finely chopped chives

Wash the chicken feet and boil in lightly salted water until tender, about 30 minutes. Drain and leave to cool.

Place in a large glass bowl. Add the cucumbers, onions, pepper, lime juice, chadon beni and chives with 2 cups water. Stir well, so that the chicken feet are covered with the marinade. Cover and let stand at room temperature for 3–4 hours, stirring to keep all pieces exposed to the marinade.

Serves 8

Green fig souse

8 green figs or green bananas

oil

¼ cup fresh lime juice

½ cup cool water

1 large onion, thinly sliced

4 garlic cloves, minced

1 hot pepper, seeded and thinly sliced

salt and freshly ground black pepper

2 cucumbers, peeled and thinly sliced

Place the green figs in plenty of water in a non-reactive heavy saucepan. Add a little oil and boil for about 15 minutes until tender. Remove and cool, then peel and slice.

Place the fig slices in a glass bowl. Add all other ingredients except the cucumber. Pour on enough boiling water to just cover the figs.

Cool then refrigerate overnight.

Add the cucumber slices 15 minutes before serving.

Serves 6

Cucumber souse

10 cucumbers, peeled and thinly sliced

juice of 3 limes

¼ cup white vinegar

1 hot pepper, minced

½ cup thinly sliced chives

2 onions, thinly sliced

¼ cup finely chopped chadon beni (cilantro)

salt and freshly ground black pepper

Place the cucumbers in a glass bowl. Add all the other ingredients, stir and cover.
Refrigerate for 1–2 hours.

Serves 10

'*Chows are lip-puckering, mouth-burning addictive snacks. Trinis are famous for making a 'chow' with anything – mango, pommecythere, pineapple and even citrus fruits!*'

Mango chow

This is a master recipe to be used and adjusted according to your taste. When you slice the mangoes be sure to keep the seed and enjoy the last juicy bits later!

4 half-ripe mangoes, peeled and sliced off the seed

1 hot pepper, chopped

¼ cup white vinegar

1 tsp salt

1 tsp minced garlic

Mix all the ingredients together and let sit for about 30 minutes before using.

Indian delicacies

For the complete Indian delicacy experience you'll need to head down south to the bustling village of Debe. Located on the main road you'll see a few small huts, each bearing the vendor's name, each a mirror image of one another. Hungry customers hover around glass cases filled with deep-fried aloo (potato) pies, doubles, saheenas (split pea and spinach fritters), kutchorie and phulorie (split pea fritters), baiganee (eggplant and split pea fritters), eagerly trying to decide what they should order. To garnish any of the above you'll need an assortment of mango or tamarind chutneys and pepper sauces which are also available and made in-house. A simple order is filled within minutes as large pots of oil are constantly frying one of the above delicacies to ensure a good supply.

The back kitchens of some of these outlets reveal large basins filled with soft shaggy-looking doughs. This dough envelops many pies that are sold. Another set of basins are filled with the saffron-flavoured dough which will become the bara for the doubles. Huge pots of tender channa (chickpeas) are kept warm – this is the filling for the doubles and is becoming increasingly popular as an extra with the aloo pies.

Then there is the making of the saheena. Huge dasheen leaves are covered with an uncooked split pea paste, then rolled up jelly-roll style, sliced, and deep-fried. When done it is slathered with your choice of pepper or chutney and enjoyed smoking hot.

‘Vendors around the country begin selling doubles from early morning and continue late into the night. They're up at the crack of dawn mixing, slicing, kneading and frying in preparation for the day's business of Indian delicacy sales. What started off as a simple operation, selling doubles from carts around the towns of Trinidad, has spawned an industry. You can spot their carts or small white vans throughout the island from as early as 6.30 am, then on through the day, providing an early morning breakfast, late morning snack or after school/work fuel for many Trinidadians.’

The iconic Brooklyn Bar in Port of Spain, noted for its doubles vendors

Doubles

vegetable oil for deep-frying

chutney and pepper sauce, to serve

Bara

2 cups flour

½ tsp salt

½ tsp turmeric or saffron powder

1 tsp freshly ground black pepper

1 tsp dried yeast

½ tsp sugar

1 tsp ground roasted geera (cumin)

about 1 cup water

Filling

2 tbs curry powder

1 tbs vegetable oil

4 garlic cloves, minced

1 hot pepper, seeded and chopped

1 onion, chopped

8 oz chickpeas (channa), soaked overnight and drained

½ tsp ground roasted geera (cumin)

¼ cup chopped chadon beni (cilantro)

Make the bara by combining all the dry ingredients. Warm the water to 120°F. Add gradually to the dry ingredients to make a soft and shaggy dough.

Cover and leave to rise until doubled in size, about 1 hour.

To make the filling, combine the curry powder with ¼ cup water.

Heat the oil in a large pan and add the garlic, pepper and onion. Cook until fragrant.

Add the curry paste and cook until the water has evaporated.

Add the chickpeas, stir, and add 1½ cups water. Season with salt and add the geera. Cover and cook until tender, about 1 hour, adding more water to prevent sticking if all the water has evaporated.

Add the chadon beni and stir.

To cook the bara, heat some oil in a deep frying pan. With oiled fingers pinch off pieces of dough about the size of a table-tennis ball. Stretch the dough into a thin circle and deep-fry in the hot oil until it floats to the top and is puffed.

Drain and sandwich with the curry channa filling. Serve with chutney and pepper sauce.

Makes about 12

'When consuming Indian delicacies you must exercise caution – some claim the name 'doubles' stems from the fact that this East Indian-inspired sandwich is so addictive you must have at least two!
How to eat doubles: Some hungry persons can be observed biting straight into the doubles, eating it as you would a sandwich. Others would use one hand to hold the doubles and the other to hold the top bara or bake to scoop and carry the channa filling into their mouths. Either way would finish with licking one's fingers!'

Baiganee

1 lb split peas, washed and soaked overnight

2 garlic cloves, minced

1 tsp saffron powder

¼ tsp baking soda

2 tsp baking powder

2 tbs flour

1½ tsp salt

1 tsp pepper sauce

1 eggplant, cut into ½-inch slices

vegetable oil for deep-frying

Drain the split peas and grind in a food processor or food mill until the consistency is smooth.

Add the garlic, saffron powder, baking soda, baking powder, flour, salt and pepper sauce. Leave to rest for 1 hour.

If the mixture seems too dry add a little water.

Salt the eggplant and let stand for 15 minutes.

Rinse and pat dry.

Heat some oil in a wok or deep frying pan.

Using your fingers or a small knife, carefully coat the eggplant slices on both sides with the split pea mixture. Deep-fry immediately until golden brown.

Drain and serve with mango chutney.

Makes about 24

Samosas

vegetable oil for deep-frying

Dough
- **1½ cups all-purpose flour plus 1 tbs**
- **½ tsp salt**
- **½ tsp baking powder**
- **1½ tbs vegetable oil**

Filling
- **1 tbs vegetable oil**
- **1 onion, finely chopped**
- **2 tsp garam masala powder**
- **½ tsp chilli powder**
- **1 tbs minced ginger**
- **2 garlic cloves, minced**
- **1 cup frozen green peas**
- **1 lb potatoes, boiled and cut into small cubes**
- **2 tbs lime juice**

Sift the flour and add the salt and baking powder. Stir in the oil and add water, a little at a time, to form a dough. Knead well and set aside. Rest for 30 minutes.

Knead the dough again and form into 16–20 even-sized balls. Cover.

Make a flour paste by combining 1 tablespoon flour with water to form a thick paste. Reserve.

To make the filling, heat the oil in a medium sauté pan. Add the onion and sauté until tender, 4–5 minutes.

Add the garam masala powder, chilli powder, ginger and garlic. Stir and fry until fragrant, about 2 minutes. Add the green peas and stir. Cook for a few minutes more until the peas are tender.

Add the potatoes and season with salt to taste. Cook until all the ingredients are well combined.

Remove from the heat, add the lime juice and stir well. Leave until cool.

To assemble the samosas, roll each ball on a lightly floured surface into a thin circle, 4–5 inches diameter. Cut across to the centre and apply the flour paste along the straight edges. Bring the two corners together, overlapping slightly to make a cone. Secure by pressing the pasted edges together.

Fill the cone with the filling. Apply flour paste to the open mouth and seal the edge. Prepare all the samosas the same way.

Heat some oil in a deep frying pan. When it is moderately hot, deep-fry the samosas, a few at a time, until golden brown.

Drain on paper towels and serve hot or cold with chutney.

Makes 16–20

Vendor's baiganee

Aloo pies

Dough

2 cups all-purpose flour

2 tsp baking powder

½ tsp salt

2 tbs butter or shortening

Filling

1 lb potatoes, peeled and cut into quarters

2 garlic cloves, minced

2 tsp ground roasted geera (cumin)

1 pimento pepper, seeded and chopped

½ Congo pepper, seeded and chopped (optional)

1 small onion, finely chopped

¼ cup finely chopped chives

vegetable oil for frying

Make the dough by combining the flour with the baking powder, salt and butter. Add water to make a soft but pliable and non-sticky dough. Knead into a ball and let rest.

Meanwhile, boil the potatoes with a little salt until tender. When cooked, drain and crush well with a potato masher.

Add the garlic, geera, peppers, onion, chives and salt and freshly ground black pepper. Taste and adjust the seasoning.

Divide the dough into eight pieces. Roll each piece into a ball and let rest for 5 minutes.

Roll each ball of dough into a 5-inch circle. Place about 1–2 tablespoons of filling onto the lower half of the circle. Bring the upper portion over the lower portion to cover in a half-moon shape.

Seal and continue with the remaining dough balls.

Heat some oil in a frying pan and shallow-fry the pies until golden brown.

Drain and serve warm with chutney.

Makes 8

' *This pie has become so popular that vendors now offer cooked channa as an optional extra.* '

Aloo pie with channa

Quick saheena

I love saheena. For me the best saheena is one loaded with lots of dasheen bush, just held together with ground seasoned dhal, then fried to crisp perfection!

1 lb split peas, washed and soaked overnight

2 garlic cloves, minced

1 tsp saffron powder

¼ tsp baking soda

2 tsp baking powder

2 tbs flour

1½ tsp salt

1 tsp pepper sauce

1 bunch young dasheen bush

vegetable oil for deep-frying

Drain the split peas and grind in a food processor or food mill until the consistency is smooth.

Add the garlic, saffron powder, baking soda, baking powder, flour, salt and pepper sauce. Allow to rest for 1 hour.

If the mixture seems too dry add a little water. Beat with a wooden spoon, to incorporate air and lighten the mixture. Let stand.

Meanwhile, clean the dasheen bush by removing the tips of the leaves, stems and veins. Wash thoroughly and chop finely. Blanch the dasheen bush in a large pot of boiling water for a couple of minutes, until it turns bright green.

Combine the split pea mixture with the dasheen bush.

Heat oil in a deep-fryer. Drop the saheena mixture by heaped teaspoonfuls into the hot oil and gently flatten with the back of a spoon. Fry until golden brown or until the saheena float to the top of the oil.

Drain and serve immediately with tamarind or mango chutney.

Makes about 72

Rolled saheena

1 cup split pea powder

1 tsp saffron powder

1 tsp salt, or to taste

1 tsp freshly ground black pepper

1 onion, grated

2 garlic cloves, minced

1 lime

1 large bunch dasheen bush, stems and tips of leaves removed (about 6–8 leaves)

1 tsp baking powder

1 cup flour

vegetable oil for frying

Combine the split pea powder, saffron, salt, black pepper, onion and garlic. Add enough water to make a soft spreadable paste. Squeeze the juice from half the lime over the mixture and beat with a wooden spoon. Cover until ready for use.

Bring a large pot of water to a boil. Squeeze the juice from the remaining half-lime into it. Place the dasheen leaves into the water and boil until the leaves become pliable, about 3 minutes. Gently remove the leaves and let cool. (If you overcook the leaves, they will break when you are using them later on.)

On a large surface, spread the cooled leaves open and overlap to make a rectangle about 24 by 30 inches. Gently spread the split pea mixture over the leaves, making a thin covering and leaving a border of about 1 inch around the edge.

Starting at a long end, roll the leaves up jelly-roll style, tucking the ends into the roll as you go. Tie with string and steam the roll for about 15 minutes.

Remove and leave to cool.

Season the flour with salt and freshly ground black pepper.

Cut the dasheen roll into ¾-inch slices and dredge the slices in the seasoned flour.

Fry the dasheen slices in some hot oil and serve with chutney.

Makes about 20

Rolled saheena

Phulorie

1 lb split peas, washed and
   soaked overnight

2 garlic cloves, minced

1 tsp saffron powder

¼ tsp baking soda

2 tsp baking powder

2 tbs flour

1½ tsp salt

juice of ½ lime

vegetable oil for deep-frying

Drain the split peas and grind in a food processor or food mill until the consistency is smooth.

Add all the remaining ingredients together with some freshly ground black pepper. Allow to rest for 1 hour.

If the mixture seems too dry add a little water. Beat with a wooden spoon to incorporate air and lighten the mixture. Let stand for about 30 minutes.

Heat oil in a deep-fryer and drop the phulorie mixture by teaspoonfuls into the hot oil. Fry until golden brown or until the phulorie float to the top of the oil.

Drain and serve immediately with tamarind or mango chutney.

Makes about 72

Kutchorie

1 lb split peas, washed and
   soaked overnight

3 tsp baking powder

½ tsp saffron powder

¼ cup flour

1 tsp pepper sauce

4 garlic cloves, minced

1 tsp salt

vegetable oil for deep-frying

Drain the peas and grind in a food processor.

Add the remaining ingredients and form the mixture into 2-inch balls.

Flatten each ball and deep-fry in hot oil on medium heat until puffed and dark golden. Drain on paper towels.

Makes about 24

Soups, salads *and* vegetables

The soups of our islands are thick and hearty, usually made with a base of split peas and finished off with provisions and dumplings, a substantial one-pot meal. Saturday is soup day in Trinidad and Tobago, and a bubbling pot may be found on the stovetop of many a local home. The most popular soup is sancoche, made with beef, or salted beef, provisions and dumplings – it's thick, peppery and satisfying.

Other bean soups are popular as well, especially dhal, the Indian split pea soup that enjoys equal popularity in homes and at lunch outlets around the country. We seem to have a love affair with gelatinous textures, as is showcased in our cow heel and chicken foot soup. Oxtail soup, with the addition of dumplings (no Trini soup or fish stew would be complete without the addition of a few dumplings), is another popular hearty soup.

Our salads are simply made, mainly with lettuce, cucumbers, tomatoes and, sometimes, watercress, which can be found each weekend at the markets. Mayonnaise-based salads, like macaroni and potato salads, are popular, as is coleslaw.

The weekend markets display a colourful array of locally grown vegetables, fruits and provisions. The most popular are melongene (eggplant), carailli, bodi, green beans, pumpkin, lettuce, tomatoes, watercress, cucumbers, beetroot, carrots, christophene, seim, cauliflower, spinach, callaloo bush. Displayed with these are a variety of fresh herbs, grown on the hills of Paramin, peppers, sweet and hot, and flavourings of onions and garlic.

Our more popular fruits range from sweet bananas and figs to orange-fleshed paw paws, sugary sweet pineapples, seasonal mangoes, citrus, seductive sapodillas and caimate, five fingers (carambola), pommeracs, tamarind and passion fruits. When mangoes are in season I love to peel and slice an almost ripened mango into my salads.

Dried peas and legumes are used extensively in our cuisine, peas often being incorporated into a rice dish as in our cookups, pelaus and kitcheree. Stewed peas are served almost daily to accompany plain boiled or steamed rice. The more popular varieties are red beans, black eye, lentils, gub gub (small navy beans) and split peas, yellow and green.

Marabella Market

Sancoche

This can be made into a vegetarian soup by omitting the beef, replacing the beef stock with vegetable stock, and adding 1 cup chopped carrots to the recipe.

1 lb stewing beef with bones

1 tbs minced chives

4 garlic cloves, minced

2 lb mixed provisions (sweet potatoes, yams, eddoes, cassava)

2 tbs vegetable oil

2 onions, chopped

3 tbs chopped celery

2 pimento peppers, seeded and chopped

¼ cup fresh thyme

1 cup yellow split peas

6 okra, sliced

1 cup chopped pumpkin

8 cups beef stock

1 plantain, half-ripe, peeled and thickly sliced

1 hot pepper, left whole

dumplings (see below)

Season the beef with the chives and half the garlic. Peel the provisions and cut into 2-inch pieces. Place in a bowl and cover with water until ready for use.

Heat the oil in a large soup pot or Dutch oven. Add the onions, remaining garlic, celery, pimento pepper and thyme. Sauté until fragrant.

Add the beef and stir until the beef is browned. Add the split peas, okra and pumpkin and sauté, then add the stock and simmer until the split peas are cooked to a nice thickness and the beef is tender, about 1 hour. Season with salt and freshly ground black pepper.

Add the provisions, plantain and hot pepper and cook until the provisions are tender, about 30 minutes.

Drop the dumplings into the pot and cook until they have floated to the top, about 10–15 minutes. Serve hot, with or without the hot pepper.

Serves 6–8

Dumplings

2 cups flour

2 tsp baking powder

½ tsp salt

1 tsp butter

Place all the ingredients in a mixing bowl. Rub the butter into the flour until the mixture is grainy. Slowly add enough water to knead to a stiff dough. Cover and let rest for about 30 minutes.

Divide the dough into two pieces. Roll each piece into a long rope-like shape, about 12 inches in length. Cut into 2-inch lengths and drop into the boiling soup.

Note
For stiffer dumplings, add only 1 teaspoon baking powder.

Lentil soup with cornmeal dumplings

1 tbs vegetable oil

4 garlic cloves, chopped

⅓ cup chopped celery

¼ cup fresh thyme

1 large onion, chopped

½ hot pepper, seeded and chopped

1 carrot, finely chopped

1 tsp ground geera (cumin)

1 lb brown lentil peas, washed and picked over

9 cups vegetable stock or water

1 tbs butter

Heat the oil in a large stockpot or saucepan. Add the garlic, celery, thyme, onion and hot pepper. Sauté until fragrant.

Add the carrot, geera and lentils and sauté for a few more minutes.

Add the stock. Cover and simmer until the lentils are soft and melted, about 40–50 minutes. Stir well or swizzle.

Drop cornmeal dumplings into the boiling soup and cook until puffed and light, about 10 minutes. Stir in the butter and serve.

Serves 6–8

Cornmeal dumplings

1 cup flour

1 cup cornmeal

2 tsp baking powder

1½ tsp ground roasted geera (cumin)

½ tsp salt

2 tbs butter

In a bowl, combine all the ingredients. Cut the butter into the flour until the texture is grainy. Add enough water to make a pliable dough.

Gently press the dough into a circle about ¾ inch thick. Cut into small 1-inch squares and drop into the boiling soup.

Trini corn soup with dumplings

8 cups beef stock or vegetable stock

¾ cup yellow split peas, washed and picked over

1 lb English potatoes, peeled and quartered

2 onions, chopped

3 garlic cloves, minced

2 carrots, diced

⅓ cup fresh thyme, chopped

¼ cup chopped celery

⅓ cup chopped chives

1 hot pepper

4 pimento peppers, seeded and chopped

6 ears corn, cut into 2-inch pieces

dumplings (see page 68)

½ cup coconut milk (optional)

½ cup chopped chadon beni (cilantro)

Heat the stock in a large soup pot or Dutch oven. Add the split peas, potatoes, onions, garlic, carrots, thyme, celery, chives and peppers. Bring to a boil. Cover and simmer for about 1 hour until the peas are soft. Remove the hot pepper.

Purée the soup to a thick and creamy consistency and return to the pot.

Add the corn and dumplings, and coconut milk if using. Continue to cook for a further 20 minutes until the corn is cooked and the dumplings float to the surface.

Add the chadon beni, remove from the heat, taste and adjust seasonings. If the soup seems too thick you can add a little water.

Serves 6–8

Corn soup has become a part of Trinidad's street foods. At any public function or fete you can see vendors with their huge pots of soup for sale. It's especially popular at Carnival time for masqueraders and onlookers alike!

Seasoning peppers

'*Callaloo is a popular soup found on most islands, its roots steeped in African tradition. It really is a potful of greens with a good amount of fresh aromatics, seasoned up with hot peppers and enhanced with coconut milk. Crab is often added for extra flavour. The colour green may not seem appetizing but when you taste a Trinidadian callaloo, you will be hooked forever! When cooking dasheen bush leaves (callaloo) it's important to wash them first, then pinch off the leaf tips, as these may cause an allergic reaction for some. Enjoy your callaloo as a soup on its own or with rice, provisions and coo coo.*'

Callaloo soup

1 bunch dasheen bush (callaloo bush), washed and coarsely chopped

4 garlic cloves, minced

½ cup chopped West Indian pumpkin

1 onion, chopped

½ large bunch French thyme

2 tbs chopped celery

1 cup chopped chives

8 okra, sliced

1 hot pepper (habenero or Scotch bonnet), left whole

2 pimento peppers, seeded and chopped

2 whole blue crabs, cleaned and washed in lime juice

1 cup coconut milk

2 tbs butter

salt and freshly ground black pepper to taste

Put about 1 cup of water in a large heavy pot. Add the dasheen bush, garlic, pumpkin, onion, thyme, celery, chives, okra, peppers and crabs.

Bring to a boil, cover and simmer until all the ingredients are tender and very soft, about 30 minutes.

Stir in the coconut milk and cook for another 10 minutes.

Remove the whole pepper and crabs. Swizzle until smooth, stir in the butter, taste and add salt and freshly ground black pepper. Return the crabs to the pot and simmer for 5 minutes more.

Serves 6–8

Crabs for sale

Oxtail soup with cinnamon dumplings

1 tbs Trini fresh herb seasoning paste (see page 355)

2 lb lean oxtail, jointed

1 tbs vegetable oil

3 garlic cloves, minced

1 large onion, chopped

⅓ cup chopped chives

2 tbs chopped celery

1 pimento pepper, seeded and chopped

2 thyme sprigs

8 oz pumpkin, peeled and cubed

1 hot pepper, left whole

2 lb provisions (sweet potato, dasheen), cut into 2-inch pieces

Rub the herb seasoning onto the oxtail and marinate for about 30 minutes.

Add the oil to a large soup pot and sear the oxtail on both sides to brown. Add the garlic, onion, chives, celery, pimento pepper and thyme. Cover with about 8 cups water and boil until the oxtail is tender, 1 hour.

Skim off any fat and froth from the surface. Add more water if necessary and bring the soup back to a boil. Add the pumpkin and hot pepper and cook for another 15 minutes, until tender.

Add the provisions, stir, and cook for 15 minutes. Add dumplings and cook for another 10 minutes. Season with salt and freshly ground black pepper. Remove the hot pepper before serving.

Serves 4–6

Cinnamon dumplings

2 cups flour

1 tsp baking powder

1 tsp cinnamon

½ tsp salt

1 tsp butter

Place all ingredients in a mixing bowl and rub the butter into the flour until the mixture is grainy. Slowly add enough water to knead to a stiff dough. Cover and let rest for about 30 minutes.

Divide the dough into two pieces. Roll each piece into a long rope-like shape, about 12 inches in length. Cut into 2-inch lengths and drop into boiling soup.

Cowheel soup

2 lb cowheels, cleaned

1 tbs Trini fresh herb seasoning paste (see page 355)

3 garlic cloves, minced

1 large onion, chopped

⅓ cup chopped chives

1 pimento pepper, seeded and chopped

1 hot pepper, left whole

2 thyme sprigs

2 lb ground provisions, peeled and cut into 2-inch pieces

cinnamon dumplings (optional) (see previous page)

1 tsp freshly ground black pepper

Place the cowheels into a large soup pot and add the seasoning paste. Cover with about 8 cups water. Add the garlic, onion, chives, peppers and thyme. Boil until the cowheels are tender, about 2 hours.

Remove any excess fat. Add the provisions and cook until tender, about 15 minutes.

Add dumplings, if using, and cook for a further 10 minutes.

Season with the black pepper and salt to taste. Remove the hot pepper before serving.

Serves 4–6

Chicken foot soup

8 chicken feet, cleaned, or 1½ lb chicken pieces – wings, neck and back

1 carrot, sliced

1 onion, sliced

¼ cup thyme

6 garlic cloves, chopped

2 pimento peppers, seeded and chopped

½ cup chopped pumpkin

2 potatoes, peeled and cubed

8 cups water

salt and freshly ground black pepper

1 lb ground provisions, peeled and cut into 1-inch pieces

dumplings (optional) (see page 68)

Place all the ingredients except the provisions and dumplings into a large soup pot. Bring to a boil and cook on medium heat for 45 minutes.

If using chicken pieces, strain at this point then return the soup to the heat (chicken feet should not be strained as they can be enjoyed as part of the finished dish).

Add the provisions and dumplings, if using, and cook for a further 20 minutes.

Serves 4–6

Red bean soup

1 lb beef bones

2 tbs Trini fresh herb seasoning
paste (see page 355)

2 cups dried red beans, soaked
overnight

2 cups chopped pumpkin

4 garlic cloves

1 onion, chopped

1 cup chopped chives

¼ cup thyme

1 tbs chopped parsley

2 tbs chopped celery

1 hot pepper, left whole

1 carrot, chopped

1 lb ground provisions, peeled
and cut into 1-inch pieces

dumplings (see page 68)

1 tbs butter

Season the beef bones with the fresh herb paste.

Drain the red beans and place in a large saucepan. Cover with about 12 cups water and add the beef bones, pumpkin, garlic, onion, herbs, celery, hot pepper and carrot. Boil until the beans are tender, about 45 minutes.

Remove the hot pepper and season with salt and freshly ground black pepper.

Add the provisions and dumplings. The soup should be thick but if needed add a little more water.

Boil until the provisions are tender. Stir in the butter.

Serves 6

Black eye peas and coconut soup

There is no need to soak black eye peas prior to cooking.

1 cup dried black eye peas

1 cup chopped pumpkin

1 lb beef bones

4 garlic cloves, chopped

1 cup chopped chives

1 onion, chopped

¼ cup thyme

2 tbs chopped celery

1 hot pepper

2 cups coconut milk

1 lb ground provisions, peeled
and cut into 1-inch pieces

dumplings (see page 68)

Place the peas in a large soup pot. Add the pumpkin, beef bones, garlic, chives, onion, thyme, celery and hot pepper. Cover with water, about 4 cups, and boil until the beans are tender, about 30 minutes. Remove the hot pepper.

Season with salt and freshly ground black pepper. Stir in the coconut milk and bring to a simmer. Add the provisions and dumplings. If needed add a little more water. Boil until the provisions are tender.

Serves 6

stewed red beans

You can use this as a master recipe for any type of peas. There is no need to soak peas like lentils, split peas, pigeon peas or black eye – simply boil them until tender before stewing.

- **1 cup dried red beans**
- **1 tsp brown sugar**
- **2 tbs vegetable oil**
- **1 onion, finely chopped**
- **2 garlic cloves, chopped**
- **1 pimento pepper, seeded and chopped**
- **2 tbs French thyme**
- **½ cup chopped pumpkin**
- **⅓ cup tomato sauce or 2 tbs tomato ketchup**

Soak the beans the night before.

The next day, discard the water and place the beans in a pot. Cover with fresh water, add a pinch of brown sugar and boil until the beans are tender and the skins have burst, about 50 minutes.

Heat the oil in a saucepan and add the onion, garlic, pepper and thyme. Cook until the onion is very tender, about 6 minutes.

Add the pumpkin and peas, with their cooking liquid, to the pot. Stir in the remaining brown sugar and the tomato sauce or ketchup. Cook until bubbling, cover and simmer to let the flavours develop, about 20 minutes. Add salt to taste before serving.

Serves 6

Green fig salad

- **12 green figs**
- **4 garlic cloves, minced**
- **½ Congo pepper, seeded and finely chopped**
- **¼ cup apple cider vinegar or red wine vinegar**
- **juice of 1 lime**
- **½ tsp Dijon mustard**
- **¾ cup olive oil**
- **1 onion, finely sliced**
- **1 red pepper, seeded and chopped**
- **1 green pepper, seeded and chopped**
- **½ cup finely chopped mint or parsley**

Place the green figs in a non-reactive heavy saucepan. Add plenty of water and a little oil and boil for about 15 minutes until tender. Remove and cool, then peel and slice.

In a food processor combine the garlic, Congo pepper, vinegar, lime juice, mustard and salt and freshly ground black pepper. Purée until smooth. Add the olive oil and process until all ingredients are incorporated and smooth.

Toss the sliced green figs with the vinaigrette. Add the onions and green and red peppers, toss again, sprinkle with fresh herbs and serve.

Serves 4–6

Green figs

Taboulleh (parsley-wheat Salad)

This delicious salad originates from Syria/Lebanon. Make it in the morning if you want to serve it at dinnertime to allow the flavours to develop. Serve it with shish kebabs or any barbecued meat, or have it as a meal in itself.

2 cups bulgur wheat (from speciality or Syrian/ Lebanese food stores)

2 cups finely chopped fresh parsley

¾ cup chopped chives

½ cup chopped fresh mint or 2 tbs dried

6 small tomatoes, peeled, seeded and diced

½ cup fresh lemon juice

1 garlic clove, finely minced

½ cup olive oil

1 small head leaf lettuce, washed and dried

1 medium cucumber or 2 small, peeled and cubed

black olives (optional) and mint sprigs to garnish

Place the bulgur wheat in a large bowl, cover with boiling water and let stand for 1 hour, or until the bulgur has doubled in size and most of the liquid is absorbed.

Drain the bulgur and squeeze out extra moisture. Return to the bowl, fluff with a fork and add the parsley, chives, mint and tomatoes.

Make the dressing by combining the lemon juice, garlic and salt and freshly ground black pepper. Add the olive oil and whisk.

Toss the taboulleh mixture with the dressing. Refrigerate until ready to serve.

To serve, line a salad bowl with lettuce leaves. Mix the cucumber with the salad and place in the salad bowl.

Garnish with black olives, if wished, and sprigs of fresh mint.

Serves 8

A variety of seasonings

Macaroni salad

⅔ cup thick low-fat yogurt

⅓ cup low-fat mayonnaise

2 tbs flavoured vinegar

1 tsp minced garlic

2 tbs chopped sweet pickles (gherkins)

1 tbs spicy brown mustard

½ tsp salt, or to taste

1 tsp freshly ground black pepper, or to taste

8 oz dried elbow macaroni,
  cooked (4 cups cooked)

1 cup sliced chives

1 cup frozen green peas, defrosted

1 cup corn niblets

½ cup diced green pepper

½ cup diced carrots

¼ cup chopped celery

½ cup cubed cheddar cheese (optional)

2 tbs chopped parsley

In a small bowl combine the yogurt, mayonnaise, vinegar, garlic, pickles, mustard, salt and black pepper. Stir to combine.

In a large bowl combine the macaroni, chives, peas, corn, green pepper, carrots, celery and cheese, if using.

Add the mayonnaise mixture to the macaroni and toss well to coat. Chill until ready to serve. Add the parsley just before serving.

Serves 8–10

Creamy coleslaw

2 cups shredded cabbage

1 cup shredded carrot

2 tbs chopped celery

1 tsp grated onion

½ tsp sugar

½ cup mayonnaise (or more, to taste)

Combine all the ingredients and refrigerate until ready to serve.

Serves 4–6

spicy egg salad

2 hard-boiled eggs
½ tsp yellow mustard
1 tbs chopped chives
a little chopped tomato
1 tsp chopped red onion
dash of pepper sauce
1 tsp mayonnaise
salt and freshly ground black pepper (optional)

Peel the eggs and chop.
Combine with the rest of the ingredients and use as a sandwich filling.

Fills 2 sandwiches

Potato salad

1 cup mayonnaise
1 tbs vinegar
1 tbs Dijon mustard
1½ tsp salt
1 tsp freshly ground black pepper
¼ cup chopped celery
2 bell peppers, seeded and chopped
2 pimento peppers, seeded and chopped
1 cup chopped chives
2 cups steamed green peas or green beans
8 cups diced cooked potatoes (about 10 potatoes)
2 hard-boiled eggs, chopped
chopped parsley to garnish

Combine the mayonnaise in a large bowl with the vinegar, mustard, salt, and pepper.
Add the chopped celery, peppers, chives and peas. Fold in the potatoes and eggs. Mix well and taste and adjust seasonings.
Garnish with parsley.
Cover and refrigerate until ready to serve.

Serves 10–12

Easy green salad

1 small head lettuce

½ bunch watercress

1 small cucumber

1 small beet

1 small carrot

½ small red onion, thinly sliced

Vinaigrette

¼ cup red wine vinegar

1 garlic clove, minced

½ tsp salt

¾ cup olive oil

Make the vinaigrette by combining the vinegar, garlic and salt in a blender. Slowly pour in the olive oil and process to a thick emulsion. Season with freshly ground black pepper. Pour into a glass jar and refrigerate.

Wash the lettuce, dry and shred thickly. Wash the watercress and dry. Break into pieces and add to the lettuce.

Peel the cucumber and cut into julienne. Add to lettuce.

Peel the beet and carrot. Grate and add to lettuce. Add the onion and toss.

Add enough dressing to cover the vegetables and serve.

Serves 6

Cucumbers

Curried mango

6 large mangoes, preferably mango 'Rose', half-ripe stage

1 tsp saffron powder

1 tbs masala powder

1 tbs amchar masala

2 tbs vegetable oil

2 tbs granulated sugar

6 garlic cloves, minced

1 hot pepper, seeded and chopped

Wash and dry mangoes. Remove the stems and slice each mango in half, cutting through the seed. Cut each half lengthways into 1-inch wide slices.

Half-fill a medium saucepan with water and bring to a boil. Add the mangoes and cook for about 10 minutes until tender. Remove from the heat and drain.

In a small bowl combine the saffron powder, masala and amchar masala with ⅓ cup water. Stir to a smooth consistency.

Heat the oil in a medium iron or cast-iron pot. Add the sugar and heat until it has become a caramel colour. Add the curry paste and cook for a few seconds stirring constantly.

Add the garlic and pepper, stir. Add the mangoes and stir to combine with the curry paste until all the pieces are coated. Add about ½ cup water and season with salt and freshly ground black pepper.

Cover and cook for about 20 minutes, stirring occasionally and adding just a little water to prevent sticking.

Taste and adjust seasonings, adding a little more salt and sugar to balance flavours if the mango is too sour.

Serves 6–8

❛ Curried mango is popular when mangoes are in season. It is a great accompaniment to any curry and is often cooked and served at a celebratory meal or wedding feast. Foods are still sometimes served on soharee leaves (similar to banana leaves) during Hindu celebrations. ❜

Clockwise from top: Paratha roti, curried channa with potato, curried mango, smashed pumpkin with garlic and pepper

Stuffed eggplant

1 eggplant

¼ cup olive oil

2 garlic cloves, minced

1 small onion, minced

1 tomato, diced

1 green sweet pepper, diced

1 cup cooked rice

½ cup chopped fresh mint or 1 tsp dried

Preheat the oven to 350°F.

Cut the eggplant lengthways and scoop out the flesh, leaving about ½ inch inside the shell. Dice the eggplant flesh.

Place the shells cut side down in a large pan with about ½ inch boiling salted water. Cover and steam for about 3 minutes. Drain and reserve.

Heat 2 tablespoons olive oil in a sauté pan and add the garlic and onion. Sauté until fragrant.

Add the eggplant flesh and sauté for about 2 minutes.

Add the tomatoes, sweet pepper and cooked rice. Stir to combine. Season with salt and freshly ground black pepper. Stir in the mint, taste and adjust seasonings.

Divide the mixture into two and stuff into the eggplant shells. Drizzle with the remaining olive oil.

Place in a heatproof casserole dish and add about ¼ inch water. Bake for about 30 minutes until the shells are tender.

Serves 2–4

Eggplant soufflé

3 lb eggplants

2 tbs olive oil

1½ cups minced onions

3 garlic cloves, crushed

¼ cup chopped parsley

4 tbs butter

5 tbs all-purpose flour

1½ cups hot milk

3 egg yolks

½ cup coarsely grated cheese

6 egg whites

Roast, bake or steam the eggplants until just tender, about 20–30 minutes. Scoop out the flesh and set aside.

Preheat the oven to 400°F. Place a roasting pan with 1 inch of water in it on a rack in the lower middle section of the oven. Make a foil collar around the top of a soufflé dish.

Heat the olive oil in a sauté pan and sauté the onions until tender. Add the garlic and then the eggplant. Season with salt and freshly ground black pepper. Continue to cook until the eggplant is soft, about 15 minutes. Add the parsley and set aside.

Make the sauce by melting the butter in a heavy saucepan. Add the flour and cook until the mixture is smooth. Add the milk and stir continuously until thick.

Beat the yolks into the white sauce, then fold in the eggplant and the cheese and season with salt and pepper.

Beat the egg whites until stiff. Stir a quarter of them into the eggplant mixture. Delicately fold in the rest of the egg whites.

Turn the soufflé mixture into the prepared dish. Bake for 1¼ hours until risen and puffed.

Serves 8

Crispy fried eggplant

1 large eggplant

1 egg

½ cup flour

1 tbs chopped French thyme

½ tsp freshly ground black pepper

1 cup fine cracker crumbs

vegetable oil for frying

Slice the eggplant into ¼-inch thick slices. Sprinkle with salt and let stand for 15 minutes. Rinse the eggplant and pat dry with paper towels.

Beat the egg and place in a wide shallow bowl.

Place the flour on a plate and combine with the thyme and pepper. Place the cracker crumbs on another plate.

Heat some oil in a large non-stick frying pan.

Dredge the eggplant slices in flour, then dip into the egg, then roll in the cracker crumbs.

Fry in the hot oil, turning, until golden. Drain on paper towels and serve immediately.

Serves 4

'Jhingi is a long thin green vegetable resembling a cucumber. It is a member of the melon family and has a flavour resembling that of christophene or zucchini.'

Jhingi

2 tbs vegetable oil

2 garlic cloves, chopped

1 onion, sliced

1 hot pepper, seeded and chopped

2 jhingi, peeled and sliced

Heat the vegetable oil in a sauté pan and add the garlic, onion and pepper. Sauté until fragrant.

Add the jhingi and stir and fry for a few minutes. Lower the heat, cover and simmer for about 10 minutes.

Remove the lid, increase the heat and cook until any liquid has dried.

Enjoy with any meat, fish or chicken dish.

Serves 4

Cauliflower tomato casserole

1 large cauliflower, washed and cut into segments

4 tomatoes, chopped

½ cup chopped fresh herbs

½ cup cracker crumbs

2 garlic cloves, chopped

1 cup grated cheese

Preheat the oven to 375°F.

Steam the cauliflower until tender crisp, about 8 minutes.

Grease a shallow baking dish and arrange the tomatoes over the base. Sprinkle with the herbs and some salt. Place the drained cauliflower on top.

Combine the cracker crumbs with the garlic and cheese. Sprinkle over the cauliflower and bake for about 20 minutes until brown and crisp on top.

Serves 4

'*In Trinidad and Tobago we use the term 'bhaji' to describe any dark leafy vegetable cooked with aromatics – our local spinach, callaloo or dasheen bush, or bok choy (pak choi).*'

Sautéed spinach (bhaji)

Enjoy this with dhal and rice or with sada roti.

1 large bunch spinach
2 tbs olive oil
1 large onion, chopped
4 garlic cloves, chopped
1 hot pepper, seeded and chopped

Clean the spinach, remove any flowering tips and hard stems, then chop. Wash well to remove any sandy residue.

Heat the oil in a sauté pan and add the onion, garlic and pepper. Sauté until fragrant.

Add the spinach and cook until wilted. Add salt and freshly ground black pepper, cover and steam. Cook, adding as little water as possible, for about 15 minutes.

Remove the lid, increase the heat and cook until all the liquid has evaporated.

Adjust the seasonings to taste and serve.

Serves 4

Note
You may use callaloo or dasheen bush in place of the spinach. Remove the tips of the leaves, and cook in the same way but for a longer time – about 30 minutes, until completely soft. You may add about ½ cup coconut milk during cooking.

Bok choy (pak choi) may also be substituted for the spinach and cooked the same way.

Dasheen bush leaves

Curried cabbage

1 tbs vegetable oil
2 garlic cloves, chopped
½ small onion, sliced
2 tsp curry powder
1 lb cabbage, shredded

Heat the oil in a frying pan and add the garlic and onion. Cook for a few minutes then add the curry powder and cook until the mixture is almost dry.

Add the cabbage and stir well. Cook until wilted, about 5 minutes.

Season with salt and cook for a few minutes more.

Serves 4

Glazed carrots with orange

1 tbs unsalted butter
¾ cup orange juice
1 tbs minced ginger
1 lb carrots, cut into ¼-inch thick diagonal slices
¼ cup chopped parsley

Melt the butter in a medium saucepan. Add the orange juice and ginger and bring to a boil.

Add the carrots and cook until tender crisp, about 8 minutes.

Drain the carrots and save the juices. Return juices to the pan and heat until the mixture has reduced to a thick glaze. Return the carrots to the pan and toss.

Season to taste with salt and freshly ground black pepper. Sprinkle with chopped parsley before serving.

Serves 4

'Christophenes are also called choyote squash in Spanish Caribbean countries.'

Christophene gratin

1 lb christophene

8 oz cauliflower, cut into pieces

8 oz carrots, sliced

½ cup dried breadcrumbs

½ cup chopped parsley

1 tsp dried oregano

1 tsp salt

1 tsp freshly ground black pepper

⅓ cup grated parmesan cheese

1 tsp minced garlic

⅓ cup olive oil

Preheat the oven to 375°F.

Peel the christophenes, slice in half lengthways then cut into ½-inch thick pieces.

Sprinkle the vegetables with a little salt and steam for 5 minutes. Drain.

Combine the breadcrumbs with the parsley, oregano, salt, pepper, parmesan and garlic. Add 1 tablespoon oil and mix.

Lightly grease a casserole dish. Place the vegetables in the dish and sprinkle with the crumb mixture. Drizzle with the remaining olive oil.

Bake for 30 minutes until the crust is browned.

Serves 6–8

Christophene salad

1 christophene, cut into julienne and lightly steamed.

1 red sweet pepper, cut into julienne

1 cucumber, cut into julienne

1 carrot, cut into julienne

½ cup finely chopped parsley or chives

Vinaigrette

1 garlic clove

¼ cup apple cider vinegar or red wine vinegar

¾ cup olive oil

salt and freshly ground black pepper to taste

Place the vegetable strips in a salad dish.

Combine all the ingredients for the vinaigrette and pour enough over the vegetables to coat (you will not need it all). Toss.

Sprinkle with fresh parsley or chives. Refrigerate until ready to serve.

Serves 4–6

Creamy christophene

1 christophene, cut into pieces

½ cauliflower, cut into pieces

1 carrot, sliced

2 tbs unsalted butter

2 tbs all-purpose flour

1 garlic clove, minced

2 cups milk

⅛ tsp grated nutmeg

⅓ cup chopped chives

½ cup grated cheese (optional)

Preheat the oven to 350°F.

Steam the vegetables until tender. Drain and place in a greased vegetable casserole.

Melt the butter in a small saucepan. Add the flour and stir until the mixture is incorporated and becomes slack in the pan.

Add the garlic and stir. Add the milk and cook until smooth and thick.

Stir in the nutmeg, chives and cheese, if using. Season with salt and freshly ground black pepper.

Pour over the vegetables and bake until heated through, about 15 minutes.

Serves 4–6

Christophene salad

Curried seim and pigeon peas

1 tbs vegetable oil

2 garlic cloves, chopped

1 onion, thinly sliced

1 hot pepper, seeded and chopped

2 tbs curry powder mixed with ⅓ cup water

1 lb fresh seim, string removed and cut into 1-inch pieces,

1 cup cooked pigeon peas

1 tomato, chopped

Heat the oil in a sauté pan and add the garlic, onion and pepper. Cook until fragrant and the onion is beginning to turn brown. Add the curry paste and cook until the liquid has evaporated.

Add the seim and stir to combine. Add the pigeon peas and tomato and stir. Add a small amount of water and cover. Cook for 30 minutes until tender, stirring occasionally and only adding water when necessary.

Serves 4–6

Seim

Sautéed carailli (bitter melon)

1 lb carailli, cut into ½-inch pieces, seeds removed

2 tbs vegetable oil

4 onions, sliced

2 pimento peppers, seeded and chopped

6 garlic cloves, chopped

1 tomato, chopped

½ hot pepper, seeded and chopped (optional)

If wished, sprinkle the carailli pieces with salt. Leave for about 20 minutes then squeeze and rinse under cool water.

Heat the oil in a sauté pan and add the onions, pepper and garlic. Sauté until fragrant. Add the carailli, tomato and hot pepper, if using.

Cover and cook for about 15 minutes until tender, adding a small amount of water, if necessary, to prevent sticking.

Serves 4

Stuffed carailli (khalounji)

A traditional East Indian dish, the carailli is stuffed with a spicy masala mixture.

4 carailli

2 tbs vegetable oil

4 onions, finely chopped

6 garlic cloves, finely chopped

1 hot pepper, seeded and chopped

4 tbs ground masala

1 tsp salt

2 tbs ground geera (cumin)

Cut long slits in the carailli and scoop out the seeds. Remove the seed covering and reserve with the seeds.

Heat half the oil in a sauté pan and add the onions, garlic and pepper. Cook until fragrant, about 3 minutes.

Add the seeds and coverings and cook for a few minutes more. Add the masala and salt. Remove from the heat and stir in the geera.

Stuff the mixture back into the carailli and tie with string to secure.

Heat the remaining oil in a frying pan and fry the stuffed carailli lightly until brown. Add a little water, cover and cook until just tender, about 10 minutes.

Remove the lid and cook until the liquid has evaporated. Drain on paper towels and remove the string.

Slice and serve as an accompaniment to rice or roti.

Serves 6

Pickled carailli

1 small carailli

1 onion

1 carrot, sliced

1 hot pepper, seeded and chopped

2-4 cups white vinegar

Slice the carailli and remove the seeds. Slice the onion thinly.

Place the caralli and onion in a large glass jar. Add the carrot and pepper.

Pour enough vinegar into the jar to completely cover the vegetables. Add some salt.

Cover and let stand for about 2-3 days.

Serve as a pickle alongside any main dish (refrigerate after opening).

Makes 1 large jar

spicy fried okra

This okra dish is traditionally served with sada roti.

18 okra

2 tbs vegetable oil

6 garlic cloves, chopped

1 large onion, thinly sliced

1 hot pepper, halved, seeds removed

Remove the stems and tips from the okra. Thinly slice and set aside.

Heat the oil in sauté pan and add the garlic, onion and pepper. Cook until the onion is translucent.

Add the sliced okra and season with salt. Turn and cook until the okra begins to soften.

Lower the heat and cook the okra uncovered, stirring occasionally to prevent sticking – do not add water. Cook until the okra have reduced in volume and have become browned around the edges, about 20 minutes.

Taste and adjust seasoning and serve hot with sada roti.

Serves 4

steamed okra

Quarter-fill a saucepan with water. Place a steamer insert into the pan.

Bring to a boil and add a little salt. Place the washed uncut okra into the steamer and cover. Steam until brightly coloured and tender, about 10 minutes.

Remove and drizzle with olive oil.

Enjoy with stewed fish.

Curried chataigne

3 lb chataigne or breadnut

2 tbs oil

1 tbs chopped garlic

1 onion, finely chopped

1 hot pepper, seeded and chopped

2 tbs curry powder mixed with
   ¼ cup water

1 cup coconut milk

Peel the chataigne, remove the pulp and separate from the seeds. Peel the seeds by removing the outer shell. Reserve both seeds and outer shell. Cut up or break the pulp into 1-inch pieces.

Heat the oil in a sauté pan and add the garlic, onion and hot pepper. Cook until fragrant, about 10 minutes.

Add the curry paste. Let it sizzle and cook until almost dry.

Add the chataigne, stir well, season with salt and add the coconut milk. Lower the heat and cook for about 50 minutes, stirring occasionally and adding a small amount of water to prevent sticking.

When the seeds are tender the chataigne will be cooked. Taste and adjust seasoning before serving.

Serves 4

‘Chataigne is a delicious vegetable, very popular at Divali time (‘the festival of lights’).’

Veggie lo mein

1 tsp cornstarch mixed with
¼ cup water

2 tbs soy sauce

2 tbs oyster sauce

1 tbs sherry or rum

1 tsp Chinese chilli sauce

1 tsp sesame oil

12 oz thin Chinese egg noodles

1 tbs vegetable oil

3 garlic cloves, minced

1 tbs shredded ginger

1 cup julienne carrots

1 cup julienne christophene

2 cups shredded bok choy (pak
choi)

1 cup sliced mushrooms

½ cup sliced water chestnuts

1 cup baby corn

½ cup sliced chives

In a small bowl combine the cornstarch mixture, soy sauce, oyster sauce, sherry, chilli sauce and sesame oil.

Boil the noodles according to the package directions, drain and rinse.

Heat the oil in a wok or frying pan, add the garlic and ginger and stir-fry until fragrant. Add the carrots, christophene, bok choy, mushrooms and water chestnuts. Stir and fry until the vegetables are tender crisp.

Add the noodles and toss. Add the baby corn, chives and sauce and cook stirring until the noodles are coated with the sauce and heated through.

Serves 4-6

"Bodi (long beans) is used in much the same way as green beans. It can be steamed with carrots or curried or sautéed and served as a side dish."

Curried bodi

For sautéed bodi simply omit the curry powder.

2 tbs vegetable oil

½ onion, sliced

2 garlic cloves, chopped

½ hot pepper, seeded and sliced

1 tbs curry powder mixed with ¼ cup water

1 bunch bodi, tips removed and cut into 1-inch lengths

Heat the oil in a sauté pan and add the onion, garlic and hot pepper. Cook for a few minutes then add the curry paste and cook until the mixture is dry. Add the bodi, toss well and add salt.

Cover and cook for about 8 minutes.

Remove the lid and continue cooking until tender, about 5 minutes.

Serves 4

Topi tambo sauté

**1 lb topi tambo, boiled for
  15 minutes and peeled**

2 tbs vegetable oil

3 garlic cloves, chopped

juice of 2 lemons

1 tsp lemon zest

2 tbs chopped parsley

1 tbs chopped basil (optional)

Slice the topi tambo in half lengthways.

Heat the oil in a large sauté pan. When hot add the garlic and
sauté until fragrant. Add the topi tambo and toss. Remove from
the heat and stand for 5 minutes.

Add the lemon juice and return to a low heat. Continue to cook
until the lemon juice has thickened somewhat.

Season with salt and freshly ground black pepper. Sprinkle with
the lemon zest and fresh herbs, remove from the heat and serve.

Serves 4

*Topi tambo is an oblong, light
brown, hairy, thin-skinned tuber,
only available around January. The
texture resembles that of a water
chestnut. It's usually boiled in lots
of salted water until tender, about
60 minutes. Then the skin is peeled
and it can be enjoyed as a snack.*

Topi tambo

Topi tambo and vegetable stir-fry

1 tbs vegetable oil
½ tbs minced ginger
½ tbs minced garlic
1 cup cauliflower segments
1 carrot, peeled and sliced
1 large sweet pepper, cut into chunks
1 small zucchini or cucumber, sliced
8 oz topi tambo, boiled, peeled and sliced

Sauce
1 tbs oyster sauce
1 tbs soy sauce
1 tsp sesame oil
¼ cup vegetable stock or water
½ tsp sugar
2 tsp cornstarch

Mix all the ingredients for the sauce and set aside.

Heat the oil in wok, add the ginger and garlic and stir-fry until fragrant. Add the cauliflower and carrot and stir-fry for about 2 minutes.

Add the pepper and zucchini together with 1 tablespoon water to steam cook the vegetables. Add the topi tambo.

Stir in the sauce and cook until bubbling and thick.

Serves 4

Tomato choka

‘ Choka is an East Indian method of preparing vegetables. They are roasted, usually over an open flame, then combined with garlic, onions and peppers. Chokas are usually enjoyed with sada roti or as a vegetable side dish for a curry meal. Melongene choka and tomato choka are the most popular. ’

108

Tomato choka

If preferred, roast the tomatoes rather than boiling them. It will intensify the tomato flavour.

1 lb tomatoes

1 onion, finely chopped

½ Congo pepper, seeded and chopped (more or less, to taste)

2 tbs vegetable oil

3 garlic cloves, chopped

Boil the tomatoes in a medium saucepan until tender, about 10 minutes. Drain and peel.

Place the hot tomatoes in a mixing bowl and add the onion and pepper.

Heat the oil in a small frying pan to smoking. Add the garlic and cook to a sizzle or until the garlic turns light brown.

Remove and pour the hot garlic oil into the tomatoes. Mix well. Season with salt and freshly ground black pepper.

Serve with sada roti.

Serves 4

Melongene choka

This choka is even more delicious if two or three tomatoes are added: roast the tomatoes over a hot fire until tender or boil for a few minutes, peel and crush, then add to the melongene.

2 large melongenes (eggplants), 4–5 lb in total

1 onion, finely chopped

¼ cup vegetable oil

6 garlic cloves, chopped

2 pimento peppers, seeded and chopped

1 hot pepper, seeded and chopped

chopped parsley to garnish

Roast the melongenes whole on an open flame, do not puncture or cut up. Remove once they are limp and very soft.

Place on a chopping board. Remove the stem and cut directly down the middle. Using a spoon, scoop out the flesh, leaving the charred skin behind. Place in a dish and add the onion.

Heat the oil in a small frying pan and add the garlic and peppers. Cook until the garlic is just beginning to turn golden brown – any longer and the garlic will become bitter.

Pour the hot oil with the peppers and garlic into the melongene.

Combine and add salt and freshly ground black pepper to taste. Sprinkle with parsley and serve.

Serves 4

Pumpkin is enjoyed often in Trini cuisine. It's what thickens our peas, flavours up our soups and is popular as an accompaniment to Indian foods and roti when it is sautéed with onions and garlic and mashed.

smashed pumpkin with garlic and pepper

2 tbs vegetable oil

1 onion, sliced

4 garlic cloves, chopped

1 hot pepper, seeded and chopped

1 lb pumpkin, peeled and cubed

Heat oil in a sauté pan and add the onion, garlic and hot pepper. Cook for a few minutes until fragrant then add the pumpkin and stir.

Add a tablespoon of water, cover and cook on a medium heat for about 10 minutes.

Remove the lid. Mash the pumpkin, add salt and continue cooking until all the liquid has dried up. Serve warm.

Serves 4

Fried potato Indian style

This is a favourite from my childhood. Enjoy it hot with freshly made sada roti.

4 large potatoes

4 tbs vegetable oil

6 garlic cloves, chopped

1 onion, thinly sliced

1 hot pepper, seeded and sliced

Peel the potatoes, cut in half and then into very thin slices.

Heat the oil in a non-stick sauté pan and add the garlic, onion and pepper. Cook until the onion is tender. Add the potato and cook on a medium heat, turning frequently and scraping the bottom of the pan.

After about 5 minutes, lower the heat and cover. Steam cook for another 5–8 minutes.

Remove the lid, season with salt and cook until the potatoes are tender, scraping the bottom to get all the crispy browned pieces into the mixture. The potatoes should have lost a lot of their moisture and be flecked with brown.

Serve hot with sada roti.

Serves 4

Fishing in Manzanilla

Fish and seafood

Trinidad and Tobago is surrounded by the fertile Atlantic Ocean, the Caribbean Sea, the Columbus Channel and the Gulf of Paria. We are privileged to be able to fish our waters and enjoy fresh fish and seafood on a daily basis for breakfast, lunch and dinner. I remember many an early morning while holidaying in the seaside town of Mayaro, standing next to the fishermen as they pulled in their gigantic seines crammed full of all types of fish and creatures from the Atlantic.

Fish is consumed in many different forms: fresh, dried and salted, as in smoked herring and salted cod (bacalao), a gift given to us by our Portuguese ancestors. A dazzling array of fresh fish fills our fishermen's nets every day. The more popular types consumed are king fish, carite (a delicate white flavourful fish), red snapper, white salmon – another delicious white fish – ancho (a dark-fleshed, rich-tasting fish), bouchee (a dense-fleshed fish), shark, grouper – usually sold by the slice due to its large size – cutlass, a long thin fish with its tail part resembling a cutlass (large knife), herring, catfish, pompano and bonito. There are also lots of shrimp, black-shelled small conchs and crabs.

Tiny oysters are consumed in fiery tomato-based concoctions sold by street-side oyster vendors, popular mainly for the touted aphrodisiac properties! Chip chip, a tiny mollusc, is dug by the thousands from the sands on the east coast beaches from Manzanilla to Mayaro. The beach gets so overpopulated with these tiny creatures around February to May that you could simply sit on the sand and dig up a few hundred in a matter of minutes! We enjoy these either curried or in a cocktail. Cascadura and blue crabs are sold by street vendors as soon as they are caught, as are spiny lobsters.

Fish and seafood are enjoyed in many ways: fried, curried, stewed, barbecued, in hot fiery fish broths, baked and stuffed. Of course they are always tasty due to being marinated in our fresh herbs and hot peppers. Salted and smoked fish are usually prepared in fish salads (buljols) and also in accras.

River fish for sale

If there is one cooking method we Trinis have mastered it's the art of currying. We've managed through the years to curry just about anything! Why? you may ask. Because curry always tastes good and some see it as a foolproof method of flavouring foods. We have done such a great job that curried foods have become part of our culinary heritage – a real treat!

Curry is so popular on this island that manufacturers have perfected the art of what is traditionally known as 'our' very own curry powder mix. Driving past a curry factory, the aroma of roasted spice stimulates the nostrils and is a piquant reminder of this diverse and delicious heritage!

There is a great variety of powders to choose from; you'll encounter vindaloo curry, duck and goat masala, spicy and mild, to name but a few. Local curry powder is made with fenugreek, coriander, cumin, garlic, turmeric powder, ajwain and curry leaves. Colour will also differ with these powders, ranging from yellowish to greenish. The more yellow in colour the milder the taste of the curry and the larger the quantity of turmeric powder in the mix – this is a favoured curry for seafood, fish and vegetables. The 'greener' or darker the curry the more intense the flavour – better for beef, goat and duck.

Curries can be used to bring up the flavour of dips, spreads and batters. You can even add it to rice for an exotic twist. If you like the taste of curry – and who doesn't? – you'll be surprised how a little can go a long way!

Curried fish with coconut

1 lb fresh fish fillets, cut into 4 portions

1 tbs vegetable oil

2 garlic cloves, minced

1 small onion, finely chopped

2 tbs finely chopped fresh chives or spring onions, green and white parts

1 hot pepper, seeded and cut into strips

2 tbs coconut milk powder

4 tsp curry powder

½ tsp fresh lime juice

Clean and wash the fish fillets. Sprinkle lightly with salt and freshly ground black pepper.

Heat the oil in a medium sauté pan and add the garlic, onion, chives and hot pepper. Sauté until fragrant, about 1 minute.

Mix the coconut powder with ¼ cup water and add the curry powder. Stir to mix.

Add to the pot and bring to a boil. Reduce the heat and simmer for about 10 minutes.

Season with salt and pepper. Add the fish fillets and cook for about 4 minutes on each side, basting frequently with the sauce.

Remove from the heat, adjust the seasonings, sprinkle with the lime juice and serve immediately.

Serves 4

Curried fish

This dish goes well with steamed basmati rice and a cooked vegetable or fresh salad.

Adding green mango or tamarind chutney to a fish curry releases a bit of acidity, which deepens the overall flavour of the dish.

3½ lb king fish, sliced into 1-inch thick slices

2 garlic cloves, minced

2 tbs Trini fresh herb seasoning paste (see page 355)

2 tbs vegetable oil

1 small onion, finely sliced

1 pimento pepper, seeded and chopped

½ hot pepper, seeded and chopped

2 tbs curry powder

1 green mango, cut into 8, or 2 tbs tamarind chutney

1 tbs chopped Spanish thyme or chadon beni (cilantro)

½ tsp fresh lime juice

Clean and wash the fish slices, removing the small whitish substance from the side of the bone. Sprinkle the fish lightly with salt and freshly ground black pepper, season with the garlic and the herb paste. Marinate, covered, in the refrigerator for about 30 minutes.

Heat the oil in a medium sauté pan, and add the onion, pimento and hot pepper. Sauté until fragrant, about 1 minute.

Mix the curry powder with ¼ cup water and stir. Add to the pot and stir and fry until the mixture is very dry.

Add the fish slices and cook for about 4 minutes on each side, basting frequently with the sauce. Cover and simmer. The fish will release some juices. Cook for a few minutes more.

Meanwhile, if using green mango, steam the slices for 5 minutes until tender. Drain.

Add the mango or tamarind to the fish and simmer for about 5 minutes more. Taste and adjust seasoning, add Spanish thyme or chadon beni and cook for 1 more minute.

Remove from the heat and serve with lime juice sprinkled over.

Serves 4

Shrimp curry

1½ lb medium shrimp

2 garlic cloves, minced

2 tbs vegetable oil

4 tsp curry powder

1 tbs minced chives

1 tbs minced ginger

½ hot pepper, seeded and chopped

1 pimento pepper, seeded and chopped

1 tomato, chopped

2 tbs dark rum

½ cup chicken stock

Peel and devein shrimp and marinate in half the garlic, salt and black pepper. Mix the curry powder with ¼ cup water.

Heat the oil in a sauté pan, add the remaining garlic and curry paste and stir until sizzling.

Add the chives, ginger and peppers and cook for 2 minutes longer.

Add the tomato, rum and chicken stock. Add salt, cover and simmer for about 10 minutes, until the mixture is reduced by about half.

Add the shrimp and cook gently until shrimp just begin to curl, about 5 minutes.

Serve hot with steaming hot jasmine rice.

Serves 4

River fishing

Grilled carite with tomato coriander salsa

1 tsp vegetable oil

1 tbs minced chives

2 garlic cloves, minced

1 tsp ground coriander

4 carite fillets (each 5–6 oz) or any other fresh fish

1 tbs chopped chadon beni (cilantro) (optional)

Salsa

4 ripe tomatoes

½ green hot pepper, seeded and chopped

1½ tbs fresh lime juice

2 large garlic cloves, minced

2 tsp olive oil

1 tbs coriander seeds, toasted and ground.

½ tsp salt

1 tsp freshly ground black pepper

¼ cup finely chopped chadon beni (cilantro)

About 20–30 minutes before cooking mix the vegetable oil with the chives and garlic. Stir in 1 teaspoon ground coriander and add salt and freshly ground black pepper to taste.

Wash the fish and pat dry. Spread the marinade over both sides of each fillet, cover and refrigerate.

Meanwhile make the salsa. Peel, seed and chop the tomatoes. Add the hot pepper, lime juice, garlic, oil and the ground coriander. Season with the salt and pepper and set aside.

Broil the carite fillets under a preheated broiler for about 3–5 minutes on each side.

Add the fresh chadon beni to the salsa.

Serve the fish topped with the salsa. Sprinkle with fresh chadon beni if desired.

Serves 4

Coo coo and fish roll

Serve this dish as a light dinner or part of a brunch or lunch buffet.

1 onion, sliced

4 garlic cloves

1 tbs French thyme

2 blades chive, chopped

2 lb fresh fish fillets

juice of 1 lime

1 hot pepper, seeded and chopped

2 pimento peppers, seeded and chopped

½ cup chopped chives

6 Spanish thyme leaves

1 chadon beni (cilantro) leaf

½ cup low-fat mayonnaise

Coo coo

6 cups seasoned chicken stock

8 oz fresh okra, finely chopped

2 pimento peppers, seeded and chopped

2 garlic cloves, minced

3 cups yellow cornmeal

vegetable oil for coating

To prepare the coo coo, bring 5 cups chicken stock to a boil in a large saucepan. Add the okra, peppers, garlic and salt and freshly ground black pepper. Simmer for 15 minutes until the okra is tender.

Add the rest of the stock and bring back to a boil. Remove the pot from the heat.

Pour in the cornmeal, whisking vigorously to prevent lumping. Stir well and cook until the mixture becomes stiff and smooth and moves away from the sides of the pot.

Divide into two portions. Rub a generous amount of vegetable oil over the coo coo. Cover and set aside.

Bring some water to a boil in a sauté pan. Add the onion, half the garlic, the thyme and chive. Add the fish and steam for about 10 minutes until opaque and tender.

Drain and remove the fish. Pour the lime juice over then place in the bowl of a food processor. Add the peppers, remaining garlic and the herbs. Purée to a thick paste. Add enough mayonnaise to bring it to a creamy consistency.

Oil two pieces of waxed paper about 15 inches long. Place half the coo coo on top of one piece and cover with the second piece. Roll out the coo coo between the sheets of paper to about ½ inch thickness.

Spread the fish onto the coo coo and gently roll up, using the oiled paper to help. Wrap tightly in plastic and refrigerate for about 1 hour. Repeat with the remaining coo coo.

Serve at room temperature. Before serving, slice on the diagonal into ½-inch thick pieces. Serve on its own or with tomato salsa.

Serves 6–8

Garlicky flying fish fry

Flying fish native to the island of Tobago is typically sold frozen, six fillets to a pack, ready to prepare.

2 tsp salt

1 lime

2 packs frozen flying fish, defrosted, or 10 flying fish fillets

1 tbs olive oil

8 garlic cloves, minced

2 tbs minced herbs (chives, parsley, thyme)

1 tsp freshly ground black pepper

½ cup all-purpose flour

2 cups breadcrumbs or cracker crumbs

2 eggs

vegetable oil for frying

Fill a bowl with water, add the salt and squeeze the lime into the water. Soak the fish fillets in this solution for 5 minutes. Remove the fish, rinse and drain well.

Combine the olive oil with the garlic, herbs and pepper. Rub this mixture onto the fish fillets, taking care to fill the openings on the fillets with some of the mixture.

Place the flour on one plate, the crumbs on another.

Lightly beat the eggs and place in a shallow dish.

Dredge the fish in the flour. Shake off any excess, then dip in the egg. Dredge in the crumbs.

Heat the oil in a frying pan. Fry the fish for a few minutes on each side, just until golden. Drain and serve at once.

Serves 4-6

Batter-fried flying fish

2 tsp salt

1 lime

2 packs frozen flying fish, defrosted, or 10 flying fish fillets

1 tbs olive oil

8 garlic cloves, minced

2 tbs minced herbs (chives, parsley, thyme)

1 tsp freshly ground black pepper

vegetable oil for frying

Batter

1 cup all-purpose flour

½ tsp baking powder

1 egg

milk

Fill a bowl with water, add the salt and squeeze the lime into the water. Soak the fish fillets in this solution for 5 minutes. Remove the fish, rinse and drain well.

Combine the olive oil with the garlic, herbs and pepper. Rub this mixture onto the fish fillets, taking care to fill the openings on the fillets with some of the mixture.

Combine the batter ingredients, adding enough milk to mix to a smooth batter.

Dip the fish in the batter and shake off any excess.

Heat the oil in a frying pan. Fry the fish for a few minutes on each side, just until golden.

Drain and serve at once

Serves 4–6

Fish in black bean sauce

This dish is easy and quick. It is delicious whatever type of fish you use. Serve it with plain boiled basmati rice and sautéed mixed vegetables.

¼ cup rice wine

1-inch piece fresh ginger, peeled and grated

6 fish fillets, cut into 1-inch cubes

1 tsp sesame oil

2 tbs black bean sauce

1 tsp hot chilli paste

½ tsp sugar

2 tbs cornstarch plus 1 tsp

1–2 tbs vegetable oil

4 garlic cloves, chopped finely

In a small bowl mix together the rice wine and half the ginger. Add the fish and marinate for about 30 minutes.

In another bowl make the sauce by mixing together ¼ cup water, the sesame oil, black bean sauce, chilli paste and sugar.

Mix 1 teaspoon cornstarch with a little water and set aside.

Drain the fish and dredge in the remaining cornstarch.

Heat about 1 tablespoon oil in a wok. When hot add the fish a few pieces at a time and brown. Remove from the wok and drain.

Add the garlic and remaining ginger and stir-fry until fragrant. Add the sauce and stir-fry briefly.

Add the fish pieces and toss until all the pieces are covered with sauce.

Add the cornstarch mixture and stir until the sauce thickens. Remove from the heat and serve immediately.

Serves 6

Calypso shrimp

1½ lb medium shrimp, peeled and deveined

2 garlic cloves, chopped

2 tbs olive oil

½ Congo pepper, seeded and chopped

3 ripe tomatoes, chopped

½ cup chopped chives

1 tbs fresh French thyme

¼ cup golden rum (optional)

½ cup chopped basil

Sprinkle the shrimp with salt and freshly ground black pepper, and ½ teaspoon garlic.

Heat the oil in a sauté pan, add the remaining garlic and the pepper and sauté until fragrant. Add the tomatoes, chives and thyme and sauté for about 2–4 minutes until the tomatoes begin to soften.

Drop in the shrimp and sauté until pink and curled. If using rum, tilt the pan towards the flame and pour in the rum. Flambé.

Turn out onto a platter and sprinkle with the fresh basil.

Serve with steamed basmati rice and a green salad.

Serves 4

Crispy fried fish

Dried cracker crumbs make this fried fish sensational – the crust is really crisp and the fish delicious and tender!

2 lb fresh fish fillets, cut into 8 pieces

2 tbs minced chives

½ tbs minced celery

½ tbs thyme

4 garlic cloves, minced

1 tbs lime juice

1 tbs olive oil

1 tsp salt

1 tsp freshly ground black pepper

1 cup cracker crumbs

½ cup flour

1 egg, lightly beaten

vegetable oil for frying

Wash the fish. Combine the chives, celery, thyme, garlic, lime juice, olive oil, salt and pepper. Rub the marinade over the fish and let marinate for 20 minutes.

Place the cracker crumbs on one plate. Place the flour on another and season with salt. Put the egg in a shallow dish.

Dip the fish first into the flour, then into the egg, then into the crumb mixture.

Heat some oil in a frying pan and shallow-fry the fish for about 3 minutes each side until golden.

Remove from the pan, drain and serve immediately.

Serves 6–8

smoked herring buljol

4 whole smoked herring

1 lime, halved

4 tbs olive oil

2 onions, finely chopped

1 hot pepper, seeded and chopped

4 garlic cloves, chopped

6 ripe tomatoes, seeded and finely chopped

Bring a large pot of water to a boil. Drop in the fish and boil until the water turns a slightly golden colour. Remove the fish and drain. Leave to cool.

Remove the head and discard. Pull the fish off the centre bone and discard the bone. Break the fish into tiny pieces with your hand, removing as many fine bones as you can. Squeeze on some lime juice.

Heat the oil in a frying pan and add the onions, pepper and garlic.

Add the herring, toss, and add the tomatoes. Cook for a few seconds.

Serve with bakes or bread.

Serves 4-6

Crate of smoked herring

Traditionally, smoked, salted and dried fish was a popular staple in West Indian kitchens. This type of fish needed no refrigeration, so provided users with a longer shelf life than fresh fish. Today, tradition lives on as these delicacies have maintained a place in traditional and contemporary Trinidad cuisine. We see them included in fantastic fish salads, sandwiched between fried bread for a quick breakfast, and even used in fancy dips.

When buying smoked herring choose the whole fish as opposed to the fillets. These provide a more delicious flavour and appealing texture.

'Buljols are salads, made originally from salted fish – mostly cod – and mixed with onions, tomatoes and peppers. Today we can enjoy this same dish with fresh fish and smoked herring. Salted cod is available but quite expensive, so other types of salted dried fish like pollock and shark are also sold. I do prefer the salted cod.'

saltfish buljol

8 oz salted fish, preferably cod, soaked overnight (see recipe)

juice of ½ lime

4 tbs olive oil

2 large onions, chopped very finely

2 large tomatoes, thinly sliced

½ large bell pepper, seeded and cut into strips, or chopped finely

2 hard-boiled eggs

8 lettuce leaves, washed and dried

1 small avocado, sliced

Cut the saltfish into chunks and soak in warm water overnight. If the cod is very salty, change the water about three times at hourly intervals during soaking.

Drain and flake the fish. Add the lime juice to the fish and rinse. Cover with warm water again and let soak for 30 minutes.

Rinse the fish and taste for salt. If it is too salty, let soak for another 30 minutes. (Alternatively place the fish in a saucepan, cover with cold water and bring to a boil. Remove fish, taste for salt and repeat if necessary.)

Drain the fish, remove bones and flake. Place on a serving platter.

Heat half the olive oil in a non-stick frying pan. Add the onion and sauté for 2 minutes. Add the tomatoes and remove from the heat. (If you prefer raw onions you can add them to the saltfish uncooked.)

Add the onion mixture to the saltfish. Add the pepper and toss.

Peel the eggs and cut into quarters.

Mound the saltfish mixture in the middle of the platter. Place the lettuce around the saltfish, and arrange the avocado and eggs on the lettuce. Drizzle the remaining olive oil over the buljol.

Serve with fried bakes or coconut bake (see page 286), pepper sauce and additional olive oil, if desired.

Serves 6

Caribbean fish buljol

2 lb fresh fish fillet

1 tsp minced chives

1 tsp minced garlic

3 tbs olive oil

1 large onion, thinly sliced

1 pimento pepper, seeded and
  chopped

1 large tomato, chopped

2 hard-boiled eggs

lettuce leaves

2 tbs chopped chadon beni
  (cilantro)

Marinate the fish in the chives, garlic, 1 tablespoon olive oil and salt and freshly ground black pepper.

Place in a heatproof platter and broil under a preheated broiler for 4 minutes each side.

Remove and flake gently with a fork. Place in a large bowl.

Heat the remaining olive oil in a non-stick sauté pan and sauté the onion and pepper for just 1 minute.

Remove and add to the fish. Add the tomatoes and toss. Season with salt if needed.

Peel the eggs and cut into quarters.

Place the fish mixture on a platter and decorate with lettuce and egg wedges.

Season with salt and pepper; sprinkle with chadon beni.

Serves 4–6

Green fig and saltfish pie

¼ cup olive oil

2 onions, sliced

2 tbs chopped garlic

1 lb salted cod, soaked in warm
  water and rinsed about twice

1 lb tomatoes, chopped

1 hot pepper, seeded and
  chopped

1 lb green figs, boiled and
  peeled

2 tbs butter

½ cup milk

1 cup grated cheddar cheese

Preheat the oven to 350°F.

Heat the olive oil in a sauté pan and sauté the onions with the garlic until tender, about 5 minutes.

Squeeze all the excess moisture from the salted fish, add to the pan and stir and fry for a few minutes more. Add the tomatoes and hot pepper and stir. Cover and simmer for about 15 minutes.

Meanwhile, mash the figs. Add the butter and milk and season with salt.

Grease a medium casserole dish and place a layer of figs at the bottom. Cover with the saltfish then top with the remaining figs. Sprinkle with cheese.

Bake for about 20 minutes until golden.

Serves 4

Stewed saltfish

1 lb saltfish, soaked overnight (see recipe)

juice of 1 lime

4 tbs olive oil

4 onions, thinly sliced

2 garlic cloves, chopped

1 pimento pepper, seeded and chopped

1 hot pepper, seeded and chopped (optional)

1 lb ripe tomatoes, seeded and chopped

The night before, soak the saltfish in plenty of cold water with the lime juice, changing the water three times.

Heat the oil in a sauté pan and add the onions, garlic and peppers. Sauté until fragrant. Add the saltfish and stir and fry until the fish has become mixed in well with the onions in the pot.

Add the tomatoes and stir. Cover and simmer for about 15 minutes.

Serve with boiled provisions.

Serves 4

Cassava and saltfish cookup

If you have leftover stewed saltfish and some boiled cassava, the next day add some olive oil to a frying pan, heat, and add the leftover saltfish together with some sliced onions, if you prefer. Heat well, then add the cassava, cut into 1-inch pieces, and cook until the mixture is dry, turning frequently until the cassava is brown and crusty and all the pan juices have evaporated. Serve with pepper sauce and enjoy!

Maracas shark and bake with chadon beni pesto

1 lb shark fillets

2 tbs flour plus more for coating

1 tsp ground chives

1 tbs minced chadon beni (cilantro)

2 garlic cloves, minced

juice of 1 lime

vegetable oil for frying

Wash the shark in a bowl of cool water to which the flour has been added. Drain and cut into four portions. Season with the herbs, garlic and lime juice. Add salt and freshly ground black pepper. Marinate for 30 minutes.

Heat some oil in a frying pan, dredge the fish in flour and fry until golden.

Drain and serve with floats (see page 288).

Serves 4

Chadon beni pesto

20 chadon beni (cilantro) leaves

2 large Spanish thyme leaves

6 garlic cloves

1 hot pepper, seeded and chopped

juice of 1 large lime

1 tbs white vinegar

salt to taste

½ cup olive oil

Place all the ingredient except the oil in a blender and purée. Gradually add the oil and blend to make a thick emulsion.

'A visit to Trinidad's famous Maracas beach will reveal many food huts all selling the hearty fish sandwich called 'shark and bake', served with the famous 'chadon beni sauce'. Maracas is a popular weekly 'liming' spot for locals. You can smell the shark and bake frying as you approach the beach. No need to pack lunch as the variety of food huts ensures there is something for everyone. In addition to shark they also offer shrimp and fish. Fried float is the 'bread' that holds this fish sandwich together, and there is a vast variety of toppings to choose from: chadon beni sauce, pepper sauce, garlic sauce, tamarind sauce, sliced cucumbers, tomatoes, pineapple, shredded cabbage and lettuce.'

shrimp and fish burgers with chadon beni mayo

1 lb small shrimp, peeled and deveined

8 oz fresh fish fillets

1 tsp minced garlic

2 tbs minced chives

1 tsp Dijon mustard

½ tsp allspice powder

salt to taste

1 egg yolk

⅓ cup fresh breadcrumbs

olive oil for frying

chadon beni mayo (see page 352)

Mince the shrimp and fish in a food processor, then stir in the rest of the ingredients.

Form into six 3-inch patties.

Heat some olive oil in a frying pan and pan-fry for about 2 minutes each side.

Serve in burger buns topped with lettuce, tomato and chadon beni mayo.

Makes 6

Grilled fillet of king fish with lime, pepper and onion relish

1 lb king fish fillets (about 4)

1 tsp minced garlic

1 tbs minced chives

1 tbs fresh French thyme

2 tbs olive oil

Marinate the fish in the garlic, herbs and olive oil and season with salt.

Cook on a hot grill for about 3 minutes per side.

Serve on crusty buns topped with lime, pepper and onion relish.

Serves 2–4

Lime, pepper and onion relish

1 onion, chopped

2 garlic cloves, minced

½ hot pepper, seeded and chopped

¼ cup chopped parsley

juice of 2 large limes

1 cup boiling water

2 tbs olive oil

Combine the first four ingredients in a bowl and stir in the lime juice. Season with salt and freshly ground black pepper.

Pour on the boiling water then cover and leave for 5–10 minutes.

Stir in the olive oil and spoon over the hot fish sandwich.

Jerked fillets of mahi mahi with roasted red onions

Mahi mahi is most popular in Tobago, where many fine restaurants serve it up as their fresh fish of the day.

6 mahi mahi fillets (each 4–6 oz and about 1 inch thick)

2 tbs olive oil

1 large red onion, thinly sliced

Jerk marinade

3 tbs allspice berries, ground

2 hot peppers (habenero or Scotch bonnet), seeded and chopped (or more, to taste)

8 blades chive or spring onions, green and white parts

1 large onion, chopped

8 garlic cloves

2-inch piece fresh ginger

⅓ cup fresh thyme

½ tsp grated nutmeg

1 tsp cinnamon

½ tbs freshly ground black pepper

2 tbs lime juice

⅓ cup vegetable oil

Preheat the oven to 400°F.

Process all the marinade ingredients in a blender or food processor to a smooth paste.

Wash the fish and drain well. Combine 6 teaspoons of jerk marinade with the olive oil. Rub 1 teaspoon of jerk mixture onto each fish fillet. Let marinate for 10 minutes.

Place the fish into a greased baking dish and arrange the onion on top.

Bake for about 10–12 minutes, until the fish is tender and flakes easily with a fork.

Serves 4–6

'*Lambie come from large conch shells and can be purchased frozen from grocery stores. Small black-shelled conchs can be bought, uncleaned, from the fish market. Both make great curries and fritters.*

To prepare lambie/conch: *Wash in several changes of water and drain. Squeeze the juice of a lime onto the lambie and cover with water. Remove from the water, drain and place on a chopping board. Remove the skin by cutting it with a knife or tearing it away from the body of the lambie. This is an easy process – you need to remove all the dark and orange-coloured skin. Place in more cool water with lime juice. When ready to cook, cut into 3-inch pieces and pound until the flesh is about ¼–⅛ inch thick. Chop finely and use in your favourite recipe.*'

Curried lambie

Curried lambie

This is a popular dish served by the Store Bay ladies in Tobago, often accompanied by large flat dumplings, referred to as 'cow tongue' dumplings.

1 lb lambie (conch), skin removed, pounded and chopped

1 lime

½ cup chopped chives, minced

1 tsp minced garlic

2 tbs vegetable oil

2 small onions, sliced

1½ tbs curry powder mixed with ¼ cup water

1 hot pepper, seeded and chopped

1 tbs chadon beni (cilantro)

Wash the lambie and squeeze the juice of half a lime over. Add the chives and garlic and let stand for 30 minutes.

Heat the oil in a sauté pan and add the onion. Sauté until almost brown, then add the curry paste and stir and fry until all the water has evaporated.

Add the lambie and hot pepper and stir well. Cook for a few minutes uncovered, then cover and cook on a low heat for about 20 minutes, adding a little water when necessary to prevent sticking.

Sprinkle with chadon beni and serve with the remaining lime.

Serves 4

Lambie fritters

1 lb lambie, cleaned and finely chopped

1 tsp minced garlic

½ tsp salt

½ cup flour

1 tsp baking powder

1 hot pepper, seeded and chopped

½ cup chopped chives

1 small onion, chopped

2 tbs thyme

about ½ cup milk

vegetable oil for frying

Place the lambie in a food processor and process to a very fine texture, or chop very finely by hand.

Combine with the garlic and salt and add the flour, baking powder, hot pepper, chives, onion and thyme.

Add enough milk to make a soft batter-like dough.

Heat the oil in a frying pan and drop in the mixture by spoonfuls. Fry until golden brown and puffed.

Serve with green mango chutney.

Makes 15–20

Baked stuffed snapper

You can try this recipe with smaller snappers as well, or with any type of fish you may prefer – any way it's great!

- **2 tbs minced chives**
- **3 garlic cloves, minced**
- **1 tbs olive oil**
- **3½ lb whole snapper, cleaned**
- **1 tbs melted butter**

Stuffing

- **2 tbs butter**
- **½ cup finely chopped onion**
- **½ cup finely chopped sweet pepper**
- **½ cup finely chopped chives**
- **1 tsp minced garlic**
- **1 tbs fresh thyme**
- **2 pimento peppers, finely chopped**
- **1 cup fresh breadcrumbs**
- **2 tbs chopped capers or olives**
- **1 egg, beaten**
- **⅓ cup grated cheese**

Combine the chives with the garlic and olive oil. Rub the mixture over the fish and sprinkle with salt and freshly ground black pepper. Refrigerate until ready to cook.

To make the stuffing, melt the butter in a large sauté pan. Add the onion, pepper, chives, garlic, thyme and pimento. Sauté until fragrant.

Add the breadcrumbs and stir to combine. Mix in the capers or olives.

Combine the beaten egg with the cheese. Stir into the stuffing mixture and leave to cool.

Preheat the oven to 350°F.

Fill the cavity of the fish with the stuffing. Close and hold together with metal skewers.

Brush the fish with melted butter and sprinkle with black pepper. Place in a baking dish and cover loosely with a 'tent' of foil.

Bake for about 40–45 minutes until the fish is cooked.

Serves 4–6

'*I still have memories of walking along Mayaro beach as a little girl, collecting chip chip from below the surface of the wet sand in my plastic bucket. It's a sight one can still see on our east coast beaches. Chip chip are tiny molluscs, housed in a triangular hinged shell, that only surface at one time of the year. Once collected, like oysters, they must be prepared immediately if they are not to be frozen.*

__To prepare chip chip:__ First wash well to remove any sand, then plunge them briefly into a pot of boiling water or dry-roast them in a heated pot. Either way the chip chip will open, revealing the salmon-coloured creature inside. Remove the soft chip chip from the shell, then pass over a fine sifter or strainer to remove any excess sand. Wash thoroughly again and use in chip chip cocktail, accras or curries. The water that chip chip has been boiled in is said to have great aphrodisiac properties as well!'

Chip chip cocktail

1 lb chip chip

2 tbs fresh lime juice

⅓ cup tomato ketchup

½ hot pepper, minced

2 garlic cloves, minced

1 tbs Worcestershire sauce

2 tbs finely chopped chadon beni (cilantro)

salt to taste

shredded lettuce, to serve

Combine all the ingredients in a small glass bowl. Taste and adjust seasonings. You may need a little more lime juice – it should have a good acid balance.

Serve in stemmed glasses with a little shredded lettuce at the base.

Serves 6–8

Hot and spicy pepper crabs

2 lb fresh crab, cleaned and each chopped into two

1 tbs minced garlic

2 tsp salt

2 tsp fresh lime juice

2 tbs vegetable oil

1 tbs chopped garlic

2 tbs Chinese chilli garlic sauce

1 hot pepper, chopped

¼ cup chopped chives

Sauce

1 tbs oyster sauce

1 tbs tomato ketchup

½ tsp granulated sugar

1 tsp sesame oil

Season the crab with the minced garlic, salt and lime juice. Refrigerate for about 30 minutes.

Combine the sauce ingredients and set aside.

Heat a large sauté pan or wok and add the vegetable oil. Add the chopped garlic, chilli garlic sauce and hot pepper. Stir and fry until fragrant.

Add the crab to the wok and stir and fry until they turn reddish in colour. Cover and steam cook for 15 minutes. Add the sauce ingredients, stir-fry for a few minutes more.

Remove from the pot to a serving platter and sprinkle with chives.

Serves 4

Chives

'Curry crab with dumplin's' is a Tobago speciality and a must try! It is generally sold by the Store Bay ladies in Tobago. The dumplings are typically large flat dumplings – 'cow tongue' dumplings. They are cooked separately and served alongside the curried crab. You can do it this way but I have found that when the dumplings are made a little softer, cut a bit smaller, then simmered with the curried crab they become juicy and succulent.

Traditional curried crab with dumplings

6 blue crabs, or any other type, cleaned

4 garlic cloves, minced

juice of 1 lime

2 tbs vegetable oil

1 onion, chopped

1 hot pepper, seeded and chopped

3 tbs curry powder mixed with ½ cup water

4 cups coconut milk

¼ cup chopped chives

about ¼ cup chopped chadon beni (cilantro)

Dumplings

2 cups flour

1 tsp baking powder

½ tsp salt

1 tsp butter

To prepare the dumplings place all the ingredients in a mixing bowl and rub the butter into the flour until the mixture is grainy. Slowly add enough water to knead to a stiff dough. Cover and let rest for about 30 minutes.

Season the crabs with salt and freshly ground black pepper, half the garlic and the lime juice. Let stand for 30 minutes.

Heat the oil in a large sauté pan, and add the remaining garlic, onion and hot pepper. Cook for about 1 minute. Add the curry paste and cook until thick. Add the crabs and stir to cover with the curry mixture.

Add the coconut milk and sprinkle with the chives and chadon beni. Cook until bubbling, cover and simmer, stirring occasionally, for about 20–30 minutes.

Divide the dumpling dough into two pieces. Roll each piece into a long rope-like shape about 12 inches in length. Cut into 2-inch lengths.

Drop the dumplings into the crab mixture, cover and steam for a further 10 minutes, turning the dumplings once. If the mixture seems too dry add a little more coconut milk or some stock.

Sprinkle on more chadon beni if necessary. Taste and adjust seasonings before serving.

Serves 4–6

Trinidadian stewed fish

6 fish fillets, king, salmon or carite (each about 4 oz)

2 tbs Trini fresh herb seasoning paste (see page 355)

2 tbs chopped Spanish thyme

4 tbs French thyme

1 tsp salt

2 tbs vegetable oil

2 garlic cloves, chopped

½ onion, finely chopped

1 pimento pepper, seeded and thinly sliced

2 tomatoes, chopped

white wine or stock (optional)

chopped parsley to garnish

Wash the fish. Rub with the seasoning paste, Spanish thyme, French thyme and the salt. Let stand for about 15 minutes.

Heat the oil in a medium sauté pan and add the garlic, onion and pimento. Sauté until the garlic turns fragrant and the onion is translucent. Add the tomatoes and cook for about 15 minutes until the tomatoes are very soft and have lost their acidity. You may deglaze the pan at this point, if wished, with a little white wine, stock or water.

Add the fish fillets and turn once to coat with the sauce. Cover and cook for 4 minutes, until the fish is opaque. Remove the lid and check the fish; the oil in the sauce should be beginning to separate.

Adjust the seasonings, remove from the heat and sprinkle with parsley. Serve hot.

Serves 4

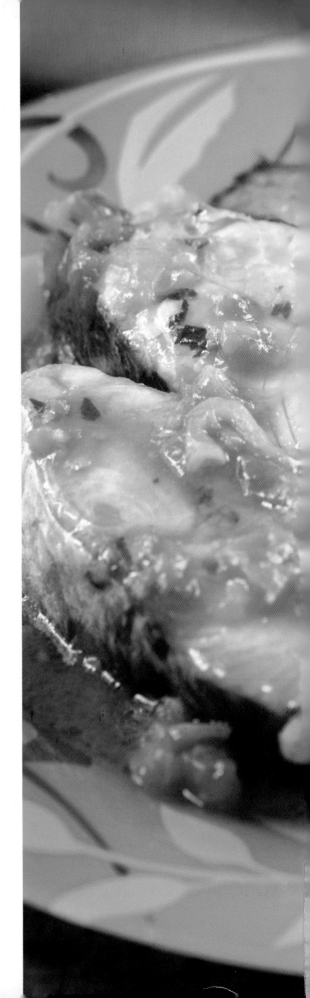

Curry fried fish

This is an East Indian-inspired recipe. Fish slices are seasoned then dredged in a mixture of flour and curry powder and fried. It is typically eaten with dhal, rice and spinach (bhaji).

6 king fish slices, about ¾ inch thick

1 tbs minced garlic

1 tbs minced chives

1 tsp salt

1 tsp freshly ground black pepper

¾ cup all-purpose flour

1 tbs curry powder

vegetable oil for frying

lime wedges, to serve

Wash the fish, rub with the garlic and chives and season with the salt and pepper.

Combine the flour with the curry powder on a plate.

Heat some vegetable oil in a frying pan. Dredge the fish in the flour mixture and shallow-fry for a few minutes on each side until golden.

Drain. Serve hot with lime wedges.

Serves 4–6

Chinese pepper shrimp

This is one of the most popular shrimp dishes ordered at Chinese restaurants. The shrimp is cooked with the shell on in a hot and spicy sauce.

12 jumbo shrimp, deveined with shells on

1 tsp salt

about 2 tbs vegetable oil

1 tbs chopped ginger

1 tbs minced garlic

½ cup chopped chives

Sauce

3 tbs tomato ketchup

1 tbs oyster sauce

2 tbs chilli garlic sauce

1 tsp Worcestershire sauce

1 tsp sesame oil

½ tbs soy sauce

Rub the shrimp with the salt.

Combine the sauce ingredients.

Heat 2 tablespoons oil in a wok, add the ginger and garlic and stir-fry for a few minutes until fragrant.

Add the shrimp and stir and fry until pink and curled. Remove from the wok.

Clean the wok, heat and add a small amount of oil. Add the sauce and stir until bubbling. Return the shrimp to the wok.

Remove and sprinkle with the chives.

Serves 2

Barbecued shrimp

24 large shrimp

⅓ cup olive oil

2 tsp salt

2 tsp minced garlic

1 tbs lime juice

1 tsp dried chilli peppers (red pepper flakes)

½ cup zesty barbecue sauce

Clean the shrimp. Remove the vein and shell, keeping the tail intact.

Combine the olive oil with the salt, minced garlic, lime juice and dried chilli peppers. Rub onto the shrimp. Let marinate for 15 minutes.

Grease a barbecue grill and preheat to high.

Thread the shrimp onto four metal skewers.

Grill, turning once. Cook until pink and curled.

Smother in barbecue sauce and serve immediately.

Serves 4–6

' Rosemary grows in abundance here in Trinidad and Tobago, and many locals use it for medicinal purposes (mostly for headache). I love rosemary and I love to incorporate it into my cooking whenever I get a fresh bunch at the market. '

Pan-roasted shrimp with rosemary

12 large shrimp

¼ cup olive oil

1 tsp salt

1 tbs minced garlic

2 tbs chopped rosemary

¼ cup fresh lemon juice

Clean the shrimp. Remove the vein and shell, keeping the tail intact.

Combine the olive oil with the salt, minced garlic, rosemary and lemon juice. Rub onto the shrimp. Let marinate for 15 minutes.

Preheat a stovetop grill pan. Place the shrimp in it and turn once, after about 4 minutes, when the shrimp begin to curl.

Remove and serve immediately.

Serves 2–3

Rosemary

Trinidad fish cakes

Often when I bring home a fish to fillet, I steam it whole and then remove the fillets and make fish cakes.

1 lb fish fillets, steamed

½ cup fresh breadcrumbs

½ cup finely chopped mixed herbs (parsley, thyme, basil, chives)

1 tsp Dijon mustard

1 tsp hot pepper sauce

½ tsp fresh lime juice

1 egg, lightly beaten

1 cup dried breadcrumbs

vegetable oil for frying

Flake the fish and remove any bones. Add the fresh breadcrumbs, herbs, mustard, some salt and freshly ground black pepper, the pepper sauce, lime juice and egg.

Form into cakes about 1½–2 inches in diameter.

Place the dried crumbs on a plate. Dip the cakes into the crumbs to coat completely.

Fry in hot oil until golden on both sides.

Makes 12

Oven-roasted fish with fresh herbs

On days when I get fresh fish from the market, I often prepare this dish – it's easy and, because the fish is freshly caught and has never been frozen, it's really delicious and flavourful.

1 tsp minced garlic

1 tsp minced chives

1 tsp fresh French thyme

¼ tsp allspice powder

olive oil

1 small red onion, sliced

6 fresh fish fillets, salmon, carite or king (each about 4 oz)

2 tbs lime juice

Preheat the oven to 400°F. Grease a 10-inch shallow glass baking dish.

Combine the garlic, chives, thyme, allspice powder, a drizzle of olive oil and salt and freshly ground black pepper. Rub onto the fish fillets on both sides.

Place into the baking dish and spread the red onion slices on top. Drizzle with more olive oil.

Roast the fish uncovered in the oven for 10 minutes or just until opaque. Remove at once, sprinkle with lime juice and serve immediately.

Serves 6

Creamy fish with herbs, mushroom and parmesan

1 lb fresh fish fillets, cut into chunks

1 tbs ground chives

2 garlic cloves, minced

2 tbs olive oil

1 red bell pepper, seeded and chopped

1 small onion, thinly sliced

½ cup sliced mushrooms

2 tbs all-purpose flour

1½ cups milk

¼ tsp grated nutmeg

½ tsp dried chilli peppers (red pepper flakes)

½ cup white wine

¼ cup grated parmesan cheese (optional)

2 tbs chopped Spanish thyme

1 tbs chopped chadon beni (cilantro)

lime wedges, to serve

Marinate the fish in the chives, garlic and some salt for 30 minutes.

Heat the oil in a sauté pan, add the pepper and onion and cook until fragrant, about 4 minutes. Add the mushrooms.

Sprinkle on the flour and cook until almost liquid, or the mixture slackens. Add the milk and cook until the mixture begins to thicken. Add the nutmeg and dried chilli peppers.

Add the fish, turn gently and simmer, covered, for 10 minutes. Remove the lid, stir and add the wine and cheese, if using. Cook for another 5 minutes.

Remove from the heat, add the fresh herbs and serve with lime wedges.

Serves 4

French thyme

Curried cascadura

6 garlic cloves, finely chopped

1 onion, minced

1 pimento pepper, minced

1 cup chopped chives

6 large cascaduras, scrubbed clean and washed in lime and water

4 tbs vegetable oil

1 hot pepper, seeded and chopped

1 small onion, sliced

4 tbs curry powder mixed with ¼ cup water

2-3 cups coconut milk

a pinch of sugar

Combine half the garlic with the minced onion, pimento pepper and chives.

Season the fish well by rubbing with the herb mixture and stuffing some of it into the cavity of the fish.

Heat the oil in a large sauté pan. Add the remaining garlic, the hot pepper and sliced onion and cook until fragrant. Add the curry paste and cook until the mixture becomes dry.

Add the fish and turn to cover with the curry mixture. Pour in about 2 cups coconut milk, bring to a boil. Add salt to taste and the sugar, cover and simmer, turning occasionally, for about 20 minutes.

Serve with rice.

Serves 6

'*Legend has it that if you eat curried cascadura here in Trinidad and Tobago you will return to these islands for your final days!*
Cascadura fish is caught on the many mudflats in southern Trinidad. It is a strange-looking fish with large, dark, hard scales. Once caught it is necessary to scrub it free of all the mud – a small brush will help with this. It is usually served highly seasoned and curried with coconut milk – delicious none the less!'

Prepared cascadura, seasoned and stuffed before cooking

Lobster Thermidor

When you order this dish at a fancy restaurant it's usually served in the lobster shell.

2 lb fresh lobster meat, cut into chunks

2 garlic cloves, minced

½ tsp salt

3 tbs unsalted butter

3 tbs all-purpose flour

1 cup evaporated milk

1 cup sliced mushrooms

2 egg yolks

½ cup white wine

½ cup grated parmesan cheese

½ tsp cayenne pepper

½ tsp mustard powder

Gratin

½ cup dried breadcrumbs

2 tbs butter

2 tbs chopped parsley

2 tbs parmesan cheese

salt and freshly ground black pepper

Combine the lobster meat with the garlic and salt. Set aside.

To make the sauce, melt the butter in a heavy medium saucepan. Stir in the flour and cook until smooth and almost liquid. Add the evaporated milk and cook, stirring well, until the mixture thickens.

Add the lobster and mushrooms, cover and simmer for 5 minutes.

Remove from the heat, add the egg yolks and wine. Stir to combine.

Place on a low heat and cook to warm the mixture. Do not boil or else the egg will curdle. Add the parmesan, cayenne pepper and mustard.

Spoon the lobster into buttered Thermidor dishes or shallow ramekins.

Combine all the ingredients for the gratin. Sprinkle on top of the lobster.

Place under a preheated broiler until golden on top.

Serves 4–6

Broiled lobster with lime butter

2 live lobsters, freshly caught, or 2 large frozen lobster tails

1 tsp minced garlic

olive oil

salt

Lime butter

⅓ cup butter

2 garlic cloves, minced

1 tsp chopped hot pepper (optional)

1 tbs fresh lime juice

1 tbs finely chopped chadon beni (cilantro)

salt and freshly ground black pepper to taste

To make the lime butter, melt the butter in a small saucepan. Add the garlic and pepper and cook to a sizzle until fragrant, taking care not to burn or brown the garlic.

Remove from the heat and stir in the remaining ingredients.

If using frozen lobster tails: Thaw thoroughly. Snip the backs to open the shell a little. Cut into the flesh and remove the small vein that runs through the back of the tail.

Season with the garlic and a little olive oil. Sprinkle with salt.

Heat the grill or a grill pan and add a little olive oil.

Place the tails flesh side down and grill for about 4 minutes each side.

Remove and serve with the lime butter.

If using live lobsters: Heat 3 quarts of water in a large pot. Add 2 tablespoons salt and bring the water to a boil. Plunge the lobsters into the water, head first.

Cover and heat to boiling. Reduce the heat and cook for a further 10–15 minutes.

Remove the lobsters and drain.

Place the lobsters on their backs and cut into halves, lengthways, with a sharp knife. Remove the stomach, which is just behind the head, and remove the intestinal vein which runs from the tip of the tail to the stomach. Crack the claws.

Place the tails flesh side up on a baking pan and drizzle with some of the lime butter.

Broil under a preheated broiler, 3 inches from heat, until hot, 2–3 minutes.

Remove and serve with the remaining lime butter.

Serves 2–3

'*Lobsters are caught in the Mayaro beach area. They are spiny Caribbean lobsters and when freshly caught are so delicious they hardly need any extra flavouring.*'

Lambie accras with chilli mayo dip

1 lb lambie (conch), skin removed, pounded and chopped

a splash of Angostura bitters

2 eggs

2 tbs minced garlic

1 pimento pepper, seeded and chopped

½ cup mixed chopped herbs (parsley, thyme, chives)

1 cup flour

2 tsp baking powder

1 tsp salt

¼ cup milk (optional)

vegetable oil for frying

Place the lambie into a food processor and mince. Add the bitters, eggs, garlic, pimento and herbs and incorporate into the mixture.

Place the mixture in a bowl and add the flour, baking powder and salt. Stir well to combine. The mixture should be like a paste, but not too runny. Add a little milk if it seems too dry.

Heat the oil in a frying pan and drop the mixture by teaspoonfuls into the hot oil. Fry until puffed and golden, about 5–6 minutes.

Drain and serve with chilli mayo dip.

Makes about 24

Chilli mayo dip

¾ cup low-fat mayonnaise

1 tbs creamed horseradish

1 tsp chilli powder

1 tsp pepper sauce

¼ cup chopped parsley

1 tbs lime juice

Combine all the ingredients. Stir well and serve with fritters.

saltfish accras

A traditional breakfast dish or light snack. Serve with fried bakes or floats (see pages 286 and 288) and mango or tamarind chutney.

½ lb salted cod, washed and soaked overnight in water and lime juice

juice of 1 lime

1 large onion, grated

1 pimento pepper, seeded and chopped

½ cup chopped chives

2 tbs French thyme

1 tbs chopped celery

1 cup flour

2 tsp baking powder

about ½ cup milk

vegetable oil for frying

Wash the saltfish in lime juice and water. Cut into strips and squeeze.

Place in a mixing bowl. Add the onion, pepper, chives, thyme, celery and salt and freshly ground black pepper.

Add the flour and baking powder to the saltfish and mix. Stir in enough milk to make a thick batter.

Heat the oil in a frying pan. Drop spoonfuls of the mixture – about the size of a small egg – into the pan. Fry until golden. Drain and serve.

Makes 15

shrimp accras

A popular alternative to saltfish accras and a delightful breakfast item too, served with fried bakes and tamarind chutney.

1 lb shrimp, cleaned

½ cup flour

1 tsp baking powder

1 hot pepper, seeded and chopped

½ cup chopped chives

1 small onion, chopped

2 tbs thyme

1 tsp minced garlic

½ tsp salt

vegetable oil for frying

Heat a large non-stick frying pan. Add the shrimp to the pan and dry-roast. Turn and cook the shrimp until pink and curled.

Remove and chop finely. Combine with the flour, baking powder, hot pepper, chives, onion, thyme and garlic. Season with the salt. Gradually add about ½ cup water, enough to make a soft batter-like dough.

Heat oil in a frying pan. Drop spoonfuls of the mixture into the pan and fry until golden brown and puffed.

Serve with tamarind chutney.

Makes 15–20

Fried bakes with saltfish accras

Paramin Hills

Mainly meat

A range of different meats are cooked and enjoyed in a variety of ways. The most popular cooking method for chicken and beef is stewing. Our African ancestors gave us the culinary gift of darkly caramelizing sugar to colour meats when cooking and this tradition remains very strong in all Trinidadian kitchens today. It is the foundation of a great chicken or beef stew, and also for a fantastic pelau. The other popular method of cooking comes from our East Indian ancestors – curry.

Chicken, beef, goat and duck are the most popular meats and appreciation for rabbit has developed recently. Wild meat has also grown in popularity and can be found during the hunting season – around Christmas time into Carnival. Agouti, lapp, iguana and manicou are the more popular wild meats consumed. These are cooked either curried or in a curry/stew fashion and enjoyed with boiled provisions.

Other frequently employed cooking methods are oven roasting and baking, as well as deep-frying, pan-frying and braising. Roasting on a barbecue or the more common coal pot cooking are also utilized quite a bit. Outdoor cooking on big ring burners is a popular method for large gatherings.

Marinating the meats plays a very important part of the preparation process for many of our meat dishes, and many a recipe calls for 'Trini fresh herb seasoning paste'. This is a blend of fresh herbs – usually chives, parsley, thyme and, sometimes, garlic. Trini households have their own home-made recipes and the commercial version can be purchased as well. The lush and intriguing Paramin Hills in the Northern Range are redolent with the scent of fresh herbs and this is the area that gives us our bounty of herbs for daily culinary use. Bundles of assorted fresh herbs are sold each week at our markets and supermarkets.

There is a large Hindu population on the islands that is strictly vegetarian. TVP or soya mince is a popular meat substitute for them; they also enjoy dried legumes in many forms.

Paramin farmer

stir-fried orange chicken

1 lb boneless chicken, cut into ¼-inch thick slices

½ cup cornstarch

6 tbs vegetable oil

1 tbs chopped garlic

1 tbs chopped ginger

⅓ cup roasted peanuts

¼ cup chopped chives

Marinade

2 tbs soy sauce

1 tsp cornstarch

1 tbs orange juice

Sauce

½ cup orange juice

2 tbs soy sauce

1 tbs chilli garlic sauce

2 tsp Worcestershire sauce

1 tsp sesame oil

1 tbs sugar

2 tsp cornstarch

Combine the chicken with the marinade ingredients and marinate for 30 minutes.

Combine the sauce ingredients, stir and set aside.

Remove the chicken from the marinade and dredge in the cornstarch.

Heat 4 tablespoons oil in a wok. Fry the chicken in hot oil until light golden in colour. Remove, drain and clean wok.

Heat 2 tablespoons oil in the wok. Add the garlic and ginger and stir and fry until fragrant. Add the chicken and sauce and cook until bubbling and thick. Garnish with peanuts and chopped chives.

Serve immediately.

Serves 4

Butter chicken

2 lb boneless chicken breasts,
cut into cubes

1 tbs grated ginger

4 garlic cloves, minced

2 tsp ground coriander

1 tsp chilli powder

2 tbs white vinegar

¼ cup tomato paste

½ cup plain yogurt

½ cup butter

1 large onion, minced

4 cinnamon sticks (each
2 inches)

6 cardamom pods, bruised

1 tsp salt

3 tsp paprika

2 tsp garam masala

⅓ cup cooking cream or
evaporated milk

Combine the chicken with the ginger, garlic, coriander, chilli powder, vinegar, tomato paste and yogurt. Refrigerate overnight.

Melt the butter in a sauté pan, add the onion, cinnamon and cardamom and cook until the onion is slightly browned.

Add the chicken and stir and fry for a few minutes.

Add the salt and paprika and stir well. Cover and simmer for about 15 minutes, stirring occasionally. If necessary, add a little water.

Add the garam masala. When the sauce has thickened, stir in the cream or evaporated milk and heat for a few minutes more.

Serve hot with basmati rice or roti.

Serves 4-6

'Within the last 10 years there has been increased interest in authentic East Indian foods, highlighted by the sudden growth in Indian restaurants. This recipe is one of the most popular for this type of cuisine.'

steak and pineapple kebabs

1 tbs minced garlic

2 tbs red wine vinegar

1 tsp Worcestershire sauce

1 tbs chopped rosemary

1½ lb sirloin steak, cut into 1-inch cubes

2 cups fresh pineapple chunks

1 large onion, cut into quarters

1 cup mushrooms

2 red sweet peppers, cut into 1-inch pieces

¼ cup olive oil

Mix the garlic, vinegar, Worcestershire sauce, rosemary and some freshly ground black pepper. Whisk well to combine. Pour over the steak cubes and mix well.

Cover and refrigerate for about 4 hours or overnight.

Remove from refrigerator 1 hour before cooking. Season with salt.

Preheat the broiler or grill to high.

Combine the pineapple with the vegetables. Add the olive oil and sprinkle on some salt.

Thread metal skewers with the steak, alternating with the pineapple and vegetables.

Lightly brush on any remaining marinade and place on a hot grill or under the broiler.

Grill for about 4 minutes each side or until the steak is cooked to your liking.

Remove and arrange on a serving platter.

Makes 6–8 skewers

'Fresh pineapples are available year round. Grilling them intensifies their sweetness and juiciness.'

Cheese and pepper meat loaf

This meat loaf, meant to be eaten cold, makes fabulous sandwiches the next day.

16 water biscuits or crackers

about 1 cup milk

1 lb lean ground beef

2 tbs Trini fresh herb seasoning paste (see page 355)

2 garlic cloves, minced

1 tbs fresh thyme

1 tsp freshly ground black pepper

½ tsp mustard powder

2 eggs

1 large green bell pepper, seeded and chopped

2 red pimento peppers, seeded and chopped

6 oz cheddar cheese, cubed

1 tsp salt

Preheat oven to 350°F.

Crumble the biscuits into a measuring cup; add enough milk to reach the 1-cup mark. Let stand for 15 minutes.

Place the beef in a large mixing bowl. Add the seasoning paste, garlic, black pepper, mustard powder and thyme and combine.

Lightly beat the eggs and add to the biscuit mixture.

Add this to the beef mixture and stir well to combine.

Stir in the peppers and cheese. Season with the salt. Place in a greased loaf pan and bake for 60 minutes.

Cool well before slicing.

Serves 6

stewed chicken with ginger

This is Trinidad's signature chicken dish!

3½ lb chicken

lime juice

4 garlic cloves, minced

2 tbs Trini fresh herb seasoning paste (see page 355)

1 onion, sliced

2 pimento peppers, seeded and chopped

¼ cup French thyme

1 tbs chopped celery leaves

1 tbs chopped ginger

1 tbs red wine vinegar

1 tsp salt

2 tbs vegetable oil

2 tbs brown sugar

Wash the chicken well with lime. Joint, or cut into smaller portions if desired, and drain.

Rub with the garlic and seasoning paste. Add the sliced onion and peppers, the thyme, celery, ginger, vinegar, salt and some freshly ground black pepper. Cover and marinate for about 2 hours in the refrigerator.

Heat the oil in a large pan. Add the sugar and caramelize to a dark brown colour. Add the chicken pieces one at a time, turning well to colour each piece.

Cook uncovered until the chicken starts to release its juices. Cover and simmer until cooked, about 20–30 minutes, turning occasionally. There is no need to add water, the chicken will first release juices then reabsorb them – at this point the stew should be cooked. There should be a rich brown gravy with a slight oil separation.

Adjust seasoning to taste and serve.

Serves 4

'*Pelau is another signature Trinidad dish. It's a weekly meal in any Trini household and is everyone's favourite, especially chicken pelau. Not only is it easy to make, it's also a great portable meal that is often taken along to the beach, or to cricket. Or to a Carnival Tuesday lime in Port of Spain! On Carnival Tuesday lunchtime, it is not uncommon to see a car trunk opened and in it a feast of pelau, sliced soused cucumbers and watercress salad, complete with pepper sauce to go. Around this car you will also see many people savouring their pelau, smiles on their faces!*'

Chicken pelau

3½ lb chicken, cut into pieces

lime juice

4 garlic cloves, minced

2 tbs Trini fresh herb seasoning paste (see page 355)

1 onion, sliced

2 pimento peppers, seeded and chopped

¼ cup French thyme

1 tbs chopped celery leaves

1 tbs red wine vinegar

4 tbs tomato ketchup

2 tbs vegetable oil

2 tbs brown sugar

2 cups pigeon peas

½ cup chopped pumpkin

2 cups parboiled rice

1 cup coconut milk

Wash the chicken well with lime juice. Drain. Rub with the garlic and seasoning paste. Add the sliced onion and peppers, thyme, celery, vinegar, ketchup, salt and freshly ground black pepper. Cover and marinate for about 2 hours in the refrigerator.

Heat the oil in a large pan. Add the sugar and caramelize to a dark brown colour, it will become very frothy. Add chicken pieces one at a time, turning to colour each piece.

Cook uncovered until the chicken starts to release its juices, about 5 minutes.

Add the pigeon peas and pumpkin, stir. Lower the heat and cook for about 10 minutes, covered. Add the rice and stir well. Add the coconut milk and 2 cups water. Bring to a boil, cover and simmer until cooked, about 20–30 minutes.

Stir the rice and chicken together and serve.

Serves 4

Beef pelau

1 lb stewing beef, cut into
    1-inch pieces

1 tbs Trini fresh herb seasoning
    paste (see page 355)

½ tbs vinegar

1 pimento pepper, seeded and
    sliced

1 small onion, thinly sliced

2 garlic cloves, minced

2 tbs chopped celery leaves

2 tbs French thyme

2 tbs tomato ketchup

2 tbs vegetable oil

2 tbs brown sugar

2 cups pigeon peas

2 cups rice

1 cup coconut milk

Mix the beef with the seasoning paste, vinegar, pimento, onion, garlic, celery, thyme and ketchup. Cover and refrigerate for about 1 hour.

Remove from refrigerator and season with salt and freshly ground black pepper.

Heat the oil in a medium sauté pan, add the brown sugar and let caramelize to a dark brown colour. It will become frothy.

Add the beef and turn well to cover with the caramelized sugar. Cook for about 10 minutes on a medium heat.

When the meat begins to release juices, lower the heat and cover. Cook for about 20 minutes, stirring occasionally.

Add a little water to prevent drying, if necessary. Cook for another 20 minutes, check and stir. If the beef is tender add the pigeon peas and rice. Stir well to cover with all the juices.

Add the coconut milk and 2½ cups water. Bring to a boil then lower the heat and simmer until the rice is cooked, about 20 minutes.

Adjust seasoning to taste, stir and remove from heat.

Serves 4–6

Stewed beef

2 lb stewing beef, cut into
    1-inch pieces

2 tbs Trini fresh herb seasoning
    paste (see page 355)

1 tbs vinegar

2 pimento peppers, seeded and
    sliced

1 small onion, thinly sliced

4 garlic cloves, minced

1 tbs chopped celery leaves

2 tbs fresh French thyme

2 tbs vegetable oil

2 tbs sugar

Mix the beef with the herb paste, vinegar, pimentos, onion, garlic, celery and thyme. Cover and refrigerate for about 1 hour.

Remove from refrigerator and season with salt and freshly ground black pepper.

Heat the oil in a medium sauté pan, add the sugar and let it caramelize to a dark brown colour. It will become frothy.

Add the beef and turn well to cover with the caramelized sugar. Cook for about 10 minutes on medium heat. When the meat begins to release juices, lower the heat and cover. Cook for about 20 minutes, stirring occasionally.

Add a little water to prevent drying, if necessary. Cook for another 40 minutes, check and stir. If the beef is tender remove from heat, otherwise cook for another 15 minutes. At this point you should have a rich brown gravy with a slight oil separation.

Adjust seasoning to taste, stir and remove from heat.

Serves 4–6

Stewed beef with rice and dasheen

Roasted stuffed chicken with fresh herbs

A Sunday lunch item on many a Trinidadian's table!

3½–4 lb chicken

butter

Marinade

1 tsp minced garlic

2 tbs olive oil

2 tbs minced fresh chives

6 tbs fresh French thyme

2 tbs red wine vinegar

1 tsp freshly ground black pepper

Stuffing

chicken giblets

lime juice

4 garlic cloves, minced

½ tsp freshly ground black pepper

2 tbs vegetable or olive oil

1 large onion, finely chopped

½ cup chopped chives

2 pimento peppers, seeded and chopped

1 hot pepper, seeded and chopped

⅓ cup fresh thyme

2 cups fresh breadcrumbs

2 tbs raisins

chicken stock (see recipe)

¼ cup grated cheese (optional)

¼ cup chopped parsley

Combine the marinade ingredients and rub onto the chicken. Refrigerate until ready to cook.

To make the stuffing, mince the chicken giblets and wash with lime juice. Combine half the garlic with the black pepper and some salt. Add to the minced giblets.

Heat the oil in a large sauté pan. Add the remaining garlic and onion and sauté until fragrant. Add the giblets and sauté until brown in colour.

Add the chives, pimento, hot pepper and thyme. Stir and fry for 4 minutes until all the herbs become fragrant.

Add the breadcrumbs and raisins and stir to combine. If dry, gradually add a small amount of chicken stock at a time to moisten. Stir until the stuffing comes together.

Stir in the cheese, if using, and parsley. Season according to taste and leave to cool.

Preheat the oven to 350°F.

Stuff the chicken with the cooled stuffing mixture. Close the cavity with toothpicks or string. Rub with butter.

Bake for 1½ hours, basting occasionally with the pan drippings.

Remove the bird from the oven once the juices run clear when pierced with a metal or wooden skewer.

Remove the stuffing immediately. Let the chicken stand then cut into serving pieces.

Serves 4–6

Parsley

chicken in black bean sauce

Use a good-quality black bean sauce for this delicious dish.

¼ **cup rice wine**

1-inch piece fresh ginger, peeled and grated

3 boneless chicken breasts, cut into 1-inch cubes

2 tbs vegetable oil

4 garlic cloves, chopped finely

1 tsp cornstarch

Sauce

¼ **cup water**

2 tbs black bean sauce

1 tsp sesame oil

1 tsp hot chilli paste

½ **tsp sugar**

In a small bowl mix together the rice wine and half the ginger. Add the chicken and marinate for about 30 minutes.

In another bowl mix all the sauce ingredients together.

Heat about 1 tablespoon oil in a wok. When hot add the chicken a few pieces at a time and stir-fry just until it loses its colour. Remove from the wok and clean the pan.

Heat the rest of the oil in the wok. Add the garlic and remaining ginger and stir-fry until fragrant. Add the sauce and stir-fry until fragrant.

Return the chicken to the pan and toss until all the pieces are covered with sauce.

Add the cornstarch and stir until the mixture thickens. Remove from heat and serve immediately.

Serves 6

curried chicken

3½ lb chicken, cut into small pieces

2 tbs Trini fresh herb seasoning paste (see page 355)

1 tbs wine vinegar or lime juice

2 tbs vegetable oil

1 small onion, sliced

1 tsp chopped ginger

1 tsp chopped garlic

1 hot pepper, seeded and chopped

3 tbs curry powder

2 tbs chopped chadon beni (cilantro) (optional)

Marinate the chicken in the herb paste and vinegar with some salt and freshly ground black pepper for about 30 minutes.

Heat the oil in a medium sauté pan or iron pot and add the onion, ginger and garlic. Stir and add the hot pepper. Sauté until fragrant and the onion is tender, about 2–3 minutes.

Stir the curry powder into ¼ cup water to make a paste.

Add the curry paste to the pot and let it cook, stirring well, until most of the water has evaporated.

Now add the chicken pieces one at a time, making sure they are covered with the curry sauce. Cover the pot and let the chicken release some juice. Stir and add a small amount of water at a time if necessary to prevent sticking. Continue cooking in this manner for about 30 minutes, or until the sauce seems to be slightly separating from the oil (even if this does not happen the chicken should be ready after 30 minutes).

Adjust seasoning to taste. Sprinkle with chadon beni, if using, and serve.

Serves 4

Curry duck

5 lb duck, cut into small pieces

1 lime

2 tsp salt

4 tbs duck and goat masala or curry powder

4 tbs vegetable oil

2 onions, thinly sliced

2 pimento peppers, seeded and chopped

1 hot pepper, seeded and chopped

4 garlic cloves, minced

1 tsp freshly ground black pepper

6 chadon beni (cilantro) leaves, finely chopped

Marinade

½ cup Trini fresh herb seasoning paste, freshly made (see page 355)

6 chadon beni (cilantro) leaves, ground

6 garlic cloves, minced

1 tbs plain yogurt

¼ cup red wine vinegar

1 tbs dark rum

Wash the duck in plenty of water with the juice of the lime. Drain.

Combine all the ingredients for the marinade and rub onto the duck pieces. Cover and refrigerate overnight.

Bring duck to room temperature, add the salt and combine well.

Combine the masala or curry powder with about ⅓ cup water to make a paste.

Heat the oil in a large heavy pan and add the onion, peppers and garlic. Cook until fragrant. Add the curry paste and cook until almost dry.

Add the duck, a few pieces at a time, stirring to coat with the curry paste. Add the black pepper and stir. Add half the chadon beni and cook until the duck starts to release its juices.

Add a little water. Cover the pot tightly and simmer, stirring occasionally to prevent sticking, adding a little water if necessary, for about 45 minutes until the duck is tender.

Add the remaining chadon beni and adjust seasoning to taste.

Serves 6–8

Note
If you intend to enjoy the duck as a 'cutter', or appetizer, remove the lid and increase the heat until the liquid has evaporated.

'Duck is eaten frequently on our shores and is often cooked when there is a river 'lime'. During long weekends in the dry season many holidaymakers camp out on the shores of some of our rivers. Curry duck is cooked over an open fire and is usually enjoyed with some good rum drinks!'

Lasagne

1 lb ground beef

1 tbs ground chives

2 garlic cloves, minced

1 tbs vegetable oil

2 bell peppers, chopped

3 cups tomato sauce (see opposite page)

1 tsp chopped fresh oregano or 1 tbs chopped fresh basil

6 tbs butter

4½ tbs all-purpose flour

3 cups milk

½ tsp grated nutmeg

1 packet ready-cooked lasagne sheets or unprepared sheets cooked according to directions and drained

4 cups grated mozzarella cheese

Preheat the oven to 375°F. Season the beef with the chives and garlic.

Heat the oil in a saucepan, add the beef and brown. Add the bell peppers, tomato sauce and oregano or basil. Season with salt and freshly ground black pepper. Cover and simmer, stirring occasionally, until cooked, about 20 minutes.

Meanwhile, make the white sauce. Melt the butter in a saucepan, add the flour and cook stirring constantly until the mixture is smooth and slack in consistency.

Add the milk, nutmeg and salt and black pepper to taste. Stir until thick. Remove from the heat.

Assemble the lasagne in a large baking dish, 9 by 13 inches. Spread about a third of the meat sauce in the bottom of the dish and cover with a layer of lasagne. Spread a third of the white sauce over the top and sprinkle with some cheese. Repeat the procedure, making about three layers and ending up with sauce at the top.

Cover with the remaining cheese and bake for about 30 minutes until bubbling.

Serves 8

'*Italian foods are big here, as with the rest of the world. Lasagne is very popular and the dish will often rub shoulders with a Creole meal on a Sunday!*'

Meatballs with parmesan

1 lb lean ground beef

½ cup fine breadcrumbs

1 large egg

1 large onion, finely chopped

1 tsp fresh thyme

2 garlic cloves, minced

¼ cup parmesan cheese

salt and freshly ground black pepper

¼ cup finely chopped parsley

vegetable oil for frying

1 quantity tomato sauce

Combine all the ingredients except the tomato sauce. Mix well. Shape into balls about 1–1½ inches in diameter.

Heat some oil in a medium frying pan. Fry the meatballs until golden in colour and cooked. Drain.

Heat the tomato sauce in a large pan and add the meatballs. Simmer for a further 30 minutes until tender and juicy.

Serve with spaghetti.

Serves 4–6

Tomato sauce

2 tbs olive oil

4 garlic cloves, finely chopped

2 onions, finely chopped

28-oz tin whole tomatoes, puréed

1 tsp tomato paste

½ tsp salt

¼ cup chopped fresh basil

1 cup chicken stock

2 tsp brown sugar

Heat the oil in a medium saucepan. Add the garlic and onion and sauté for about 3–5 minutes.

Add the tomatoes, tomato paste, salt, basil and some freshly ground black pepper. Add the stock and sugar. Stir and simmer for 40 minutes until thick.

Taste and adjust seasoning.

Makes about 3 cups

Stewed lamb with rosemary

6 lamb slices (from leg or shoulder), about 1 inch thick

2 tbs olive oil

1 cup chopped tomatoes

8 garlic cloves, finely chopped

1 tbs chopped fresh rosemary

Marinade

2 tbs plain yogurt

2 tbs minced chives

2 garlic cloves, minced

Mix the marinade ingredients together. Rub onto the lamb slices and marinate for 2 hours or overnight.

Heat the olive oil in a large frying pan and fry the lamb slices on both sides until the meat is nicely browned.

Add the tomatoes and garlic, and sprinkle the rosemary over the top of the meat. Cover and simmer for 1 hour or more, adding a little water at a time if necessary to prevent sticking.

Season to taste with salt and freshly ground black pepper.

Serves 6

Trini fried chicken

1 chicken, jointed

2 tbs Trini fresh herb seasoning paste (see page 355)

1 tbs vinegar

1 tsp salt

1 cup thin plain yogurt

1 cup flour

1 tsp baking powder

1 tsp paprika

1 tsp cayenne pepper

vegetable oil for deep-frying

Clean and wash the chicken joints. Pat dry. Rub with the herb paste, vinegar and salt. Combine with the yogurt and refrigerate for about 1 hour.

Combine the flour and baking powder and season with the paprika, cayenne pepper and salt and freshly ground black pepper.

Remove the chicken from the yogurt, dredge in the flour and place on a wire rack.

Heat about 1 inch oil in a large frying pan. Fry the pieces a few at a time until golden brown, about 20–25 minutes.

Serve with pepper sauce.

Serves 4–6

> *Trinidadians love fried chicken, as is evident from the numerous fried chicken chains located across the two islands. The secret to our tasty fried chicken? Fresh herb seasoning and pepper sauce!*

Jerked chicken brochettes with mango salsa

Although traditionally Jamaican, jerk has grown in popularity in Trinidad and Tobago in recent years.

4 tbs jerk marinade

2 tbs vegetable oil

2 lb boneless chicken, cut into 1½-inch pieces

Soak eight wooden skewers in water for 4 hours.

Combine the jerk marinade with the oil, add the chicken and combine. Let marinate for about 2 hours in the refrigerator.

Preheat grill, broiler or barbecue to medium.

Thread the chicken onto the skewers and place on a greased grill or under the broiler. Grill for about 10 minutes, turning once, until the chicken is cooked through.

Serve with mango salsa and a rice pilaf (see page 209).

Serves 4

Mango salsa

2 mangoes, half-ripe, preferably Julie mango or any large smooth-textured variety

1 garlic clove, minced

½ hot pepper, finely chopped and seeded (more or less, to taste)

1 tbs fresh lime juice

½ tsp salt

¼ cup chadon beni (cilantro), finely chopped

Combine the mangoes, garlic, pepper, lime juice and salt.

Let stand for 1 hour.

Add the chadon beni just before serving.

Makes about 3 cups

shepherd's pie with cheesy mashed potatoes

You can use any type of ground beef, chicken or lamb or a combination. You can incorporate some vegetables into the mix before topping with loads of creamy mashed potatoes – that way you have a wholesome all-inclusive meal. You can even freeze the leftovers, if there are any!

2 lb potatoes

¾ cup milk

¾ cup grated cheddar cheese

2 tbs butter

1 tsp salt

2 lb ground beef

2 tbs ground chives

1 tbs fresh thyme

2 tbs vegetable oil

1 onion, chopped

2 garlic cloves, chopped

2 pimento peppers, seeded and chopped

19-oz tin tomatoes, drained

Peel the potatoes and cook in boiling salted water for 40 minutes until tender. Drain and mash with the milk, cheese, butter and salt. Set aside.

Combine the beef with the chives and thyme.

Preheat the oven to 400°F. Butter a 9 x 3-inch heatproof glass casserole dish.

Heat the oil in a sauté pan and add the onion, garlic and pimento. Cook until translucent.

Add the beef and brown, then add the tomatoes, breaking them up with a fork.

Bring the mixture to a boil and season with salt and freshly ground black pepper. Cover and simmer for about 15 minutes, stirring occasionally. The mixture should have some sauce.

Taste and adjust seasonings.

Transfer the meat mixture to the prepared dish. Spread the mashed potatoes on top and bake for 30 minutes until the potatoes are browned on top.

Serves 6

'As long as I can remember, since I was a child, I have always loved shepherd's pie. It contained all the ingredients I enjoyed eating in a mouthwatering combination. I even loved to eat the leftovers, which tasted even better! For anyone who is just a little uncertain as to what exactly shepherd's pie is, well originally, as history dictates, it was a way to use up leftover meat, which was ground, seasoned (sometimes!) and then topped with mashed potatoes and baked. Today's version, or the one I've come to love, is much fresher and tastier.'

'When there is a Muslim wedding a goat will be killed and curried as part of the feast but goat meat is also consumed regularly for everyday meals.'

Curried goat

2 lb lean goat meat, cut into ½-inch cubes

⅓ cup plain yogurt

2 tbs lime juice

2 tbs minced chives

1 tbs dark rum

6 garlic cloves, minced

3 tbs duck and goat masala or dark curry powder

1 tbs vegetable oil

1 onion, chopped fine

2 hot peppers, seeded and chopped

2 pimento peppers, seeded and chopped

1 tbs minced thyme

1 tsp salt

¼ cup chadon beni (cilantro), finely chopped

Marinate the goat meat in the yogurt, lime juice, minced chives, rum, two of the minced garlic cloves and 1 tablespoon masala powder. Leave overnight.

Heat the oil in a large iron pot. Add the remaining garlic, the onion, peppers and thyme and sauté for about 4 minutes.

Mix the remaining masala powder with 4 tablespoons water.

Add to the pot and cook until quite dry. Add the goat meat and brown, stirring occasionally. Add the salt and cover, adding only a small amount of water if necessary to prevent sticking.

Cook until tender, about 1 hour. Taste and adjust seasoning, add the chadon beni and remove from heat.

Serves 4

Chadon beni

Pot roast of beef

Pot roasts are a slow-cooking process for the less tender cuts of beef. When braised in a delicious marinade and liquid the result is a wonderful roast, full of flavour. The leftovers make the best sandwiches!

12 garlic cloves, minced

3 tbs olive oil

⅓ cup fresh thyme

1 tbs Dijon mustard

1 tbs freshly ground black pepper

2 tbs red wine vinegar

1 cup red wine

3½–4 lb beef roast

3 cups thinly sliced onion

½ cup thinly sliced carrot

4 cups beef or chicken stock

1 tsp flour (optional)

Combine half the garlic with 2 tablespoons oil, the thyme, mustard, black pepper, vinegar and wine. Rub onto the roast, cover and marinate overnight in the refrigerator.

Remove roast from refrigerator. Preheat the oven to 350°F.

Heat the remaining oil in a heavy frying pan and sauté the onions with the remaining garlic until translucent. Add the carrot and sauté for a few minutes more. Remove from the pan and set aside.

Remove beef from marinade and add to the pan. Brown evenly on all sides.

Place the onion mixture into a casserole dish big enough to hold the roast, then place the browned roast on top of the onions. Add about ½ cup stock, cover and bake, basting every 20 minutes until done. Add only about ½ cup stock at a time during the roasting process. Keep the roast tightly covered at all times to prevent sticking.

The meat should be cooked in about 2 hours, but check after 90 minutes. It is done when a pronged fork will go through it fairly easily. If you taste a little it should be fairly chewy but reasonably tender. If you have a meat thermometer, a reading of 110–125°F is a medium-rare roast, very pink in the middle – this is a good reading for beef. A reading of 125–140°F is a well-done roast.

Remove the roast from the pan. The liquid that remains should be a delicious aromatic and flavourful broth. Strain the liquid and place in a saucepan. You can thicken it, if wished, by stirring in 1 teaspoon flour and cooking for another 3 minutes.

Serves 6–8

stir-fried beef with oyster sauce

3 tsp cornstarch

2 tbs oyster sauce

2 tbs soy sauce

1 tbs sesame oil

1 lb boneless beef or sirloin steak

1 tsp sugar

2 tbs vegetable oil

1 tbs minced garlic

1 tbs minced ginger

8-oz tin sliced bamboo shoots

4-oz tin mushrooms

8 oz green vegetables (bok choy/pak choi or green beans)

½ cup chicken stock or water

½ cup chives, cut into 2-inch pieces

Stir 2 teaspoons cornstarch into 2 tablespoons water. Mix with the oyster sauce, half the soy sauce and half the sesame oil. Set aside.

Trim the fat from the beef and slice with the grain into 2-inch strips. Cut strips into ⅛-inch slices across the grain.

Mix the sugar with the remaining cornstarch, soy sauce and sesame oil. Toss the beef in the marinade, put into a plastic bag and rest in the refrigerator for about 30 minutes.

Heat a wok and add half the vegetable oil. Add the garlic and ginger and stir-fry until fragrant.

Add the beef and stir and fry until the beef is brown. Remove beef from the wok and clean the pan.

Heat the remaining oil in the wok and add the bamboo shoots, mushrooms and green vegetables. Stir-fry until the vegetables are bright coloured, 2–8 minutes.

Return the beef to the pan and stir and fry until it is coated. Add the cornstarch mixture and chicken stock and stir until thickened.

Sprinkle with the chives and serve with noodles or rice.

Serves 4–6

stuffed chicken breasts

1½ lb boneless chicken breasts (about 6)

4 garlic cloves, minced

½ tsp freshly ground black pepper

2 tbs vegetable oil

1 large onion, finely chopped

½ cup chopped chives

2 pimento peppers, seeded and chopped

2 tbs fresh thyme

2 cups fresh breadcrumbs

2 tbs raisins

½ cup chicken stock

¼ cup chopped parsley

¼ cup grated cheese (optional)

2 tbs olive oil

Prepare the chicken breasts by placing each piece between two sheets of waxed paper. Pound until about ¼-inch thick. Season with half the garlic and the black pepper.

Heat the vegetable oil in a large sauté pan and add the remaining garlic and the onion. Sauté until fragrant, then add the chives, pimento pepper and thyme. Stir and fry for 4 minutes until all the herbs become fragrant.

Add the breadcrumbs and raisins and stir to combine. Gradually add the chicken stock and stir until the stuffing comes together. Add the parsley and cheese, if using. Adjust the seasoning to taste. Leave the stuffing to cool.

Preheat the oven to 350°F.

Place about 1 tablespoon of stuffing on each chicken breast. Roll each breast up and hold together with small metal skewers.

Heat the olive oil in a sauté pan and sauté the chicken breasts until brown. Remove to a heatproof baking dish and bake for 30 minutes.

Remove the chicken breasts from the dish and take out the skewers. Let rest briefly then slice and serve.

You may make a sauce using the drippings from the baking dish.

Serves 6

' There is a strong Lebanese population on our islands and their foods have only now come mainstream – lucky for those of us who love this cuisine. Probably the most popular snack along with their salads is kibbeh – Syrian stuffed bulgur croquettes with pine nuts and spices. '

Kibbeh

1½ cups fine or medium bulgur wheat

8 oz boneless lamb, cubed

1 onion, minced

vegetable oil for frying

Filling

2 tbs olive oil

1 small onion, minced

¼ tsp ground allspice

1 tsp ground cinnamon

¼ tsp ground cloves

1 tbs minced ginger

¼ tsp grated nutmeg

4 oz lean ground lamb

¼ cup chopped parsley

2 tbs lemon juice

2 tbs pine nuts, toasted

Cover the bulgur wheat with cold water and soak for 20 minutes. Drain, squeeze out excess moisture and place in a clean towel.

Place the cubed lamb, onion and some salt and freshly ground black pepper in a food processor and process for 1 minute. Add the bulgur in three batches and process for about 3 minutes, until the mixture is like a soft dough.

To make the filling, heat the oil in a frying pan and sauté the onion until soft. Add the spices and cook for 2 minutes more.

Add the ground lamb and cook for about 4 minutes.

Add the parsley, lemon juice and pine nuts. Season with salt and pepper.

With wet hands take a tablespoon of the kibbeh mixture and make it into a round ball. Flatten into a 3-inch disc.

Place a small amount of filling on the lower half of each kibbeh disc. Seal the edges and roll into an egg shape, tapering the ends to a point.

Heat some oil in a medium frying pan and shallow-fry a few at a time until golden.

Makes 15

stewed oxtail

2 lb oxtail, sliced into ¾-inch pieces

1 tbs minced garlic

2 tbs Trini fresh herb seasoning paste (see page 355)

1 tbs red wine vinegar

2 tbs vegetable oil

2 tbs brown sugar

1 large French thyme sprig

1 pimento pepper, seeded and chopped

1 large onion, chopped

¼ tsp allspice powder

4 cloves

Trim the meat of fat and season with the garlic, herb paste and vinegar. Set aside for 1 hour.

Heat the oil in a sauté pan, add the sugar and caramelize to a dark brown colour. It should look dark and frothy. Add the oxtail pieces, turning quickly to ensure even browning.

Add the thyme, pimento and onion, stir and fry well. Add the allspice and cloves, salt and freshly ground black pepper. Cook for a few minutes then turn the heat to low and cover.

Let cook until tender, about 40 minutes, basting occasionally and adding water only if needed to prevent sticking. The meat should be a deep brown colour with a rich-looking gravy.

Serves 4–6

sautéed chicken livers

These are usually enjoyed with sada roti or bake for a quick dinner.

12 fresh chicken livers, cleaned and cut in two

2 tbs unsalted butter

2 garlic cloves, finely chopped

1 small onion, chopped

2 tbs fresh lemon juice

1 tbs fresh thyme

¼ cup good-quality olive oil

Season the livers with salt and freshly ground black pepper.

Melt the butter in a small frying pan. Add the garlic and onion. Sauté until fragrant and the onions have become soft and sweet, about 5 minutes.

Add the livers and cook for about 3 minutes for pinkish livers or 5–7 minutes for well-done. They should remain moist and tender and should just be beginning to give up their juices.

With the heat still on, add the lemon juice and thyme and scrape the drippings from the pan. Add the olive oil and stir until the mixture is warm and well blended.

Serves 2–4

Garlicky roasted leg of lamb

8 garlic cloves, minced

4 tbs red wine vinegar

2 tbs Dijon mustard

2 tsp coarsely cracked black pepper

2 tbs chopped fresh rosemary or 1 tbs dried rosemary

2 tbs olive oil

4 lb leg of lamb, bone in

2 tsp salt

Place the garlic, vinegar, mustard, pepper, rosemary and olive oil in a food processor and process until combined.

Rub the marinade over the lamb, cover and refrigerate overnight.

Before roasting remove lamb from refrigerator, bring to room temperature and rub with the salt.

Preheat oven to 375°F.

Roast the lamb for 1–1½ hours or until done. Lamb is usually at its best when a meat thermometer inserted in the thickest part registers 140°F (medium-rare).

Allow the roast to rest for 15 minutes before carving.

Serves 8

BBQ chicken

4 lb chicken, cut into 8 pieces

1 tbs minced garlic

2 tbs fresh French thyme

2 tbs minced chives

1 tbs fresh rosemary (optional)

2 tbs red wine vinegar

1 tsp coarsely ground black pepper

½ cup olive oil

1 tsp salt

1 cup barbecue sauce (see page 353)

Wash the chicken pieces and dry.

Combine the garlic, thyme, chives, rosemary, if using, vinegar, black pepper and olive oil. Rub the chicken inside and out with the marinade, getting under the skin if possible. Cover and refrigerate for 2 hours or overnight.

Preheat the barbecue to medium setting. Remove the chicken from the marinade and add the salt.

Grease the grill and place the chicken on it.

Cook for about 30 minutes, turning the chicken frequently and extinguishing any flare-ups with a spray bottle filled with water.

Brush with barbecue sauce, turn once again and serve immediately.

Serves 4

BBQ is big on this island and is sold at many fast-food huts and tents around the island. Popular offerings are chicken, lamb and fish. They are sold with sides of green salad and a choice of macaroni, potato salad, fries or rice.

BBQ steak

1 tbs minced garlic

1 tbs Worcestershire sauce

1 tsp Dijon mustard

1 tbs coarsely ground black pepper

¼ cup olive oil

6 rib-eye steaks, 1 inch thick

1 cup barbecue sauce (see page 353)

Combine the garlic, Worcestershire sauce, mustard, black pepper and olive oil. Pour over the steaks and leave to marinate for about 1 hour.

Preheat the barbecue to high, grease the grill and place the steaks on it.

Grill for about 4 minutes each side – when blood begins to pool at the surface of the steak, flip over and cook for a few minutes more to desired stage of doneness.

Brush with the barbecue sauce and serve immediately.

Serves 6

BBQ lamb chops

8 lamb shoulder or loin chops

barbecue sauce (optional)

Marinade

4 garlic cloves, minced

2 tbs honey

2 tbs soy sauce

2 tbs minced fresh herbs (thyme, basil, chives)

1 tbs lemon juice

Combine all the ingredients for the marinade and rub onto the chops. Marinate for 4 hours or overnight.

Preheat the barbecue to medium hot. Grease the grill and place the lamb on it. Baste with a zesty barbecue sauce, if desired, and cook, turning once, for 5–6 minutes on each side, or until desired doneness.

Serves 4

Chinese fried chicken

1 bottle dark soy sauce

3 lb chicken, left whole

3 cups vegetable oil for deep-frying

Pour the soy sauce over the chicken, cover and let marinate for a few hours in the refrigerator, turning occasionally.

Remove from the refrigerator and drain.

Heat the oil in a wok. After about 5 minutes place the chicken whole into the oil and turn.

Cover and let cook for about 20 minutes. Remove the lid, turn again and allow the chicken to crisp up a little.

When fully cooked, remove and drain.

Serves 4–6

Vegetarian

Chickpea burgers

2 cups cooked chickpeas
   (channa)

4 blades chive

½ onion

1 egg

2 tbs all-purpose flour

1 tbs fresh oregano or French
   thyme

½ tsp paprika

1 tsp ground roasted geera
   (cumin)

1 tsp pepper sauce

1 tsp salt

olive oil for frying

Place all the ingredients into the bowl of a food processor. Pulse, stopping once or twice to scrape down the sides. Stop when the mixture is still coarse in texture but holds together when pressed between the fingers.

Form into four to six patties, depending on the size you prefer.

Heat the olive oil in a non-stick frying pan over medium-high heat. Add the patties and pan-fry until golden, about 4 minutes. Flip over and cook for 2–4 minutes more.

Drain and serve in whole-wheat buns or pitta bread with yogurt sauce, lettuce and tomatoes.

Serves 4

Pigeon pea patties

1 tbs olive oil

1 onion, chopped

1 garlic clove, chopped

1 large potato, boiled

1 lb fresh pigeon peas,
   precooked, or 14-oz tin pigeon
   peas, drained

1 tbs thyme

1 tbs chopped chives

⅓ cup chopped fresh basil

½ hot pepper, seeded and
   chopped

1 cup dried breadcrumbs

1 egg

¼ cup vegetable oil

Heat the olive oil in a small frying pan. Add the onion and garlic and cook until soft, about 3–4 minutes.

In a large mixing bowl mash the potato well until very creamy – this will help the patties hold together. Add the pigeon peas and the onion and garlic from the frying pan.

Add the thyme, chives, basil and pepper. Stir well to combine. Season to taste with salt and freshly ground black pepper.

Form the mixture into about 10 balls and set aside.

Place the breadcrumbs on a plate and season with salt and pepper. Lightly beat the egg and place in a shallow dish.

Flatten the pigeon pea balls into patties about 2½ inches in diameter. Dip each patty into the egg and dredge in crumbs.

Heat the vegetable oil in a large frying pan and shallow-fry the patties for 2 or 3 minutes on each side until golden.

Makes about 10

Lentil burgers

⅔ cup milk

1 cup fresh breadcrumbs

1 cup cooked lentils

1 large onion, minced

2 garlic cloves, minced

½ cup chopped celery

2 pimento peppers, seeded and chopped

1 tsp roasted geera (cumin)

1 tsp chilli powder

salt to taste

olive oil for frying

flour for dredging

Combine the milk with the breadcrumbs and let stand for 5 minutes.

Combine all the other ingredients in a bowl. Add the breadcrumb mixture and mix with a spoon. The mixture should hold together.

Form the mixture into patties with your hands, approximately 2 inches across.

Heat some olive oil in a frying pan. Dredge the patties in flour and pan-fry in the hot oil for 2 or 3 minutes on each side until golden.

Makes 8

Veggie burgers

2 cups soya mince (textured vegetable protein)

4 black Chinese mushrooms, soaked for 30 minutes in hot water, drained and chopped

1 green bell pepper, seeded and chopped

2 pimento peppers, seeded and chopped

2 garlic cloves, minced

1 onion, minced

about 1 cup fresh breadcrumbs

½ cup grated cheese

⅓ cup chopped chadon beni (cilantro)

⅓ cup chopped basil

⅓ cup chopped parsley

salt and freshly ground black pepper

1 egg yolk (optional, see recipe)

2 tbs olive oil for frying

Soak the soya mince for about 30 minutes.

Rinse in a strainer under plenty of running water. Squeeze the mince well and place in a mixing bowl.

Add the rest of the ingredients. If the mixture seems a little wet, add some more breadcrumbs; if too dry, add an egg yolk. Form the mixture into 3-inch patties with your hands.

Heat the olive oil in a frying pan and pan-fry the patties for 2 or 3 minutes on each side until golden.

Makes 6

Curried channa with potato

1 cup chickpeas (channa),
  soaked overnight

2 tbs vegetable oil

4 garlic cloves, chopped

1 onion, sliced

½ hot pepper, seeded and
  chopped

3 tbs curry powder mixed with
  ¼ cup water

2 potatoes, cubed

Drain the chickpeas, place in a saucepan, cover with water and boil until tender, about 40 minutes. Drain.

Heat the oil in a heavy sauté pan. Add the garlic, onion and pepper and cook for a few minutes until fragrant. Add the curry paste and cook until the mixture is almost dry.

Add the channa and potato, stir well. Add a little water and cook at a simmer until the potato is tender, about 20 minutes.

Serves 4

Note
You can make this without the potatoes. Simply add the channa and a little water to the cooked curry paste and simmer for about 15 minutes.

Scarlet ibis

Provision plate

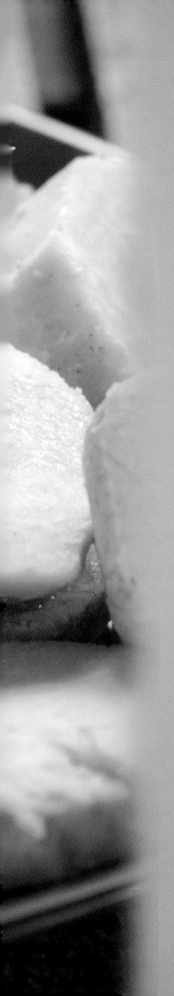

Rice, coo coo and provisions

Rice and provisions are mealtime staples here in Trinidad and Tobago. Rice is often served plain boiled or steamed accompanied by stewed peas or dhal though fancy rice dishes or rice pilafs have become more popular through the years.

All types of provisions and breadfruit are enjoyed – mostly plain boiled as an accompaniment to stewed fish, saltfish or meats. Dasheen, eddoes, cassava, yams and sweet potatoes are the most available and the most popular. The deliciousness of these provisions allows them to star without fancy dressings at any meal table. I have come to love plain boiled cassava with just a drizzle of olive oil. Dasheen is peeled, boiled and sliced and marries well with callaloo. Eddoes, like cassava, are enjoyed with saltfish. Yams, due to the dry texture, are usually best either mashed or made into crusty yam cakes. Sweet potatoes can be enjoyed in chips, plain boiled, roasted and in croquettes.

There is no specific way to prepare any provision; they can be used interchangeably and will make a delicious accompaniment to any meat or fish dish, and even stand on their own, as in the ubiquitous breadfruit oiled down. They are all stars in our hearty Trini soups.

Then there are plantains. These do not fall into the provision category but do bring big and bold flavours to our meals. They are eaten plain boiled or, when fully ripened, fried, made into casseroles, even baked with cinnamon and orange juice for added sweetness at our tables. A local speciality of pound plantains is still enjoyed. There is no specific time to serve plantains – for me, I can eat them with my meals every day!

Coo Coo is another major starch, part of our culinary heritage from our Spanish ancestors. It is cornmeal cooked with okra and aromatics, and sometimes coconut milk, rolled into a ball, cooled, sliced and served with stewed fish and/ or callaloo.

Provisions

Cassava

Yams

Eddoes and dasheen

All provisions need to be boiled in plenty of water. They will be cooked after about 30 minutes or when tender to a tester.

Cassava must be peeled and then boiled. It can also be peeled and frozen for future use.

Dasheen, yam and tannia should be peeled and then boiled. Sometimes dasheen will turn a slight tinge of lavender or blue. This is normal and depends on the type of dasheen. There is a specific type called 'blue' dasheen which is synonymous with Tobago cuisine, hence their food is often termed 'blue food'.

Eddoes and sweet potatoes can be boiled with or without the skin; sweet potatoes can be wrapped in foil and oven-roasted.

Sweet potato French fries

2 lb sweet potatoes
vegetable oil for frying

Peel and cut the sweet potatoes into French fry shapes.

Heat the oil in a large frying pan.

Dry the sweet potatoes and fry in the hot oil until golden and crisp. Be careful when stirring not to break the fries.

Drain on paper towels and serve.

Serves 4

Tannia cakes with fresh herbs

Tannia is a cousin to the African yam. It is very white and very tender.

4 tannias

1 tbs unsalted butter

1 tbs chopped fresh chives

1 garlic clove, minced

2 tbs flour

½ cup toasted breadcrumbs

1 egg, lightly beaten

vegetable oil for frying

1 tbs chopped fresh parsley

Boil the tannias in enough salted water to cover until cooked and tender.

Peel, cut into small pieces and mash with a potato masher.

Add the butter, chives and garlic and season to taste with salt and freshly ground black pepper.

Form the tannia mixture into cakes about 2 inches in diameter.

Place the flour on one plate, the breadcrumbs on another. Put the egg in a shallow dish.

Dredge the cakes in the flour then dip into the beaten egg and coat with breadcrumbs.

Fry in hot oil until golden brown on both sides.

Drain on paper towels and sprinkle with chopped parsley before serving.

Makes 8

Note

For a lighter dish: Place the tannia cakes on a non-stick baking tray and bake at 450°F for about 10 minutes on each side until crusty

To make yam cakes follow the above recipe, using 2 lb yams instead of the tannias.

Cassava dumplings

1 lb cassava, peeled

1 tbs chopped parsley

1 tbs chopped fresh thyme

2 tbs all-purpose flour

1 tsp baking powder

1 tsp brown sugar

½ cup milk

½ tsp salt

olive oil, to serve

Either place the cassava in the bowl of a food processor and process until a fine paste is obtained or grate the cassava on the fine side of a grater.

Add the chopped herbs to the cassava, place in a large mixing bowl and add the flour, baking powder, sugar and some salt. Add the milk a little at a time and knead to a firm but not hard dough.

Form the dumplings into 2-inch oblong shapes using a teaspoon to help you.

Bring a large pot of water to a boil, add the salt and when boiling drop in the cassava dumplings.

Cook until they float to the top of the pot, remove and serve hot, drizzled with olive oil, with salted fish or any stew-type meat dish.

Makes 16–24

Cassava sauté

1 lb cassava, peeled and cut into 3-inch pieces

2 tbs vegetable oil

2 onions, sliced

2 pimento peppers, seeded and cut into strips

½ Congo pepper, seeded and chopped

2 garlic cloves, chopped

¼ cup chopped celery

¼ cup chopped parsley

2 tbs fresh thyme

Place the cassava in a saucepan, cover with water, add a pinch of salt and boil until tender, 20–25 minutes. Drain and cool.

Cut the cassava into 1-inch pieces, split in half and remove the centre fibre.

Heat the oil in a large non-stick frying pan and add the onion, peppers and garlic. Sauté until fragrant.

Add the cassava and turn and toss until the cassava pieces become coated with the onion and garlic mixture. Add the celery, parsley and thyme and season with salt and freshly ground black pepper. Continue cooking over a medium heat, scraping the bottom of the pan to prevent sticking.

Cook for 10 minutes or until the cassava pieces are golden in colour. Adjust seasoning to taste before serving.

Serves 4–6

Sweet potatoes

Roasted garlic and sweet potato croquettes

1 head garlic

olive oil

2 lb sweet potatoes

¼ cup butter

2 eggs

½ cup milk

½ cup flour

1 cup dried breadcrumbs

vegetable oil for frying

Preheat the oven to 400°F.

Slice the top from the garlic head, drizzle with a little olive oil, place in a roasting pan and wrap in foil. Roast for 1 hour then let cool.

Squeeze the garlic from the base and the pulp should come right out. Set aside.

Boil the sweet potatoes until very soft, about 40 minutes, depending on size.

Peel and mash well. Add the butter, one beaten egg, milk and roasted garlic cloves and stir to combine. Season with salt.

Place the flour on a plate and the breadcrumbs on another. Beat the remaining egg in a shallow dish.

Roll the potato into 1½-inch balls. Dredge in the flour, then dip into the beaten egg, then roll in the crumbs.

Heat some oil in a large frying pan and fry the croquettes until golden.

Makes 8–12

'Breadfruit is aptly named as history dictates that it once served as a main source of nourishment for slaves brought to the Caribbean to work on the sugar plantations. It originates from the South Pacific and the trees were brought from Tahiti to Jamaica and St Vincent by Captains Bligh and Cook in 1793. It has since spread throughout the Caribbean and we are now blessed with this delicious and versatile fruit. If you're unfamiliar with how to deal with breadfruit don't be intimidated by it as it cooks in about 30 minutes and lends itself to many delicious ways of preparation.

This irresistible provision with its unique flavour and texture produces the ubiquitous breadfruit oiled down when simmered in a coconut milk broth, fired up with hot peppers and flavoured with local herbs. An oiled down (oil down, run down, mettagee) is certainly one of the most delicious local dishes around. Whether breadfruit is whipped, baked, fried, sautéed, souffléd or scalloped it's a cook's dream ingredient because of its versatility.

Breadfruits are more readily available these days. There are two types – the yellow breadfruit tends to be the favourite because the flesh has a creamier texture and flavour than the white breadfruit, which tends to be a little drier. However they are both really wonderful when used in any of the following recipes! Remember, breadfruit is a good source of complex carbohydrates and is rich in vitamins A, B and C.'

Breadfruit oiled down

- **3 lb breadfruit**
- **2 tbs vegetable oil**
- **1 cup chopped onion**
- **1 tbs chopped garlic**
- **1 Congo pepper, seeded and chopped, plus 1 whole Congo pepper (optional)**
- **2 large pimento peppers, seeded and chopped**
- **¾ cup chopped chives or spring onions, green and white parts**
- **2 tbs chopped fresh thyme**
- **3 cups fresh coconut milk**
- **2 tsp salt**
- **1 tsp freshly ground black pepper**

Peel and cut the breadfruit into 2-inch pieces.

Heat the oil in a large heavy frying pan. Add the onion, garlic, chopped pepper, pimentos, chives and thyme. Sauté until fragrant, for about 4 minutes.

Add the coconut milk, salt and pepper and bring the mixture to a boil. Lower the heat and add the breadfruit. Drop in the whole Congo pepper at this point, if using.

Cover the pan and simmer for about 25–30 minutes until all the coconut milk has been absorbed and the breadfruit is cooked and tender. There should be only a small amount of coconut oil at the bottom of the pan when the breadfruit is cooked.

Serves 6–8

Buying breadfruit

Choose breadfruit that's not too green, with a relatively smooth skin. Breadfruit that is yellowish on the outside is probably overripe and won't be as delicious.

Cooking breadfruit

Always try to prepare the breadfruit on the day you bought it. If you can't, then leave it overnight in a bucket filled with water and prepare it the next day.

You can steam cook the breadfruit whole. Place in a deep saucepan, half-fill with water, then cover and steam for about 45–60 minutes, depending on size. When the breadfruit is tender it's cooked.

If you don't want to use all the uncooked breadfruit at once just cut it in half and refrigerate the unused portion for just a couple of days wrapped in plastic wrap. Freezing uncooked breadfruit is not recommended.

Breadfruit Creole

1 medium breadfruit

2 tbs olive oil

1 cup chopped onion

3 garlic cloves, chopped

1 hot pepper, seeded and chopped (more or less, to taste)

2 pimento peppers, seeded and chopped

2 tomatoes, chopped

1 tbs fresh thyme

1 tbs chopped celery

Cut the breadfruit into quarters, remove the core and place in a saucepan. Cover with water and cook for about 20–30 minutes until tender.

Drain, peel and cut into 1-inch cubes.

Heat the oil in a large heavy frying pan and sauté the onion, garlic and peppers until tender. Add the breadfruit and stir to combine. Add the tomatoes, thyme and celery and cook, stirring occasionally until all the ingredients are tender, about 10 minutes. Season with salt and freshly ground black pepper.

Serves 6

Creamy breadfruit pie

3 lb breadfruit

about ¾ cup milk

¼ cup butter

½ cup grated carrot

2 tbs chopped parsley

½ cup grated cheese

Preheat the oven to 375°F.

Peel and core the breadfruit and cut into eighths. Place in a saucepan and boil in plenty of salted water.

Remove and drain when the breadfruit is very tender. Mash with a potato masher.

Warm the milk with the butter and add to the mashed breadfruit – more milk may be needed to give a creamy consistency.

Add the carrot and parsley and season to taste with salt.

Place in a greased glass ovenproof dish and top with the cheese. Bake until golden on top.

Serves 8

Breadfruit and saltfish roll

As an alternative the above breadfruit mix can be rolled out to a rectangle 12 by 10 inches, spread with saltfish sautéed with onions, peppers and tomatoes, rolled up jelly-roll style and baked in a preheated 375°F oven for 30 minutes.

Slice and enjoy as a light lunch or as an addition to a breakfast or brunch table.

Breadfruit chips

These can be serves as an appetizer with an avocado or tomato salsa or as a side dish in place of French fries.

1 medium breadfruit

vegetable oil for frying

Peel and cut the breadfruit into quarters, remove the core and slice each quarter lengthways into ¼-inch thick slices.

Heat the oil in a deep frying pan. When hot, drop the breadfruit slices into the oil and fry in batches turning occasionally until golden in colour on both sides.

Drain and sprinkle with salt.

Serves 6

Breadfruit turnovers

2 lb breadfruit, peeled and cut into quarters

1 tsp salt

¼ cup melted butter

¾ cup flour

1 cup fine toasted breadcrumbs

1 egg, lightly beaten

Filling

2 tbs vegetable oil

2 garlic cloves, minced

1 small onion, minced

½ carrot, finely chopped

½ cup mixed fresh herbs, finely chopped

8 oz ground chicken or beef (or both)

⅓ cup chopped parsley

Boil the breadfruit in plenty of water with the salt until tender, 20–30 minutes. Drain.

While the breadfruit is still hot, mash and add the melted butter and ¼ cup flour. Combine until the mixture begins to stay together, knead for a few minutes, cover and set aside.

Heat the oil in a sauté pan, add the garlic and onion and sauté for a few minutes. Add the carrot and the mixed herbs.

Add the chicken or beef and cook until tender, about 15 minutes. Season with salt and freshly ground black pepper.

Remove from the heat, add the parsley and leave the mixture to cool.

Preheat the oven to 375°F.

Flour a work surface and roll out the breadfruit dough to about ¼-inch thickness. Stamp out circles using a 3-inch cutter.

Place about 1 tablespoon filling on the lower half of each circle. Fold over and seal with a fork.

Put the remaining flour on one plate and the breadcrumbs on another. Put the egg in a shallow dish.

Dust the turnovers with flour, brush with beaten egg and roll in the breadcrumbs.

Bake for about 15 minutes until golden.

Makes about 10

Roasted stuffed breadfruit

Delicious as a light meal with a fresh salad.

1 large yellow breadfruit

1 lb ground beef

2 tbs Trini fresh herb seasoning paste (see page 355)

2 tbs chopped celery

2 garlic cloves, minced

2 tbs vegetable oil

1 small onion, minced

1 hot pepper, seeded and chopped

2 pimento peppers, seeded and chopped

Remove the top of the breadfruit and set aside. With a sharp knife, remove the heart, or centre, only.

Season the beef with the herb paste, celery, garlic and some salt.

Heat the oil in a sauté pan, add the onion and peppers, and sauté for a few minutes. Add the beef and cook for about 20 minutes until tender.

Stuff the breadfruit with the beef mixture. Put the top back onto the breadfruit and wrap in foil.

Place on a preheated open grill or barbecue and roast for 1 hour until tender.

Slice into quarters and serve.

Serves 4-8

Okra rice with coconut

2 oz salted cod

2 tbs vegetable oil

1 large onion, chopped

4 garlic cloves, chopped

1 hot pepper, seeded and chopped

2 pimento peppers, seeded and chopped

12 okra, sliced

2 tomatoes, chopped

2 cups rice

3 cups chicken or vegetable stock

1 cup coconut milk

Soak the salted cod in cool water for about 30 minutes. Drain and shred into pieces.

Heat the oil in a large sauté pan. Add the onion, garlic and peppers and sauté until fragrant.

Add the shredded cod, stir then add the okra and cook for about 5 minutes.

Add tomatoes and stir well. Then add the rice and turn to coat the grains with the oil and flavourings. Pour in the stock and coconut milk and stir to combine.

Bring to a boil, then cover and cook for about 20 minutes until the rice grains are tender.

Season with salt before serving.

Serves 6-8

Black eye peas and rice cookup

1 tbs vegetable oil

1 onion, chopped

1 tbs chopped celery

1 tbs chopped thyme

1 tbs chopped garlic

2 pimento peppers, seeded and chopped

1 tomato, chopped

1 cup cooked black eye peas

1 cup parboiled rice

2 cups vegetable or chicken stock

½ cup coconut milk

2 tsp salt

1 hot pepper, left whole

Heat the oil in a heavy medium saucepan. Add the onion, celery, thyme, garlic and pimento pepper. Sauté until fragrant and the onion is tender then add the tomato and cook for 1 minute more.

Add the black eye peas and rice and turn to coat. Pour in the stock and coconut milk and bring to a boil.

Season with the salt and some freshly ground black pepper. Add the hot pepper and turn the heat to low. Cover and steam until cooked, about 20 minutes. Remove the hot pepper before serving.

Serves 4

Spiced rice pilaf with chickpeas and pine nuts

3 tbs vegetable or olive oil

1 large onion, finely chopped

1 garlic clove, chopped

1 tsp ground cinnamon

½ tsp turmeric powder

½ tsp paprika

14-oz tin chickpeas

⅓ cup pine nuts, toasted

1½ cups parboiled rice

3¾ cups chicken stock

½ cup raisins or currants

Heat the oil in a saucepan, add the onions and garlic and sauté until tender, about 4 minutes.

Add the cinnamon, turmeric and paprika, stir, and add the chickpeas. Add the pine nuts and combine then add the rice and sauté with the spices so that all the grains are coated.

Add the chicken stock and stir well. Season with salt and freshly ground black pepper. Add the raisins, bring to a boil and cover and simmer until the rice is tender.

Fluff with a fork before serving.

Serves 4–6

split pea kitcheree

Kitcheree is a split pea and rice cookup. Sometimes about 2 oz of salted cod is added to the rice dish in the first stage of cooking. If you are doing this just soak the cod for about 20 minutes, then squeeze the water out and shred finely.

½ cup yellow split peas, washed and picked over

2 tbs vegetable oil

1 large onion, sliced

2 garlic cloves, chopped

2-inch stick cinnamon

2 cloves

½ tbs chopped ginger

½ tsp saffron powder or turmeric

1 cup parboiled rice

2½ cups vegetable or chicken stock

Boil the split peas in a saucepan of water for about 10 minutes. Drain.

Heat the oil in a saucepan. Add the onion, garlic, cinnamon, cloves and ginger.

Add the saffron and cook for a few minutes then add the split peas and rice. Stir and fry for a few minutes more.

Add the stock, bring to a boil and simmer for about 20–30 minutes.

Season with salt, fluff with a fork and serve.

Serves 4

Exotic beef biryani rice

2 lb boneless beef, cut into cubes

4 garlic cloves, minced

1 tbs minced ginger

1 hot pepper, seeded and chopped

2 tsp ground coriander seeds

2 tsp ground roasted geera (cumin)

½ tsp turmeric powder

½ cup plain yogurt

2 cups parboiled rice

2 tbs vegetable oil

2 large onions, sliced

2 x 3-inch pieces cinnamon

6 cardamom pods, bruised and opened

2¼ cups beef stock

1½ cups frozen green peas

⅓ cup currants or raisins

2 large tomatoes, cut into wedges

½ cup toasted almonds, halved

2 tbs chopped chadon beni (cilantro) (optional)

Combine the beef with the garlic, ginger, pepper, coriander, geera, turmeric and yogurt. Cover and refrigerate for about 1 hour.

Wash the rice and drain.

Heat the oil in a large pan and add the onion, cinnamon and cardamom. Sauté until the onions are almost browned at the edges.

Add the beef and stir well. Cover and simmer until the beef is tender, about 45–60 minutes, adding just a little water at a time if necessary to prevent sticking.

Add the rice and stir well then add the stock and peas. Simmer for another 20 minutes, until the rice is cooked. Stir in the currants and tomatoes.

Before serving add almonds and chadon beni, if using.

Serves 4-6

'Biryanis have become popular in Trinidad and Tobago due to the growth in the number of authentic Indian restaurants here.'

Callaloo rice

2 tbs vegetable oil

1 tbs chopped garlic

1 onion, finely chopped

½ hot pepper, seeded and chopped

1 pimento pepper, seeded and chopped

3-4 callaloo leaves, chopped

1 cup parboiled rice

1 cup coconut milk

1 cup vegetable or chicken stock

Heat the oil in a saucepan and add the garlic, onion and peppers. Sauté for a few minutes.

Add the callaloo and stir well. Cover and cook until tender, about 10 minutes.

Stir in the rice then pour in the coconut milk and stock. Bring to a boil and lower the heat to a simmer. Cover and cook until the rice is tender, 20 minutes.

Serves 4

spinach rice with coconut (bhaji rice)

2 tbs vegetable oil

1 large onion, minced

2 garlic cloves, minced

1 pimento pepper, seeded and chopped

½ hot pepper, seeded and chopped

4 cups fresh spinach leaves, cleaned, washed and chopped

1 tsp salt

1 tsp freshly ground black pepper

½ tsp grated nutmeg

1 cup parboiled rice

1 cup coconut milk

1½ cups vegetable or chicken stock

Heat the oil in a medium saucepan. Add the onion, garlic and pimento and cook for a few minutes, taking care not to burn.

Add the hot pepper and stir. Add the spinach, combine then lower the heat, cover and cook until the spinach is tender.

Season with the salt, black pepper and grated nutmeg.

Add the rice and stir to combine. Pour in the coconut milk and stock and cook until boiling. When holes appear at the top of the rice, cover and simmer for 20 minutes.

Serves 4

Above: Callaloo bush

Opposite: Spinach rice

Pigeon pea cookup

2 tbs vegetable oil

½ cup chopped onion

1 tsp chopped garlic

2 pimento peppers, seeded and
  chopped

½ hot pepper, seeded and
  chopped

½ cup chopped pumpkin

1 cup parboiled rice

3 tbs tomato sauce

1 tsp salt

1 cup cooked pigeon peas or
  14-oz tin pigeon peas, drained

1½ cups chicken or vegetable
  stock

⅓ cup chopped chives

1 tsp butter

Heat the oil in a saucepan, add the onion and garlic and sauté for a few minutes until golden,

Add the peppers and pumpkin and stir to combine well. Cook for about 5 minutes then add the rice, tomato sauce and salt. Stir well.

Add the pigeon peas and stir then pour in the stock, stir and bring to a boil.

Season with salt and freshly ground black pepper, add the chives, stir, cover and simmer for 20 minutes.

Add the butter, fluff with a fork and serve.

Serves 4–6

'Fried rice can be a major part of many a special meal or a Sunday lunch even when there aren't any other Chinese-inspired dishes on the table.'

Vegetable fried rice

3 tbs vegetable oil

2 eggs, lightly beaten

1 tbs minced garlic

1 tbs minced ginger

1 onion, finely chopped

1 carrot, finely chopped

1 pimento pepper, seeded and chopped

2 tbs chopped celery

5 cups cold cooked rice, separated with a fork

2 tbs soy sauce

1 tsp sesame oil

Heat a wok or large frying pan, add 1 tablespoon oil and heat until hot. Add the eggs and fry over high heat until set. Flip and break up with a spoon. Remove from the pan.

Heat the remaining oil in the wok, add the garlic and ginger and stir-fry until fragrant.

Add the onion, carrots, pepper and celery and continue to cook until the vegetables are tender.

Return the egg to the pan, add the rice and stir-fry until heated thoroughly.

Add the soy sauce and sesame oil, toss to coat evenly. Serve at once.

Serves 6–8

Corn pie

1⅓ cups fresh or tinned corn

2 tbs butter

2 tbs all-purpose flour

1 cup milk

1 garlic clove, finely minced

2 large eggs, lightly beaten

a pinch of sugar

2 tbs grated cheese

Here is an all-time favourite, enjoyed by adults and children alike. There are many variations on this recipe, but to me corn pie is the ultimate in comfort food!

Preheat the oven to 350°F. Lightly grease a 9-inch baking dish.

If using fresh corn, lightly steam the kernels until tender. If using tinned corn, drain.

Melt the butter in a medium saucepan, stir in the flour and cook over medium to low heat until the mixture is fairly liquid. Add the milk and continue cooking, stirring constantly until the mixture thickens.

Remove from the heat and add the corn and garlic and salt and freshly ground black pepper. Add the eggs and stir until well combined.

Adjust seasoning to taste and add a pinch of sugar to enhance the sweetness of the corn. Turn the corn mixture into the prepared baking dish and sprinkle with the grated cheese.

Bake for about 40–50 minutes until the pie is golden and puffed.

Serves 4

Note
For a lighter pie use skimmed milk.

215

Macaroni pie

1 lb macaroni

2 eggs

2 cups evaporated milk

1 lb cheddar cheese, grated

½ cup cracker crumbs

¼ cup butter

Preheat the oven to 375°F.

Break stick macaroni into 2-inch pieces. Boil the macaroni in plenty of water, according to the packet directions. Drain.

Beat the eggs with the milk and stir in the cheese. Add the drained macaroni and combine.

Combine the cracker crumbs with the butter, adding some more grated cheese if liked.

Pour the macaroni mixture into a greased 12-inch glass baking dish. Sprinkle with the crumb mixture.

Bake for 30 minutes until set, and golden and crusty on the top.

Serves 4–6

'For many Trinidadians macaroni pie is the only 'pie' they know! It is a definite on many Sunday lunch tables. Traditionally it is made with stick macaroni but elbow may be used instead.'

Creamy green fig pie

12 green figs
½ cup milk
¼ cup butter
½ cup grated cheese

Preheat the oven to 375°F.

Boil the figs until tender, about 20 minutes.

Warm the milk with the butter.

Drain the figs, peel and mash. Add the milk and butter and salt to taste. If the figs seem to be dry add a little more milk; it should have the consistency of firm mashed potatoes.

Sprinkle with cheese and bake until the cheese is melted and lightly browned.

Serves 4–6

To boil green figs

Place the figs unpeeled in a non-reactive saucepan. Cover with a lot of water, add a little salt and 1 tablespoon vegetable oil to the pot. (This prevents the pot from darkening, as figs contain a lot of iron, some of which is released during cooking.) Bring to a boil and continue boiling until the figs feel tender when a metal skewer is inserted into the centre. Drain.

Peel by removing the top and bottom ends and peeling off the skin, which should come away easily.

To peel uncooked figs

Run the tip of a sharp knife down the length of a fig, making a ¼-inch incision. Repeat at about ½-inch intervals around the fig. Oil your fingers and, using your thumb, move it along the cuts you have just made, lifting the skin as you go. Continue until all the skin has been lifted off.

' Plantains are very popular throughout the Caribbean and are used frequently in our cuisine. They can be boiled, fried or baked and the green plantains are used to make chips to snack on. '

Plantain casserole

¼ cup olive oil

4 almost ripe plantains, peeled and sliced lengthways

Filling

2 tbs vegetable oil

1 onion, chopped

1 pimento pepper, seeded and chopped

2 garlic cloves, chopped

½ cup chopped fresh herbs

1 lb ground beef or chicken

½ cup tomato sauce

⅓ cup chopped olives

2 tbs raisins

1 tsp salt

½ tsp freshly ground black pepper

½ cup grated parmesan cheese

Preheat the oven to 350°F. Lightly grease a 10-inch pie plate or large shallow glass heatproof dish.

Heat the vegetable oil in a large frying pan and add the onion, pimento and garlic. Sauté until fragrant. Add the herbs and combine.

Add the meat and cook until it loses its pinkness then stir in the tomato sauce, olives, raisins, salt and pepper. Cover and simmer for about 20 minutes, adding a little water to prevent sticking.

Meanwhile, heat the olive oil in a frying pan and fry the plantains until golden on both sides. Remove and drain. (Alternatively you can bake the slices in the oven at 350°F for 10 minutes.)

Line the prepared dish with half the plantains and spoon the meat mixture on top. Cover with the remaining plantains, sprinkle with the cheese and bake for 20–30 minutes.

Serves 4–6

Pound plantain

Serve this as an accompaniment to fish or meat stews.

2 large green plantains, unpeeled

1 large ripe plantain, unpeeled

butter (optional)

Boil the plantains until tender – ripe ones will need about 20 minutes; green about 40 minutes.

Peel and remove the threads. Pound in a mortar with a pestle until smooth, adding a little hot water if needed. Add salt to taste.

Form into either several round balls or one large ball. Butter if you wish then slice or cut into squares and serve in a glass serving dish.

Serves 6

Honey-glazed plantains

1 large ripe but firm plantain

¼ cup honey

2 tbs lime juice

½ tsp cinnamon

Preheat the oven to 400°F. Grease an ovenproof baking dish.

Peel the plantain and slice into 4-inch lengths, about ¼ inch thick. Arrange in the prepared dish.

Combine the other ingredients and brush some onto the plantains.

Bake for 10 minutes, turn and brush with the remaining honey mixture. Bake for another 8 minutes.

Serves 4

To peel plantains

Slice off both ends and cut the plantain in half. Make a shallow slit down the side of the skin and use your fingers to lift the skin off the flesh – it should come away easily.

Oven-baked plantains

2 almost ripe plantains
2 tbs vegetable oil
1 tsp cinnamon

Preheat the oven to 375°F. Grease an ovenproof baking dish.

Peel the plantains and slice lengthways. Place in the prepared dish and brush with the vegetable oil. Sprinkle with the cinnamon.

Bake for 15 minutes until tender, turning once if necessary.

Serves 4

Fried plantains

2 ripe plantains
vegetable oil for frying

Peel the plantains and slice into ¼-inch thick slices.

Heat some oil in a frying pan. When hot add the plantains and shallow-fry until dark golden on both sides. Drain on paper towels and serve.

Serves 4

'The smell of ripe plantains frying is absolutely delightful: the sugar in the plantains begins to caramelize as they fry, an aroma that always escapes the kitchen to the outdoors – a sure sign that lunch is being cooked in that household!'

Fried plantains

Coo coo

1 cup chicken stock or water
8 oz fresh okra, finely chopped
4 pimento peppers, seeded and chopped
2 garlic cloves, minced
2 cups coconut milk
3 cups yellow cornmeal
butter

Bring the stock or water to a boil in a large Dutch oven. Add the okra, peppers, garlic and salt and freshly ground black pepper. Simmer for 15 minutes until the okra is tender.

Add the coconut milk and return to a boil.

Pour in the cornmeal, whisking vigorously to prevent lumping. Stir well and cook until the mixture becomes stiff and smooth and moves away from the sides of the pot.

Generously butter a bowl. Put the coo coo in the bowl and shake it around to form a ball. Let set.

Slice and serve.

Serves 6

Note
If preferred, instead of rolling the coo coo into a ball in a bowl simply pour it into a shallow glass serving dish and cut into squares before serving.

*‘ Callaloo is synonymous with coo coo,
the dish that has become so popular
that bite-sized pieces of coo coo are often
served with a callaloo dip at cocktail
parties! Coo coo is also a delightful
accompaniment to stewed fish, a
tradition that has remained strong. ’*

Pink poui in bloom

Coconut lily

Cakes, pastries, desserts and ice creams

We are indeed a cake-loving nation; everyone loves a great butter cake – or sponge cake, as we lovingly refer to it. Trinidad sponge cake is simply the traditional 1:2:3:4 cake: it is often served with ice cream as a quick dessert, it occupies prime space on an afternoon tea plate and is indeed the ubiquitous birthday cake. This sponge cake is often marbled with pink food colouring and/or chocolate. It can be frosted or served up as it is or the mixture made into cupcakes.

Coconut, pineapples and bananas are all popular flavours used in our cakes and desserts, while currants roll is a popular pastry in our local bakeries. As the years have moved on we have embraced lots of different cakes, but sponge cake stands up the best to our tropical weather conditions, though cream cakes and elaborate dessert cakes are often ordered or found on fancy restaurant menus.

Fruit cakes and black Christmas cakes are immensely popular. Many black cake recipes remain family secrets and recipes are handed down from generation to generation. Black cake has its roots steeped in the English tradition of pudding-making at Christmas time. A black fruit cake is cooked at a very low temperature (about 250–325°F) and is baked in a cake tin lined with heavy brown paper thereby somewhat steaming the cake in the oven. Fruits are chopped and 'soaked' in a liquid often made with a combination of alcohol: rum, cherry brandy, port or brandy – the longer the soak the more redolent the cake of the spirits.

A black cake should not be eaten straightaway, usually a week should elapse between baking and eating. The fruits tend to release their juices into the cake after baking; more spirits are drizzled onto the cake for a few days after – both of which contribute to a tender, melt-in-your-mouth cake. This after-baking process is called 'allowing your cake to ripen'.

Wedding cakes are black fruit cakes. Often the bride retains the top tier of the cake and enjoys it on her first wedding anniversary – the cake having been wrapped in traditional marzipan before being frosted, thereby preserving it.

The four most popular desserts on this island are ice cream, crème caramel, cheesecake and Black Forest cake. Any local restaurant will have these items on their dessert menus, and although there are other desserts infused with local flavours these are always winners!

Traditional sponge cake

1 cup very cold butter

2 cups granulated sugar

3 cups all-purpose flour

5 tsp baking powder

4 eggs

1 cup milk

2 tsp vanilla extract

Measure out all the ingredients and set them aside. Preheat the oven to 350°F. Grease the sides of two 9-inch cake pans. Line the bases with waxed paper, grease the paper and flour the pans. Shake out any excess flour.

Cut the butter into chunks and place in a mixing bowl. The butter must be as cold as possible.

Cream the butter until light in colour, but still cold. Then add the sugar and cream until light – take your time here; use your fingers to feel whether the sugar has dissolved.

Sift the flour three times. Add the baking powder.

Add the eggs to the creamed mixture one at a time, beating well between additions. You must incorporate the eggs slowly; the mixture should be light and fluffy before you add the next egg. If the mixture seems somewhat loose and rather 'eggy', or appears curdled, you must beat a little more.

Combine the milk with the vanilla.

Add the flour in three additions, folding in alternately with the milk, beginning and ending with the flour.

Spoon the batter evenly into the cake pans, and bake for 35–40 minutes, until the cakes pull or shrink away from the sides of the pans. Do not open the oven door during baking or the cakes will fall.

Remove the cakes from the oven, cool in the pans for 5 minutes, then invert onto cooling racks, remove lining paper and place right side up.

Makes 2

Banana and pineapple cake

4 eggs

1 cup brown sugar

2⅔ cups vegetable oil

3 cups cake flour

1 tsp cinnamon

½ tsp grated nutmeg

3 tsp baking powder

1 tsp baking soda

2 bananas

juice of 1 orange

8-oz tin crushed pineapple, well drained

1 tsp vanilla extract

1 tsp orange zest

1 cup chopped walnuts

Preheat the oven to 350°F. Grease and flour two 8-inch layer cake pans.

Using an electric mixer, beat the eggs until fluffy. Add the sugar and beat until thick and creamy. Add the oil and slowly beat for about 2 minutes more.

Sift together the flour, spices, baking powder and soda.

Mash the bananas and combine with the orange juice, pineapple, vanilla and orange zest.

Fold in the flour alternately with the banana mixture in three additions, beginning and ending with flour. Fold in the walnuts.

Spoon into the prepared cake pans and bake for 35–40 minutes until risen and firm to the touch.

Remove from the oven. After 5 minutes remove from the pans and leave to cool on racks. Frost with cream cheese frosting.

Cream cheese frosting

2 x 8-oz packages cream cheese

3 cups icing sugar, sifted

Cream the cheese then add the icing sugar. Cream.

Spread half the frosting onto the first cake, place second cake on top and then top with the remaining frosting.

Toasted coconut cake

1 cup finely grated fresh coconut

1 cup unsalted butter

1 cup granulated sugar

2⅓ cups cake flour

2 tsp baking powder

½ tsp cinnamon

4 large eggs

¼ cup fresh orange juice

1 tbs grated orange zest

½ tsp orange or vanilla extract

Preheat the oven to 325°F. Line, grease and flour the base and sides of a 9-inch cake pan.

Spread the coconut onto a baking tray and lightly toast for about 5 minutes, just until the coconut is dry and beginning to turn colour – don't let it brown. Crumble lightly with your fingers.

Cream the butter until light and add the sugar a tablespoon at a time, beating well until the sugar is dissolved and the mixture is fluffy.

Sift the flour with the baking powder and cinnamon.

Add the eggs one at a time to the creamed mixture, beating well between addition.

Combine the orange juice, orange zest and orange or vanilla extract.

Combine the coconut with the flour mixture.

Fold in the flour alternately with the juice in three additions, beginning and ending with flour.

Spoon the batter into the prepared pan and bake for about 50 minutes until a wooden pick inserted through the centre comes out clean.

Cool on a wire rack for 6 minutes then turn out of the pan, remove lining paper and finish cooling on a rack.

'When I was a little girl, one of my favourite treats was the coconut tea cake my mother used to bake for us. I remember waiting patiently as the cake came out of the oven, out of the tin and finally, still warm, into my cupped hands. Feathery light, golden yellow with specks of grated coconut, redolent with the butter and spices that made up that cake, each piece for me was a taste of heaven.

For years I tried to locate the recipe, sifting through her numerous handwritten recipes, many tattered and discoloured from age and frequent use, but alas I came up empty-handed. Still determined, I proceeded to check every cake cookbook in my possession until I discovered one recipe that seemed comparable to what may have been hers.

A few trial bakings later and some recipe and method adjustments and I think I have at least come close to that memorable cake from my past. My recipe may not yield a cake as feathery light as my mother's but each time I bake this cake and inhale the rich aromas from the oven, each time I taste it, I'm happy knowing that I'm reliving a little of my past.'

Chocolate cake

1 cup butter

2 cups granulated sugar

2¼ cups all-purpose flour

4 tsp baking powder

1 tsp baking soda

1 cup cocoa powder

4 eggs

2 tsp vanilla extract

1 cup milk

Preheat the oven to 350°F. Grease the sides and bases of two 9-inch cake pans and line with waxed paper.

Cream the butter and sugar until light and fluffy and doubled in volume.

Sift the flour three times. Add the baking powder and soda. Sift the cocoa and combine with the flour.

Add the eggs one at a time to the creamed butter mixture, making sure to beat well between additions – the batter must be fluffy.

Add the vanilla to the milk.

Add the flour to the batter alternately with the milk in three additions, beginning and ending with the flour/cocoa mixture.

Spoon the batter evenly into the prepared pans and bake for 35–40 minutes until done and the cake pulls away from the sides of the pan.

Cool on a wire rack.

Makes 2

Coconut chiffon cake with lemony coconut drizzle

1 cup finely grated fresh coconut

2¼ cups cake flour, sifted

1 tbs baking powder

½ tsp salt

5 egg yolks

1 whole egg

1⅓ cups granulated sugar

½ cup vegetable oil

⅔ cup orange juice

6 egg whites

¼ tsp cream of tartar

Preheat the oven to 325°F. Grease a 10-inch angel food pan.

Place the coconut onto a baking tray and toast for about 10 minutes until dried.

Finely chop ½ cup of the dried coconut in a food processor and combine with the flour. (Reserve the remaining coconut for the drizzle topping.) Add the baking powder and salt.

Place the egg yolks and whole egg into a mixer bowl with beaters or whisk attachment and beat until frothy. Add 1 cup sugar gradually and beat until thick, fluffy and light in colour.

Slowly pour in the oil in a steady stream and continue beating for about 1 minute longer.

Divide the flour mixture into three parts and add to the yolk mixture alternately with the orange juice, beginning and ending with flour.

Wash and dry the beaters and beat the egg whites with the cream of tartar until frothy. Gradually add the remaining sugar and beat to a soft meringue.

With a large spatula fold a quarter of the yolk mixture into the whites and then fold the whites into the yolk mixture in four additions, taking care not to over fold.

Gently pour or spoon the batter into the prepared pan.

Bake for 60–65 minutes until springy to touch.

Invert the cake and cool completely in the pan before removing.

Lemony coconut drizzle

4 cups icing sugar, sifted

4-6 tbs fresh lemon juice

coconut to decorate (see recipe above)

Combine the icing sugar with the lemon juice until the texture is thick but soft. Drizzle onto the cake and sprinkle with coconut.

Traditional marble cake

3 cups cake flour

1 tbs baking powder

½ tsp salt

1 cup butter

2 cups granulated sugar

4 large eggs

1 tsp vanilla extract

1 cup milk

¼ cup cocoa powder, sifted

pink food colouring

Preheat the oven to 350°F. Grease and flour two 9-inch cake pans.

Sift the flour three times and add the baking powder and salt. Set aside.

Using an electric mixer, cream the butter with the sugar until light and creamy, about 10 minutes.

Add the eggs one at a time, beating well between additions. Add the vanilla.

Reduce the mixer speed to medium-low or low and divide the flour into four portions. Add the flour alternately with the milk, starting and ending with the flour. Mix just until incorporated after each addition.

Combine the cocoa powder with 3 tablespoons warm water and mix well.

Remove half the batter and place in a small mixing bowl. Gently mix in enough food colouring to colour the batter to your liking.

Gently mix the remaining batter with the cocoa mixture.

Divide both batters evenly between the pans and gently swirl together.

Bake for 35–40 minutes, or until the cake pulls away from the side of the pan.

Remove from oven and cool for 5 minutes in the pans before turning out.

Frost with fluffy boiled frosting.

Makes 2

Note

If preferred, leave some of the batter uncoloured.

Fluffy boiled frosting

2 egg whites

⅛ tsp cream of tartar

1 cup granulated sugar

Using an electric mixer, beat the egg whites until fluffy but not dry. Add the cream of tartar.

Stir the sugar gently with ⅓ cup water to combine. Place in a small saucepan and bring to a boil. Boil until the mixture is bubbling and the sugar spins a thread when lifted from a fork.

Pour the sugar syrup into the egg whites with the mixer running. Continue to beat until all the syrup has been incorporated. Beat for a few minutes longer until the mixture loses some of its gloss.

Jam roll

This can be found in many bakeries, and is a popular teatime favourite. Jam roll, jelly roll – or swiss roll as it is sometimes called – also makes a great base for a trifle.

4 eggs

1 cup sugar

1 cup flour

icing sugar and coarse sugar for dusting

½ cup jam or jelly

Preheat the oven to 350°F. Butter, flour and line a 9 x 7-inch baking tray or sheet pan.

Beat the eggs until frothy. Gradually add the sugar and beat until thick and light in colour.

Add ¼ cup water and fold in the flour.

Spread in the baking tray and bake for 10–15 minutes.

Immediately invert onto a clean tea towel dusted with icing sugar and coarse sugar.

Roll up from the long side and cool completely.

Unroll, spread with the jam, and re-roll.

Wrap in foil or plastic until ready to serve.

Makes 10 slices

Pineapple upside down cake

⅓ cup butter plus 2 tbs

½ cup granulated sugar

2 eggs

1½ cups all-purpose flour

2½ tsp baking powder

1 tsp cinnamon

½ cup pineapple juice

1 tsp vanilla extract

¼ cup brown sugar

14-oz tin pineapple rings, drained, juice reserved

9 maraschino cherries

Preheat the oven to 350°F.

Cream ⅓ cup butter with the granulated sugar until light and fluffy.

Add the eggs one at a time, beating well between additions.

Sift the flour with the baking powder and cinnamon.

Add to the butter mixture alternately with the pineapple juice and vanilla, making sure your last addition is flour.

Melt 2 tablespoons butter in a 9-inch heatproof cake pan, add the brown sugar and stir to melt. Do not brown.

Remove from the heat. Arrange the pineapple rings in the cake pan and place a cherry in each pineapple ring,

Pour on the cake batter and bake for 35 minutes.

Remove from the oven and invert onto a serving plate,

Serve warm with thick cream.

Serves 8

Currant cherry cake

1 lb currants

8 oz sultanas

8 oz halved glacé cherries

½ tsp mixed essence

½ cup cherry brandy

2 cups all-purpose flour

2 tsp mixed spice

2 tsp baking powder

1 cup unsalted butter

1 cup brown sugar

5 eggs

Preheat the oven to 300°F. Line the base and sides of a 9-inch round cake pan with three layers of paper.

Wash the currants and sultanas and air-dry.

In a mixing bowl combine the currants, sultanas, cherries, mixed essence and cherry brandy.

Sift the flour into another bowl and combine with the mixed spice and baking powder.

Using an electric mixer, cream the butter with the sugar just until combined.

Add the eggs one at a time, beating only until combined between each addition.

Fold in the flour mixture alternately with the fruit mixture.

Spread evenly into the prepared pan and bake for about 2½ hours until done.

Leave to cool in the pan and then cover tightly with foil.

This cake will keep for up to 3 months.

Nutmeg-scented banana streusel cake

½ cup unsalted butter

1 cup brown sugar

2 eggs

2 cups cake flour

1 tbs baking powder

1 tsp grated nutmeg

½ cup milk

2 bananas, mashed

1 tsp vanilla extract

Streusel topping

½ cup chopped nuts

4 tbs brown sugar

2 tsp cinnamon

Preheat the oven to 350°F. Grease and flour a 9-inch cake pan.

Cream the butter with the sugar until light. Beat in the eggs, one at a time.

Combine the flour with the baking powder and nutmeg.

Combine the milk with the bananas and vanilla.

Add the flour alternately with the milk. Spoon into the prepared pan.

Combine the ingredients for the streusel and sprinkle on top of the cake.

Bake for 30 minutes. Let cool in pan for 5 minutes then remove.

Pumpkin spice cake

3 cups all-purpose flour

1 tsp baking soda

2 tsp cinnamon

1 tsp grated nutmeg

¼ tsp allspice powder

¼ tsp ground cloves

1 tsp powdered ginger

½ tsp salt

1 cup unsalted butter

1½ cups sugar

½ cup brown sugar

3 eggs

2 cups finely grated (uncooked) pumpkin

2 tsp vanilla extract

icing sugar to decorate

Preheat the oven to 325°F. Grease and flour a 12-cup bundt pan.

Sift the flour then add the baking soda, cinnamon, nutmeg, allspice, cloves, powdered ginger and salt.

Cream the butter with the sugars until light and fluffy. Add the eggs one at a time, beating well.

Add the flour mixture alternately with the pumpkin.

Stir in the vanilla.

Spoon into the baking pan and bake for about 60 minutes until a tester inserted near the centre comes out clean.

Cool for 20 minutes in the pan before turning out.

Sprinkle with icing sugar.

Serves 10–12

Light Christmas fruit cake

This light fruit cake is delicious and is sure to be enjoyed by kids and grown-ups alike!

1 cup butter

1 cup granulated sugar

4 eggs

2 cups all-purpose flour

½ cup raisins, minced or chopped

½ cup glacé cherries, finely chopped

½ cup mixed candied peel

½ cup chopped walnuts or almonds (optional)

Preheat the oven to 325°F. Grease, line and flour a 9-inch round pan.

Using an electric mixer, cream the butter and sugar until light and creamy, about 5 minutes. Add the eggs one at a time, beating well between additions.

Sift the flour and combine with the fruits and nuts, if using.

Fold the flour mixture into the butter mixture.

Pour the batter into the prepared pan.

Bake for about 1½ hours.

Leave in the pan until cool.

Old-fashioned black cake

1 cup mixed candied peel

2½ cups raisins, chopped

2 cups currants, chopped

8 oz pitted prunes, chopped

1 cup each red and green glacé cherries, halved

1½ cups dark rum or cherry brandy

1¾ cups all-purpose flour

1 tsp cinnamon

¼ tsp grated nutmeg

¼ tsp allspice powder

½ tsp ground cloves

1 tsp baking powder

a pinch of salt

1 cup unsalted butter

1 cup brown sugar

3 eggs

2 tsp vanilla extract

2 tbs molasses

2 cups pecans or walnuts, chopped and toasted

brandy or rum for 'nursing' cake after baking

Line two 9 x 5-inch loaf pans or 9-inch round cake pans with a double layer of brown paper. Grease the last layer and flour.

In a large bowl combine the mixed peel, raisins, currants, prunes and cherries. Pour on the rum and let soak overnight or up to a week.

Drain. Divide the fruits in two. Mince half and combine with the unminced half.

Preheat the oven to 250°F.

Combine the flour with the cinnamon, nutmeg, allspice, cloves, baking powder and salt.

Using an electric mixer, cream the butter with the sugar until light and fluffy. Add the eggs one at a time, beating well between each addition. Add the vanilla and molasses.

Fold in the flour mixture.

Fold in the fruit mixture and the nuts.

Turn the batter into the prepared pans and bake for 2½–3 hours until a tester comes out clean.

Leave in the pans until cool.

Pour a tablespoon of brandy or rum over the cakes after baking. Wrap cakes in parchment or waxed paper and store in a cake tin. Repeat the addition of brandy or rum daily for about a week.

Makes 2

Trinidad black cake

1 lb 4 oz raisins

8 oz currants

12 oz sultanas

8 oz pitted prunes

4 oz mixed candied peel

1⅔ cups dark rum

1⅔ cups cherry brandy

2 cups butter

1 lb brown sugar

6 eggs

3 cups all-purpose flour

3 tsp baking powder

1 tsp mixed cinnamon and allspice powder

4 oz glacé cherries, halved

8 oz chopped walnuts

2 tsp mixed essence

brandy or rum for 'nursing' cake after baking

Seed the fruits and cut up all except the cherries into approximate ¼-inch pieces.

Combine the rum and cherry brandy and add the raisins, currants, sultanas, prunes and peel to the mixture.

Let soak overnight or for 1 week – or longer if preferred.

Preheat the oven to 300°F. Grease and line two 9-inch cake pans with waxed paper. Grease and flour the paper.

Cream the butter and sugar until light and fluffy. Add the eggs one at a time, beating well after each addition.

Sift together the flour, baking powder, cinnamon and allspice.

Drain the fruits and reserve the liquid. Mince the fruits and add to the creamed mixture. Add the halved cherries and nuts.

Fold the flour into the mixture alternately with the reserved liquid. Add the mixed essence and mix well.

Divide the cake batter between the prepared baking pans.

Bake for 2–2½ hours.

Leave to cool in the cake pans. Pour a tablespoon of brandy or rum over the cakes after baking. Repeat daily for about a week.

The cakes will keep, well wrapped and in a covered tin, for about a year.

Makes 2

Note
To make a non-alcoholic version of this cake, soak the fruits in grape juice for just 1 week. The cake will need to be refrigerated a few days after baking.

The best currants roll

This is a traditional pastry, still very popular in bakeries.

3 cups good-quality seedless currants, washed and dried

1 tsp cinnamon

¼ cup granulated sugar

2 tbs melted butter

⅓ cup toasted breadcrumbs

1 egg, beaten lightly

1 tbs brown sugar

Pastry

3 cups all-purpose flour

¾ cup shortening

¼ cup cold butter

1 tbs vinegar

To make the pastry, place the flour in a large bowl. Cut the shortening and butter into the flour until it looks like large peas.

Combine the vinegar with ⅓ cup cold water. Sprinkle the liquid evenly over the flour mixture and gather together loosely. It will be very rough.

Turn the dough out onto a floured surface and pat into a rough rectangle. Roll into a rectangle about 10 by 16 inches. Fold the long ends of the dough into the centre and then fold in half like a book. With the smooth end on your left, roll into another rectangle and fold a second time. Turn the dough as before, and roll and fold a third time.

Refrigerate dough for about 30 minutes. Wrap until ready to use.

Preheat the oven to 375°F.

Combine the currants with the cinnamon and sugar.

Roll the pastry out to a rectangle 12 by 20 inches and about ¼ inch thick.

Brush with the melted butter and sprinkle with the breadcrumbs. Distribute the currant mixture evenly over the top.

Beginning at a long end, roll up jelly-roll style, seal the ends and place on a baking tray, seam side down.

Brush with the beaten egg and sprinkle with the brown sugar.

Bake for 45–50 minutes until golden.

Remove from the oven, cool slightly, then slice the log diagonally into pieces about 1½ inches in width.

Place back on the baking tray and return to the oven for a further 10 minutes.

Remove and cool on racks.

Makes 10–12 pieces

Mango turnovers

4 half-ripe Julie mangoes, cut into small cubes

1 tsp cinnamon

1 tbs flour

2 tbs granulated sugar plus more to sprinkle

1 quantity flaky pie dough (see below)

1 egg, lightly beaten

Preheat the oven to 400°F.

Combine the mangoes, cinnamon, flour and sugar in a large bowl.

Roll the dough to ¼-inch thickness and cut into 4-inch squares using a pastry cutter or small knife.

Place about 1 tablespoon of mango filling in the lower corner of a square, moisten the edges of the pastry with water and bring the upper piece over to cover the filling. Press with the tines of a fork to seal – you should have a triangle. Brush with beaten egg and sprinkle with granulated sugar. Place on a baking tray. Repeat until all the pastry has been used.

Bake for 10–15 minutes until light golden.

Let cool and remove gently from the baking tray.

Makes about 12

Flaky pie dough

2¾ cups all-purpose flour

1 tsp salt

2 oz cold unsalted butter

5½ oz shortening

½ cup iced water

Place the flour and salt in the bowl of a food processor.

Cut the butter and shortening into small pieces and drop onto the flour.

Pulse in the food processor until the mixture resembles fine crumbs.

Add a little iced water and pulse a few times. Add more water and pulse again. Continue until the mixture has curds and clumps and sticks together when pressed between your fingers.

Remove and form into a ball.

Wrap and chill for at least 2 hours before using.

Coconut cookies

¼ cup butter

½ cup sugar

1 egg

¼ tsp Angostura bitters

½ cup finely grated coconut

2 cups all-purpose flour

2 tsp baking powder

½ tsp baking soda

⅓ cup milk

glacé cherries to decorate

Preheat the oven to 375°F.

Cream the butter with the sugar. Add the egg and beat. Add the bitters and coconut.

Mix the flour with the baking powder and soda. Add to the creamed mixture alternately with the milk. Stir to combine.

Drop the batter by teaspoons onto a greased cookie sheet. Flatten slightly with a fork.

Decorate with the cherries.

Bake for 10–15 minutes until lightly golden around the edges.

Makes about 20

'*Coconut tarts are a long-time favourite of many Trinis. The 'tarts' are really pastry pockets, filled with a sweet and juicy coconut filling that is finger lickin' good! The trick is not to overcook the coconut.*'

Coconut tarts/ turnovers

You can enjoy these with a pastry dough or a sweet leavened dough as in the daisy ring recipe (see page 310).

1 cup grated coconut

1 cup granulated sugar

2 cloves, ground

1 tsp cinnamon

1 quantity flaky pie dough (see previous page)

1 egg, beaten

Add the coconut and sugar to a large shallow saucepan and cook on medium heat until the mixture begins to bubble and liquefy a little. Add the spices and continue to cook, stirring frequently, for about 10–15 minutes until the mixture comes together. You can add a small amount of water if necessary to prevent sticking.

When the coconut is cooked yet still juicy remove and let cool.

Preheat the oven to 400°F.

Roll out the pastry to about ¼ inch thickness and cut out rounds 4 inches in diameter.

Place 1 tablespoon of filling on the bottom half of each pastry round, leaving an edge of about ½ inch around the filling.

Bring the top half over the coconut to cover it, crimp the edges and seal with a fork.

Repeat until all the pastry and coconut is used. Brush the tarts with beaten egg.

Place on a baking sheet and bake for 15–20 minutes or until the pastry is golden brown.

Makes about 12

Bread pudding

1 cup boiling water

⅓ cup raisins

2 cups full-cream milk

4 eggs

½ cup granulated sugar

2 tsp vanilla extract

½ tsp freshly grated nutmeg

6 oz good-quality bread

Preheat the oven to 350°F. Butter an 8-inch baking dish.

Pour the boiling water over the raisins and allow to soak for 10 minutes.

Heat the milk in a saucepan.

In a mixing bowl beat the eggs with the sugar. Add the milk, vanilla and nutmeg.

Sprinkle half the raisins in the bottom of the prepared baking dish.

Thinly slice the bread and arrange the slices in a single layer in the dish.

Sprinkle with the remaining raisins and pour the milk mixture over.

Bake in a bain marie for about 50–60 minutes.

Let cool a little until warm, then serve.

Serves about 8

Mango lime pie

This is a delicious way to use up an abundance of mangoes when in season.

3½ oz ginger snaps

2 tbs melted butter

4 egg yolks

1 cup condensed milk

1 tsp lime zest

½ cup lime juice

½ cup mango purée

whipped cream, to serve (optional)

Preheat the oven to 325°F.

Place the ginger snaps in the bowl of a food processor and process to fine crumbs. Add the melted butter and pulse together.

Press the mixture into the bottom of a 9-inch pie plate. Bake for 5 minutes until set.

Increase the oven heat to 350°F.

Using an electric mixer beat the egg yolks until light and fluffy. Add the condensed milk and lime zest and mix on low speed until combined. Add the lime juice and mango purée, and mix well.

Pour the mixture into the pre-baked shell and bake for 20–30 minutes until the centre of the pie is firm and dry to the touch.

Chill thoroughly until ready to use. Serve with whipped cream if desired.

Serves 6-8

*'Simple baked custard is both nutritious and delicious.
I enjoyed many a serving when growing up!'*

Baked custard

4 eggs
⅓ cup sugar
1½ cups milk
1 tsp vanilla extract
¼ tsp grated nutmeg

Preheat the oven to 350°F.

Beat the eggs in a bowl with the sugar and milk. Stir in the vanilla and nutmeg.

Strain the mixture and pour into a greased pie dish.

Place the pie dish into a shallow pan of water and bake for 30 minutes until a knife inserted into the centre comes out clean.

Remove and cool. Invert before serving.

Serves 6–8

Caramel custard

½ cup sugar plus ⅓ cup
3 eggs, lightly beaten
a pinch of salt
1 tsp vanilla extract
2½ cups milk

Make the caramel: heat ½ cup sugar in a saucepan over low heat until the sugar is melted and caramel-coloured. Pour the caramel into a 9-inch round dish, tilting the dish to evenly coat the base. Set aside.

Preheat the oven to 350°F.

Make the custard by mixing eggs with the remaining sugar, salt and vanilla. Stir in the milk and mix.

Pour the custard mixture into the caramel-coated dish. Place the dish in a shallow pan of water and bake for about 45 minutes or until a knife inserted into the centre comes out clean. Cool and chill.

Invert onto a serving platter and serve with the caramel sauce.

Serves 6

Baked custard

sweet rice

I love this dish – the rice becomes very creamy and wonderful, and it's great served warm or chilled.

½ cup short-grain or arborio rice

⅔ cup water

7½ cups milk

2 cardamom pods

¾ cup sugar

1 tablespoon toasted almonds, coarsely chopped

⅓ cup raisins

Soak the rice in ½ cup water for 30 minutes. Add the remaining water and boil the rice in the water until all the liquid has dried up. Remove the pot from the heat.

Add the milk and cardamom pods to the rice and stir well.

Simmer on low heat for 1½ hours, stirring occasionally to ensure the rice does not stick to the bottom and sides of the pan.

Add the sugar, stirring constantly over low heat until the sugar is dissolved and the rice is of a creamy consistency.

Remove from the heat. Remove the cardamom pods.

Serve in individual bowls garnished with toasted almonds and raisins.

Serves 8

Irresistible cheesecake

2 cups graham cracker or digestive cookie crumbs

4 tbs sugar

⅓ cup melted butter

Filling

2 lb cream cheese at room temperature

1 cup granulated sugar

4 tbs flour

6 eggs

1 tsp vanilla extract

1 cup sour cream

Preheat the oven to 325°F.

Make the crust by combining the crumbs with the sugar and melted butter. Press into the base and partly up the sides of a 9- or 10-inch springform pan.

Bake for 5 minutes then remove and set aside.

Beat the cream cheese in a large mixing bowl until there are no lumps.

Add the sugar and flour and combine. Beat in the eggs one at a time until well combined and the mixture is smooth. Add the vanilla.

Fold in the sour cream then pour the mixture over the prepared crust. Bake for 50–60 minutes.

Run a knife around the rim of the pan to loosen the cheesecake. Cool completely before removing from the pan. Chill for 4–6 hours before serving.

Serves 12–15

Note
You can wrap foil around the pan during baking to prevent any liquid from dripping through the seam of the pan.

Christmas trifle

1 jam roll, sliced (see page 238)

½ cup dark rum

4 cups mixed fruit (any type) or 28-oz tin peaches or fruit cocktail.

1 cup slivered toasted almonds

maraschino cherries

Custard

¾ cup custard powder

1 cup granulated sugar

3 cups milk

2 tsp vanilla extract

1 cup whipping cream plus more to decorate (optional)

Combine the custard powder and sugar in a medium saucepan. Gradually stir in the milk.

Cook over a low heat and stir until the mixture thickens. Whip to remove any lumps.

Remove from the heat and stir in the vanilla. Cover the surface with plastic wrap and refrigerate.

Meanwhile, beat the cream until it forms soft peaks. Fold into the custard.

Place a layer of jam roll slices in a large trifle bowl or individual glasses. Sprinkle on some rum, spoon a layer of custard on top, followed by a layer of fruits. Repeat with another layer of jam roll, rum, custard and fruit. Repeat until all jam roll is used, finishing with a layer of custard and fruit.

Decorate with additional whipped cream, if desired, and top with the almonds and some cherries.

Serves 10

Bananas flambé

3 tbs butter

1 tbs brown sugar

1 tsp cinnamon

3 ripe bananas, peeled and sliced in half lengthways

1 tbs dark rum

shredded coconut to decorate

Melt the butter in a large frying pan. Add the sugar and cinnamon and stir well.

Add the banana halves and sauté for about 2 minutes.

Raise the heat. Slightly turn the frying pan in towards the heat, but away from your face. Pour on the rum and tilt the pan into the flame. The bananas should light! That's flambé!

Top with shredded coconut and serve with ginger vanilla ice cream.

Serves 4

Tropical fruit salad

½ cup granulated sugar
juice of 1 lime
2 cups cubed watermelon
2 oranges, segmented
2 cups seedless grapes
2 cups pineapple chunks
2 cups almost ripe papaya
2 cups almost ripe Julie mango
2 bananas
mint leaves to decorate

Boil the sugar in 1 cup water until melted. Leave until cool then add the lime juice.

Place all the fruits except the bananas into a large glass bowl. Pour the cooled syrup over and refrigerate.

Slice the bananas and add just before serving. Decorate with mint leaves.

Serves 10

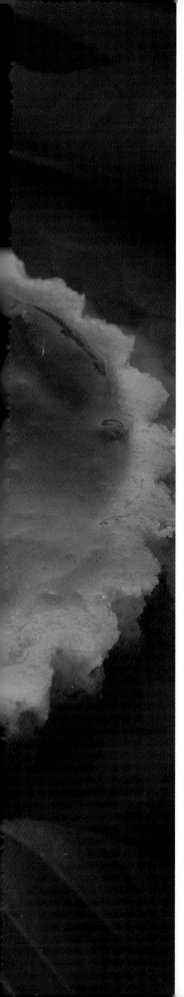

Guava pineapple cheesecake with guava pineapple glaze

15 digestive cookies
4 tbs melted butter
1 lb cream cheese
½ cup granulated sugar
4 eggs
1 tsp vanilla extract
1 cup guava pineapple juice
4 tbs all-purpose flour
4 tbs sour cream

Preheat the oven to 350°

Crush the cookies finely in a food processor. Add the melted butter and combine.

Press the mixture into the bottom of a 10-inch round springform cake pan. Bake for 5 minutes then remove from the oven.

Using an electric mixer, beat the cream cheese until creamy. Add the sugar, eggs and vanilla. Beat until smooth then add the guava pineapple juice, flour and sour cream and beat for a few minutes more. Pour into the cookie crust.

Bake for 40 minutes until the cheesecake is slightly puffed.

Allow to cool then spread with guava pineapple glaze.

Refrigerate for 4 hours or overnight.

Serves 10–12

Guava pineapple glaze

1 cup guava pineapple juice
¼ cup guava jam
2 tsp fresh lime juice

In a small saucepan combine the guava pineapple juice and the jam. Stir together and cook until thick, about 15–20 minutes.

Stir in the lime juice.

Chill then spoon onto the chilled cheesecake.

Lemon meringue tartlets

Rough-skinned lemons are very abundant in Trinidad and Tobago and make delightful desserts.

Pastry
  1 cup flour
  a pinch of salt
  1 tbs sugar
  ½ cup butter
  about 2 tbs iced water

Filling
  1⅓ cups granulated sugar
  2½ tbs cornstarch
  ½ cup milk
  1 cup lemon juice
  2 egg yolks

Meringue
  2 egg whites
  ¼ cup granulated sugar
  a pinch of cream of tartar

Make the pastry by placing the flour, salt and sugar in a mixing bowl. Add the butter and cut into the flour until the mixture resembles fine crumbs. Add iced water as needed and bring the mixture gently together with your hands.

Form into a ball. Wrap in plastic wrap and refrigerate for 1 hour or more.

Preheat the oven to 400°F.

Roll the dough into a circle ¼ inch thick. Fit into six small 3-inch tartlet pans or a pie plate. Prick the pastry, cover with a piece of foil, fill with dried beans and bake for 15 minutes. Remove foil and beans and bake for a further 10 minutes or until golden.

Leave until cool.

To make the filling, combine the sugar and cornstarch in a heavy saucepan. Add the milk and lemon juice and whisk to remove any lumps. Add the egg yolks.

Cook over a gentle heat until the mixture is thick, about 6–8 minutes (you may use a double boiler here).

Remove from heat, cover with a piece of plastic wrap directly on the surface to prevent a skin from forming, and leave to cool.

Reduce oven temperature to 350°F.

To make the meringue, beat the egg whites with the sugar until frothy. Add cream of tartar and continue beating until the mixture is glossy and forms peaks easily.

Fill the pre-baked pie shells with the lemon filling and top with meringue. Bake for 15 minutes until golden. Refrigerate until ready to serve.

Serves 6

'Home-baked cookies are not a huge part of our snack culture, although our local biscuit company has cornered the market with its sweet and savoury offerings. When I made thumbprint cookies as a child, the choice of jams was not as vast as today and I often filled them with guava jam and used crushed peanuts on the outside – a delicious combination!'

Thumbprint cookies

1 cup unsalted butter
⅓ cup brown sugar
⅓ cup granulated sugar
2 eggs, separated
1 tsp vanilla extract
2½ cups all-purpose flour
a pinch of salt
1 cup finely chopped nuts (peanuts, hazelnuts or almonds)
1 cup jam or jelly

Preheat the oven to 350°F. Butter and flour baking trays.

Cream the butter until light. Beat in the sugars. Add the egg yolks and vanilla and beat until blended.

Combine the flour and salt and add to the batter. Stir until a dough-like consistency is formed. Shape the dough into 1-inch balls.

Lightly beat the egg whites in a shallow bowl. Place the finely chopped nuts in another shallow dish.

Roll each ball of cookie dough in the egg white and then roll lightly in the nuts.

Place on the prepared trays about 1 inch apart. Press the centre of each cookie in slightly, using your thumb or index finger.

Bake for 9–12 minutes, or until the cookies are lightly browned.

Gently press the indentations again and let the cookies cool on racks.

When cooled, spoon a little jam or jelly into the centres.

Makes about 48

> *Mammy apple is also called mamey sapote. It is a delicious large, orange-fleshed, fibrous fruit with a flavour resembling peaches. It is not widely available; nonetheless it can be enjoyed fresh or cooked.*

Mammy apple cake

1 large mammy apple
2½ cups all-purpose flour
⅔ cup butter
¾ cup granulated sugar
2 eggs
2 tsp baking powder
½ tsp baking soda
1 tsp cinnamon
1 cup milk
1 tsp vanilla extract

Preheat the oven to 350°F. Grease and line a 9-inch springform pan or pie plate.

Peel the mammy apple by scoring the skin in sections and tearing it off without cutting into the fruit. Scrape off the thin brown skin which covers the fruit ensuring that all is removed. Cut the fruit off the core and slice into uniform pieces. Set aside.

Mix ⅓ cup flour with 1 tablespoon butter and 2 tablespoons sugar. Combine and set aside.

Cream the remaining butter with the remaining sugar until light and creamy. Add the eggs one at a time, beating well between additions.

Sift together the remaining flour, the baking powder, soda and cinnamon.

Combine the milk with the vanilla.

Add the flour and milk alternately to the creamed mixture.

Pour the batter into the prepared pan or plate. Arrange the mammy apple on top of the batter and sprinkle with the reserved flour/sugar mixture.

Bake for about 40 minutes until a wooden pick inserted into the centre comes out clean.

Stewed mammy apple

2 large mammy apples
1 cup sugar
2 tbs lemon juice

Prepare the mammy apples as for mammy apple cake (see above).

Boil the sugar in a saucepan with 1 cup water until dissolved. Add the mammy apple and continue to cook on a low heat until tender, about 15–20 minutes.

Add the lemon juice and remove from the heat.

Serve as a dessert with ice cream, yogurt or on its own.

Serves 4

Pineapple cheesecake slices

Crust
- **1 cup crushed cookies**
- **2 tbs melted butter**

Filling
- **1 lb cream cheese**
- **¾ cup sugar**
- **2 eggs**
- **2 tbs flour**
- **14 oz-tin crushed pineapple, drained**

Preheat the oven to 250°F.

Crush the cookies to a fine texture, add the butter and mix.

Press into the bottom of a 9-inch springform pan and refrigerate.

Beat the cream cheese until smooth and add the sugar and eggs. Beat well then stir in the flour and pineapple.

Pour into the cookie crust.

Bake in a bain marie for 35–40 minutes.

Remove from the oven and allow to chill before slicing.

Serves 10

Nutty mocha ice box cake

This is an updated version of the traditional mocha ice box cake, which was a lot sweeter. I like this version, and it will win you great reviews!

- **6 oz cream cheese, softened**
- **1 cup icing sugar**
- **2 egg yolks**
- **¼ cup dark rum**
- **2 tbs extra-strong instant coffee granules**
- **2 cups whipping cream**
- **one 9-inch butterless sponge cake (see opposite page)**
- **1 cup chopped toasted walnuts**
- **2 oz unsweetened chocolate, grated**

Beat the cream cheese with an electric beater until smooth. Add the sugar and egg yolks and beat to a smooth consistency. Refrigerate.

Warm 1 tablespoon of the rum. Dissolve the coffee in the rum.

Beat the cream until it forms soft peaks.

Fold the remaining rum into the whipped cream, and the whipped cream into the cream cheese mixture.

Slice the sponge cake across into three layers.

Place one layer, cut side up into a springform pan. Brush the surface with the coffee mixture. Spoon a third of the cream cheese mixture onto the cake and spread gently.

Top with another cake layer, brush with rum and spoon another third of the cream cheese mixture on top.

Place the final cake layer on top, brush with rum and spread with the remaining cream cheese mixture. Sprinkle with the chopped nuts and grated chocolate.

Cover well with plastic wrap and refrigerate (or freeze) until ready for use. If frozen, remove from the freezer and place in the refrigerator before serving.

Serves 8

Butterless sponge cake

5 eggs
1 cup granulated sugar
1 cup all-purpose flour
½ tsp baking powder

Preheat the oven to 350°F. Line, butter and flour a 9-inch cake pan.

Using an electric mixer, beat the eggs until frothy. Add the sugar gradually and beat until thick and increased in volume, until the batter forms a ribbon on itself.

Fold in the flour, baking powder and 2 tablespoons warm water.

Pour into the cake pan and bake for 35 minutes.

Let cool in the cake pan for 5 minutes, then remove from the pan and cool on a rack.

Ice creams

Trinidadians love ice cream – it's the ultimate dessert, and the most welcome refreshing snack for young and old. We share our love for this creamy delight with many other countries; it's probably the most popular dessert or frozen treat worldwide. Some ice-cream makers boast over 100 flavours to choose from, an indication of ice cream's huge popularity.

Local ice creams have come of age with lots of tropical flavours on offer: soursop, barbadine, coconut, passion fruit, guava, nutmeg, mango, pineapple, coffee – even Guinness – to name a few!

Home-made ice cream

Luscious, creamy, ice cream is a real dream to enjoy if you can get a good-quality one from the supermarket's frozen food shelf, but it's even more of a dream if you make it at home. Great ice cream begins with a good custard base and to that you can add any fruit, fruit purée, nut, or any flavouring agent, to create your own delectable concoction. Never add thickeners to the custard base as this may sometimes result in a powdery mouth-feel to your ice cream.

If you don't have an ice-cream maker, simply chill the ice-cream mixture, then pour it into a large but shallow baking pan and place into the freezer. When the ice cream just begins to freeze, from the sides to the centre, remove it from the freezer, place the contents into a blender or beat it with an electric mixer (don't beat it back to liquid form). This will incorporate some air into the ice cream. Then spoon it into a container and place it back in the freezer to freeze.

Mango-lemon ice cream

This ice cream is particularly creamy and delicious. It's a good way to use up bruised or overly ripe mangoes, so when mangoes are in season there's no better time to try this recipe. Remember, everyone loves home-made ice cream!

2 cups diced ripe mango flesh

¼ cup fresh lemon juice

1 cup sugar

2 cups milk

5 egg yolks

1 cup heavy cream

Combine the mango with the lemon juice and ¼ cup sugar in a medium-sized glass bowl. Refrigerate until ready to use.

Scald the milk in a heavy saucepan.

In a large mixing bowl whisk the egg yolks and the remaining sugar. Whisk in the scalded milk. Return the mixture to the saucepan and cook uncovered over medium heat until the mixture thickens and coats the back of a wooden spoon. Make sure it does not boil or the eggs will curdle.

Strain the custard in a bowl and cool.

Add the cream to the custard and mix until the mixture is smooth.

Add the mango mixture to the custard and stir. Taste the mixture and adjust the sugar if you like.

Put the mixture into an ice-cream maker and proceed according to the manufacturer's instructions.

Serves 6

Ripe mango

Coconut ice cream

This is the number-one flavour (see photograph page 267)! Though soursop comes in a close second!

4 tbs instant custard powder

1 cup full cream milk

½ cup granulated sugar

4 cups fresh coconut milk (from 2 dried coconuts)

1 cup heavy cream

395-g tin condensed milk

1 tsp vanilla extract

Combine the custard powder, milk, sugar and coconut milk in a heavy saucepan. Heat gently and cook until thick.

Cool, then stir in the cream, condensed milk and vanilla.

Pour the mixture into an ice-cream maker and proceed according to the manufacturer's instructions.

Makes 8 cups

To make fresh coconut milk

Crack open a coconut and remove any liquid inside. With a strong knife remove the coconut flesh from the hard covering. The flesh will come away if you slide a knife between the flesh and the covering. Place the flesh in a blender with 1 cup hot water. Blend until finely grated or puréed.

Line a strainer or sieve with a thin tea towel and pour the coconut mixture into this. Squeeze the milk out of the towel. The coconut husk that remains in the towel should be very dry; if not, squeeze some more.

1 coconut will yield 1 cup coconut milk

Rum-infused ice cream

6 egg yolks

½ cup granulated sugar

2 cups full-cream evaporated milk

2 cups whipping cream

¼ tsp grated nutmeg

2 tbs grated orange zest

¼ cup rum

Beat the egg yolks with the sugar until light. Add the evaporated milk and cook over low heat until thick. Be careful not to boil. Let the mixture cool.

Lightly whip the cream and fold into the cooled custard mixture. Add the nutmeg and orange zest. Stir in the rum and chill the mixture.

Place in an ice-cream maker and proceed according to the manufacturer's instructions.

Makes 6 cups

Pineapple ice cream

4 eggs

1 cup granulated sugar

2 cups milk

1 tsp vanilla extract

1 cup heavy cream

**1 cup drained crushed
  pineapple**

Beat the eggs with the sugar until thick.

Heat the milk and combine with the sugar and eggs. Add the vanilla and return to the heat. Cook until the custard is thick and coats the back of a wooden spoon. Do not boil.

Remove from the heat, strain and cool slightly.

Stir in the cream and pineapple. Chill for 4 hours.

Place in an ice-cream maker and proceed according to the manufacturer's instructions.

Makes 4 cups

Passion fruit sorbet

This is a delicious and refreshing fat-free dessert.

2 cups sugar
1 cup passion fruit pulp
1 tbs lime juice

Make a sugar syrup by boiling the sugar in 3 cups water. Cool overnight.

Combine the passion fruit pulp with the lime juice and cooled sugar syrup.

Pour into an ice-cream maker and proceed according to the manufacturer's instructions.

Serves 8–10

Passion fruit ice cream

4 egg yolks
1 cup granulated sugar
2 cups milk
1 tsp vanilla extract
1 cup heavy cream
1 cup passion fruit purée

Beat the egg yolks with the sugar until thick.

Heat the milk and combine with the sugar and eggs. Add the vanilla and return to the heat. Cook until the custard is thick and coats the back of a wooden spoon. Do not boil.

Remove from the heat, strain and cool slightly.

Stir in the cream and passion fruit purée. Chill for 4 hours.

Place in an ice-cream maker and proceed according to the manufacturer's instructions.

Makes 4 cups

Guava ice cream

15 guavas

4 egg yolks

½ cup granulated sugar

1 cup full-cream milk

⅔ cup condensed milk

1 tsp vanilla extract

¾ cup heavy cream

Wash the guavas and cut into quarters. Place in a saucepan, add 2 cups water and simmer for about 40 minutes until tender.

Pass through a food mill with any remaining liquid. Leave to cool.

Make a custard by whisking the egg yolks with the sugar. Add the full-cream milk and cook over a double boiler until the mixture is thick and coats the back of a wooden spoon.

Remove from the heat and stir in the guava mixture, condensed milk, vanilla and cream. Refrigerate until cold.

Pour the mixture into an ice-cream maker and proceed according to the manufacturer's instructions.

Makes 4 cups

Ponche de crème ice cream

4 egg yolks

½ cup granulated sugar

2 cups full-cream or evaporated milk

2 cups whipping cream

¼ tsp grated nutmeg

2 tbs grated orange zest

¼ cup rum

Beat the egg yolks with the sugar until light. Add the milk and cook over a low heat until thick. Be careful not to boil.

Leave the mixture to cool.

Lightly whip the cream and fold into the chilled custard mixture. Add the nutmeg and orange zest. Stir in the rum and chill the mixture.

Place in an ice-cream maker and proceed according to the manufacturer's instructions.

Makes 6 cups

Soursop ice cream

4 tbs instant custard powder

1 cup full-cream milk

½ cup granulated sugar

4 cups fresh soursop pulp (from 2 soursops)

1 cup heavy cream

395-g tin condensed milk

1 tsp vanilla extract

Combine the custard powder, milk and sugar in a heavy saucepan. Heat gently and cook until thick. Leave until cool.

Stir in the soursop pulp, cream, condensed milk and vanilla.

Pour the mixture into an ice-cream maker and proceed according to the manufacturer's instructions.

Makes 6 cups

Note
To make soursop pulp, peel the soursops, remove the seeds and cut up the flesh. Place in a blender with 2 cups water and purée.

Breads, bakes and *pancakes*

Breads both sweet and savoury are a huge and integral part of the culinary landscape. The breads enjoyed on the islands indeed reflect a marriage of influences from our past. Cassava breads made from grated and dried cassava, rotis and bakes are all indigenous to our islands, given to us by our Carib, East Indian and African ancestors respectively.

East Indian rotis are enjoyed by all from breakfast to dinner, as are Creole bakes, both fried and roasted. Roadside food shops sell sada roti and bake sandwiches for breakfast. Bake and saltfish, cheese, sausage and eggs are normal offerings as much as sada with aloo (potato), carailli (bitter melon), pumpkin, bodi and tomato and melongene chokas – to name but a few. These local 'breads' make the whole carbohydrate experience so much more exciting. They are also very easy to duplicate at home so we never run out of choice!

Hops bread, native to Trinidad and Tobago, is our version of French bread – hard and crusty on the outside, light on the inside. It's baked daily by bakeries and is usually served up as a 'quart' or 10 rolls to go. Most other breads enjoyed are traditional loaves like white or whole-wheat. Recently, multigrain breads have been appearing in bakeries.

Sweet yeasted breads appear in our bakeries in the form of coconut sweet breads, rolls and turnovers. Stewed coconut, flavourful and juicy, is often used as a filling and is also rolled into many dough-based confections. Bananas are another popular ingredient and are used in breads, muffins and breakfast treats.

Pone, a dense coconut and provision pudding, is enjoyed any time of day as a snack. It's a treat that really has maintained popularity through the years!

Paratha roti

6 tbs softened butter or ghee

**4 tbs vegetable oil and 4 tbs melted butter, or
8 tbs melted ghee**

Dough

4 cups all-purpose flour

1 tbs butter, softened

1 tsp salt

4 tsp baking powder

To make the dough, combine the flour with the butter, salt and baking powder.

Add enough water to knead to a very soft dough, cover and rest for 30 minutes.

Divide the dough into eight pieces and form each piece into a ball.

Roll out each ball of dough into a 6-inch round, place about ¾ tablespoon butter onto the round and spread to the ends.

Cut the dough in half from the middle of the top edge, leaving a 1-inch uncut portion at the base. Starting from the top right-hand side portion, roll the dough all the way to the bottom and up the left side so that it resembles a cone. Tuck the end under and push the pointed part into the dough, flatten slightly and rest for a further 30 minutes.

Combine the oil with the butter.

Lightly flour a surface, roll each piece of prepared dough into a 10-inch circle and cook on a hot baking stone. Turn, brush with the oil mixture, turn again, and brush again. Cook until it balloons or bubbles on the surface then remove. This should take about 3–4 minutes in total.

Beat the roti with your hands or a wooden spatula to break and flake. Serve with any curried dishes.

Makes 8

Paratha roti (*left*) and dhalpourie roti

'*Pepper roti is usually eaten on the eve of a Hindu wedding. When the wedding food is being prepared by family members, the roti is enjoyed as an accompaniment to the drinks that are served up as part of the festivities of the wedding preparation.*'

Pepper roti

2 tbs vegetable oil and 2 tbs melted butter or 4 tbs melted ghee

Dough

4 cups all-purpose flour

1 tbs softened butter

1 tsp salt

4 tsp baking powder

Filling

4 tbs melted butter

2 tsp ground roasted geera (cumin)

1 tsp ground hot pepper

2 tbs minced chadon beni (cilantro)

1 tbs minced garlic

salt

To make the dough, combine the flour with the butter, salt and baking powder.

Add enough water to knead to a very soft dough, cover and rest for 30 minutes.

Divide the dough into eight pieces and form each piece into a ball.

Combine the filling ingredients and set aside.

Roll out each ball of dough into a 6-inch round. Place about ¾ tablespoon filling mixture onto the dough and spread to the ends.

Cut the dough in half from the middle of the top edge, leaving a 1-inch uncut portion at the base. Starting from the top right-hand side, roll the dough all the way to the bottom and up the left side so that it resembles a cone. Tuck the end under and push the pointed part into the dough, flatten slightly and rest for a further 30 minutes.

Combine the oil with the butter.

Lightly flour a surface, roll each piece of prepared dough into an 8-inch circle and cook on a hot baking stone. Turn, brush with the oil mixture, turn again, and brush again. Cook until it balloons, then remove.

Beat the roti with your hands or a wooden spatula to break and flake. Serve with any curried dishes.

Makes 8

Note

Pepper roti is now made with a filling of mashed potato seasoned with Indian spices and pepper. This filling is spread onto one piece of rolled dough, and is then topped with another piece of rolled dough of the same size. The ends are pressed together and this is baked on a baking stone (tawah).

Pepper roti on baking stone (tawah)

Dosti roti

4 cups all-purpose flour

1 tbs softened butter

1 tsp salt

4 tsp baking powder

½ cup ghee or butter

Combine the flour with 1 tablespoon softened butter, the salt and baking powder.

Add enough water to knead to a soft dough, cover and rest for 30 minutes.

Divide the dough into eight pieces and form each piece into a ball. Let rest for 15 minutes.

Divide each loya (dough ball) into two and flatten slightly. Spread some ghee onto half the pieces, then cover with another flattened loya, like a sandwich. Press together, cover and let rest for 30 minutes.

Melt the remaining ghee.

Lightly flour a surface, roll each piece of prepared dough into an 8–10-inch circle and cook on a hot baking stone. Turn, brush with ghee, turn again and brush with ghee. Cook until it balloons, then remove.

Split the dosti into two and wrap in a tea towel. Serve with any curried dishes.

Makes 8

Pizza

1 cup tomato sauce

1 tsp pizza seasoning plus more for finishing

1 tsp minced garlic

2 tbs vegetable oil

½ cup sliced mushrooms

½ cup sliced green or red bell pepper

½ cup sliced onion

½ cup tinned pineapple pieces, drained

2 cups grated cheese

Dough

2½–3 cups all-purpose flour

2 tsp instant yeast

1 tsp sugar

½ tsp salt

2 tbs olive oil

1 cup warm water (105–115°F)

Make the dough by combining 2 cups flour with the yeast, sugar and salt.

Add the oil and water and knead to a soft dough, adding a little more flour to make it smooth and pliable.

Cover and let rest for about 30 minutes.

Preheat the oven to 400°F. Grease a large baking sheet.

Combine the tomato sauce and pizza seasoning. Set aside.

Divide the dough into two pieces. Roll each piece into an 11-inch circle. Dimple the surface and place on the baking sheet.

Combine the garlic with the oil and spread over the dough. Spread with the tomato sauce and top with the vegetables and pineapple.

Sprinkle with pizza seasoning and the grated cheese.

Cook until the cheese is melted and the pizza is lightly browned around the edges, 20–25 minutes.

Makes 2

Delicious garlic bread

1 large loaf French bread, unsliced

¼ cup butter

2 tbs olive oil

2 tsp minced garlic

¼ cup grated parmesan cheese (optional)

1 tbs finely chopped chives

Preheat the oven to 400°F.

Slice the bread lengthways into two pieces.

Soften the butter and combine with the olive oil, garlic and some salt.

Spread the butter and garlic mixture evenly onto the two cut sides of the loaf. Sprinkle with the parmesan cheese, if using, and the chives.

Replace the top half onto the bottom. Wrap the loaf in foil and bake in a hot oven for about 10 minutes until heated through.

If you prefer a crusty loaf, then open the foil after 10 minutes, lower the temperature to 350°F and bake the bread for a further 5–10 minutes, uncovered, to crisp up the crust.

Remove from the oven and slice.

Serves 6

Whole-wheat oatmeal bread

1 tbs instant yeast

1 tbs brown sugar

1½ cups rolled oats

3 cups whole-wheat flour

2 tsp salt

2 cups milk, warmed to 105°F

½ cup melted unsalted butter

3–3½ cups bread flour

Combine the yeast, sugar, oats, whole-wheat flour and salt in the bowl of an electric mixer.

Add the milk and melted butter and beat on medium speed until the mixture is well combined.

Add the remaining flour, ½ cup at a time, to make a soft but pliable dough. (Take care not to add too much extra flour as the oats will absorb moisture during the rising process and so the dough may become dry.)

Continue kneading by hand or by machine until smooth and pliable, about 4 minutes.

Cover and let rise in a greased bowl until doubled in volume, about 45 minutes.

Preheat the oven to 400°F.

Form into two loaves and place in greased bread pans. Cover and let rise for another 20–30 minutes.

Bake the loaves for about 35 minutes until golden.

Makes 2 large loaves

Sada roti

4 cups all-purpose flour
4 tsp baking powder
1 tsp salt
1 tsp butter

Combine the flour with the baking powder and salt.

Rub the butter into the flour and add enough water to make a firm dough.

Turn the dough onto a lightly floured surface and knead for about 5 minutes until smooth.

Divide the dough into four pieces and form each piece into a smooth ball.

Cover with a damp towel and let rest for 15 minutes.

Heat a baking stone until hot.

Roll out the balls of dough to about ½ inch thickness.

Place one on the heated baking stone and cook until small bubbles appear on the surface. Turn over the roti and continue to cook for about 4 minutes longer.

Using pot holders or a towel pull the baking stone away from the fire towards you to expose the open flame or heat element. Push the roti onto the open flame and swiftly turn it around so that it begins to balloon.

Remove from heat and wrap in towels. Repeat for the other three rotis.

Makes 4

This is indeed the East Indian equivalent of bread! The recipe largely resembles that of the original chapati roti from India, reflecting our Eastern influences. Sada is sold at breakfast stops across the island and is usually sandwiched with a myriad of vegetable fillings, from pumpkin to carailli. It's made in most homes at breakfast time, and sometimes at dinner when it's enjoyed with chokas like tomato or eggplant.

Dhalpourie roti

8 oz yellow split peas

½ tsp saffron or turmeric powder

3 garlic cloves

3 tsp ground roasted geera (cumin)

4 cups all-purpose flour

2 tsp baking powder

1 tsp salt

½ cup melted butter or ghee

Place the split peas in a pot, cover with water, add the saffron and garlic and bring to a boil. Lower the heat and boil for about 15–20 minutes until the peas are tender and cooked but not mushy.

Drain in a colander and let cool.

Grind the peas to a fine consistency using a food processor or food mill. Season with some salt and the geera.

Combine the flour with the baking powder. Add the teaspoon of salt. Mix in enough cool water to make a soft pliable dough. Cover and let rest for 30 minutes.

Divide the dough into eight pieces. Form into smooth balls and cover. Leave for 20–30 minutes.

Pat each piece of dough into a 3-inch circle. Cupping the dough in your hands, fill the cavity with the dhal, about 1½ tablespoons. Bring the sides of the dough together at the top and pinch together so that the filled dough becomes a smooth ball. Repeat.

Heat a baking stone. Roll the filled roti dough into an 8-inch circle about ⅛–¼ inch thick.

Place on the heated baking stone. Cook until bubbles appear on the surface.

Flip the roti and brush with melted butter. Turn again and brush with butter. The roti should balloon, which means it is cooked. Remove and repeat with the remaining pieces of filled dough.

Makes 8

'The delightful dhal-filled roti that envelops a good curry gives us what we call a 'wrap roti'. Some refer to dhalpourie as roti skins but the true name is dhalpourie roti. Roti shops across the island serve this roti filled with our choice of curried chicken, beef, goat, shrimp, lambie or vegetables.'

Wrap roti

Potato roti (aloo poori)

3 cups all-purpose flour

3 tsp baking powder

1 tbs softened butter plus ½ cup melted butter or ghee

1 cup cool water

Filling

8 oz potatoes

½ cup finely chopped chives

2 garlic cloves, minced

1 tsp salt

1 tsp freshly ground black pepper

½ tsp pepper sauce (or more or less, to taste)

¼ cup chopped chadon beni (cilantro)

1 tbs ground roasted geera (cumin)

To make the dough, combine the flour and baking powder. Add the softened butter and rub it into the flour until it is combined. Add the water and knead to a soft dough.

Cover and let rest for 30 minutes.

Meanwhile, boil the potatoes and mash to a smooth consistency to prevent lumps.

While still hot add the chives, garlic, salt, black pepper, pepper sauce, chadon beni and geera. Mix well.

Divide the dough into six equal pieces.

Flatten each piece in the palm of your hand to about a 3-inch circle and cup the dough. Put about 3 tablespoons of the potato mixture in the centre and fold the dough over to cover the potato, as if forming a dinner roll.

Repeat with the remaining pieces of dough and allow to rest for 15 minutes.

Heat a baking stone or tawah.

On a lightly floured board gently roll the roti as thin as possible without letting it burst, about ¼ inch thickness.

Place the roti on the hot tawah and when tiny bubbles appear on the surface quickly turn over. Brush the cooked side with melted butter and turn again, brushing the other side with butter, and pressing the edges to ensure even cooking. At this point the roti should have many large bubbles and should be cooked. Do not allow to brown too much. Remove, wrap the roti in clean tea towels to keep warm and repeat for the other rotis.

Makes 6

I grew up enjoying my mother's fine rotis. This aloo poori, or potato roti, was and still remains one of my favourites. You won't find this in any eating establishment, but you'll most certainly find it in many an East Indian home!

Roast bake

4 cups all-purpose flour

4 tsp baking powder

1 tsp brown sugar

2 tsp salt

4 tbs shortening

butter for finishing

Combine the flour with the baking powder, brown sugar and salt. Rub in the shortening until the mixture resembles fine crumbs.

Add enough water to knead to a firm dough. Cover and let rest for 30 minutes.

Preheat the oven to 375°F.

Knead the dough into a smooth ball and roll out into a 9-inch circle. Prick with the tines of a fork, spread a little butter on the top and place on a baking tray.

Bake for 30 minutes until golden on top and the underneath is brown and crisp.

Serves 4–6

' Roast bake is the one I grew up eating, quick and easy and delicious with just about everything. This bake was originally made on an open fire, hence the name 'roast' bake, or on top of a stove either on a baking stone or inside a pot, which is why it is also sometimes referred to as 'pot' bake. If making on top the stove, simply heat the baking stone and place the bake onto the stone. Flip the bake over, lower the heat and keep turning while cooking. It will be ready in about 30 minutes. '

Coconut bake

This coconut bake is delicious, and can be enjoyed with a fish salad for breakfast or simply with butter and cheese.

1 cup coconut milk

4½ cups all-purpose or bread flour

2 tsp instant yeast

¾ tsp salt

1 tbs brown sugar

¼ cup butter or shortening

¼ cup freshly grated coconut

Warm the coconut milk to about 120°F.

Place the flour, yeast, salt and brown sugar into a work bowl.

Add the butter and rub it into the flour until the mixture resembles fine crumbs. Add the grated coconut and mix.

Pour in enough coconut milk to make a firm dough. If more liquid is needed add a little water.

Turn the dough out onto a floured surface and knead lightly until smooth. Divide into two pieces and roll each piece into an 8-inch circle. Prick with a fork and place onto baking sheets. Let rest for 20 minutes.

Preheat the oven to 400°F.

Bake for 15–20 minutes.

Makes 2

Note
For a lighter bake omit the coconut and use water in place of the coconut milk. You may also use one-third whole-wheat flour and two-thirds baker's flour.

Fried bakes

These bakes are golden and crisp on the outside, light and almost hollow on the inside. They are the perfect breakfast bread to be enjoyed with fish salads or eggs.

4 cups all-purpose flour

1 tsp salt

4 tsp baking powder

1 tsp brown sugar

1 tbs shortening

vegetable oil for frying

Combine the flour, salt, baking powder and sugar in a bowl.

Add the shortening and rub into the flour until the mixture resembles fine crumbs.

Add just enough water to make a soft dough.

Knead on a floured surface for about 5 minutes. Let rest for 30 minutes.

Divide the dough into two pieces and divide each half into 12. Roll each piece into a ball.

Rest the dough for another 5 minutes and then roll out each ball of dough to about 3 inches in diameter.

Heat some vegetable oil in a deep frying pan. Fry the bakes, making sure that they are covered in the hot oil. Turn and fry until fully ballooned or puffed.

Remove and drain. Serve hot.

Makes 24

*'Floats is the bread that sandwiches the ever famous shark and bake.
It uses yeast as its leavening, thereby giving softer bread that will
remain soft for a while after it's cooked (see photograph page 133).'*

Floats

4 cups all-purpose flour

2 tsp instant yeast

1 tsp salt

1 tbs sugar

1 tbs shortening

vegetable oil for deep-frying

Combine the flour with the yeast, salt and sugar.

Rub in the shortening until the mixture resembles fine crumbs.
Add enough warm water to make a soft dough.

Knead for 5 minutes, then form into a smooth ball. Cover and let
rest for 30 minutes until doubled in size.

Form the dough into eight balls. Leave to rest again for 15
minutes.

Flatten the dough balls into 4-inch rounds.

Heat some oil in a deep frying pan and deep-fry the floats until
they actually float to the top of the oil. Turn and fry until golden.

Drain and serve hot

Makes 8

Delightful corn bread

**1½ cups buttermilk or 1½ cups
milk combined with 1½ tbs
lime juice (see recipe)**

1 cup cornmeal

1¼ cups all-purpose flour

2 tbs sugar

1 tbs baking powder

½ tsp baking soda

1 tsp salt

2 eggs

¼ cup melted butter

Preheat the oven to 375°F.

If not using buttermilk combine the milk with the lime juice and
let stand for 10 minutes until thick and curdled.

Combine the cornmeal, flour, sugar, baking powder, baking
soda and salt in a large bowl.

In a separate bowl beat the eggs and add the buttermilk and
melted butter.

Stir the wet ingredients into the dry ingredients until just
combined.

Spoon the batter into a 9-inch square baking pan. Bake for 30
minutes until the corn bread is done and is springy to the touch.

Let cool for 10 minutes before cutting.

Serves 4–6

Basic bread

5–6 cups bread or all-purpose flour

1 tbs instant yeast

3 tsp salt

1 tbs brown sugar

2½ cups milk

½ cup butter

2 eggs

Place 3 cups flour, the yeast, salt and sugar in the bowl of an electric mixer.

Warm the milk with the butter to 115–120°F.

Add the milk mixture to the flour, add the eggs and beat, adding enough extra flour to give a soft smooth dough.

Turn the dough onto a floured surface and knead for about 5 minutes. Place in an oiled bowl, cover and let rise until doubled in volume, about 45 minutes.

Grease two 9 x 5-inch bread pans. Divide the dough into two and shape into loaves. Place in the pans, cover and let rise for about 20–30 minutes.

Preheat the oven to 400°F.

Bake until the loaves are golden brown and sound hollow when tapped on the underside, 30–45 minutes.

Makes 2

Hops

4 cups all-purpose flour
2½ tsp instant yeast
1 tsp brown sugar
1 tsp salt
½ cup milk
1 cup warm water (110–120°F)
2 tbs vegetable oil

Combine 3 cups flour with the yeast, sugar and salt in a large mixing bowl or using an electric mixer.

Combine the milk with the water and oil, add to the flour mixture and mix well.

Add enough of the remaining flour to knead to a soft smooth dough. Knead for about 8 minutes.

Lightly oil the dough and cover with plastic. Let rise until doubled in volume, about 1½ hours.

Punch down, and divide the dough into eight equal pieces. Roll each piece into a smooth ball.

Place on a greased baking tray and let rise again until doubled in size, about 45–60 minutes.

Place in a cold oven and turn the oven temperature to 375°F. Do not preheat, just let the rolls begin baking in a cool oven. Bake for 25 minutes until dark golden.

Makes 8

'Hops is the ubiquitous Trini bread, a light, crusty, large roll that is savoured with just about anything – hops and sardines, hops and cheese, hops and smoked herring and saltfish buljols. True hops bread is supposed to be soft and light on the inside and hard and crusty on the outside. Not too much milk (or oil) is added, and the dough is mostly made with flour, water and yeast.'

Paramin bread rolls

You may use all white flour for this recipe or 2 cups whole-wheat to 3 cups white.

4–5 cups all-purpose flour

1 packet instant yeast

1 tbs sugar

2 tsp salt

1 cup chopped fresh herbs (Spanish thyme, basil, chives)

⅓ cup chopped rosemary

¾ cup melted butter

2½ cups milk, warmed to 115–120˚F

1 egg

Combine the flour with the yeast, sugar and salt. Add the herbs and stir.

Combine the butter with the milk and stir in the egg. Add to the flour mixture and stir, or knead with an electric mixer, to make a soft smooth dough.

Place in a greased bowl, cover and let rise for 50–60 minutes or until doubled in volume.

Punch down and divide the dough into 24 pieces. Roll each into a smooth ball and place on a greased baking tray.

Cover and let rise for another 40 minutes or until doubled in size.

Preheat the oven to 375˚F.

Bake the rolls for 20 minutes until golden.

Makes 24

Whole-wheat rosemary focaccia

2 cups all-purpose flour

1 cup whole-wheat flour

1 tsp salt

1 tsp sugar

3 tsp instant yeast

¼ cup olive oil

about 2 cups warm water (120°F)

cornmeal for sprinkling

2 tbs fresh rosemary, chopped

8 leaves Spanish thyme

Place the flours, salt and sugar in a mixing bowl. Add the yeast and stir. Add 2 tablespoons olive oil and combine.

Pour in enough warm water to make a very soft dough. Knead for a few minutes, brush with olive oil, cover and set aside for 1½ hours.

With oiled fingers punch down the dough, and then stretch into a 9-inch circle using the heel of your hands, lifting and pulling the dough into shape.

Place on an oiled baking tray sprinkled with cornmeal. Let rest for 30 minutes more.

Preheat the oven to 450°F.

Dimple the dough with your fingers to make small deep indentations. Drizzle with olive oil, sprinkle with salt and the herbs.

Bake for 30 minutes until golden.

Remove from the oven and serve hot.

Serves 4

Trini heavy coconut sweet bread

1½ cups finely grated coconut

¾ cup milk or water

1 tsp vanilla extract

1 egg

3 cups all-purpose flour

1 tbs baking powder

1 cup sugar

1 tsp ground cinnamon

½ tsp grated nutmeg

¼ tsp ground cloves

½ cup butter

1 cup raisins

½ cup green and red glacé cherries, chopped

¼ cup mixed peel

¼ cup currants

Glaze
> **2 tbs brown sugar**
> **2 tbs hot water**

Preheat the oven to 350°F.

Combine the coconut with ½ cup milk or water and the vanilla. Beat the egg and add.

Combine the flour with the baking powder, sugar and spices. Add the butter and blend to a crumbly texture.

Add the coconut mixture and stir well, adding a little more milk or water if needed to make a soft dough.

Add the dried fruits and stir.

Spoon the mixture into a bread pan, about 8 by 4 inches.

Bake for 50–60 minutes until a wooden pick inserted into the centre comes out clean. To glaze the bread, combine the sugar and hot water and stir until the sugar dissolves. Brush over the bread 5 minutes before it comes out of the oven.

Makes 1 large loaf

> *This bread is native to our country, dense, crumbly, and packed with juicy coconut and raisins. It is so rich and flavourful that you can enjoy it on its own.*

Easter is an occasion of big celebration on our islands and many bakeries take orders ahead of time for hot cross buns.

Hot cross buns

1 tbs active dry yeast

¼ cup warm water

1 cup lukewarm milk

⅓ cup sugar

⅓ cup melted butter

1 tsp salt

1 tsp ground cinnamon

¼ tsp ground cloves

¼ tsp grated nutmeg

2 eggs

4–4½ cups all-purpose flour

1 cup raisins

½ cup mixed peel (optional)

In a large bowl, dissolve the yeast in the water. Stir in the milk, sugar, butter, salt, cinnamon, cloves, nutmeg, one whole egg plus one egg yolk (reserve the white) and 2 cups flour. Beat until smooth.

Stir in the raisins and mixed peel, if using, and add enough of the remaining flour to make the dough easy to handle.

Turn the dough onto a lightly floured surface and knead for about 5 minutes until smooth and elastic.

Place in a greased bowl then turn over so the greased side of the dough faces up. Cover and let rise until doubled in volume, about 1½ hours.

Punch down the dough and divide into four. Cut each quarter into six equal pieces.

Shape each piece into a ball and place about 2 inches apart on a baking sheet. With scissors, snip a cross on top of each ball. Cover and let rise until doubled in size, about 40 minutes.

Preheat the oven to 375˚F.

Mix the remaining egg white with 1 tablespoon water and brush the top of the buns with the mixture.

Bake until golden brown, about 20 minutes.

Frost crosses onto the buns with powdered sugar frosting.

Makes 24

Note
If preferred, you can use an electric mixer for this recipe.

Powdered sugar frosting

1 cup icing sugar

1 tbs lemon juice

1 tsp lemon zest

Mix the sugar with the lemon juice and zest until smooth. Add a little water to thin, if necessary, ½ teaspoon at a time.

Double chocolate banana cinnamon bread

¾ cup milk

1 tbs lime juice

2 cups all-purpose flour

1 cup cocoa powder

1½ tsp baking powder

¼ tsp baking soda

½ tsp salt

1 tsp cinnamon

½ tsp grated nutmeg

½ cup butter

1 cup brown sugar

2 eggs

2 large ripe bananas, mashed

½ cup chocolate chips

Mix the milk and lime juice and let stand for 20 minutes.

Preheat the oven to 375°F. Grease and flour a 9 x 5-inch loaf pan.

Combine the flour with the cocoa, baking powder, baking soda, salt and spices.

Cream the butter with the sugar until light. Add the eggs and cream until fluffy.

Combine the mashed bananas with the milk mixture.

Add the banana mixture alternately to the butter mixture with the dry ingredients. Stir in the chocolate chips.

Bake for 55–60 minutes until a wooden pick inserted near the centre comes out clean.

Leave to cool on a wire rack.

Banana bread

⅓ cup vegetable oil

2 large eggs

1½ cups brown sugar

5 bananas, puréed

2½ cups all-purpose flour

1 tbs baking powder

a pinch of salt

1 tsp cinnamon

1 tsp grated nutmeg

Preheat the oven to 350°F.

Using an electric mixer, beat the oil with the eggs and sugar until creamy. Stir in the puréed bananas.

Combine the flour with the baking powder, salt, cinnamon and nutmeg.

Stir the egg mixture into the flour mixture.

Pour into two greased and floured loaf pans.

Bake for 50 minutes until a wooden pick inserted into the centre comes out clean.

Makes 2

Mini coconut rolls

1 cup milk

⅓ cup butter

4–4½ cups all-purpose flour

1 tbs instant yeast

2 tsp grated orange zest

1 tsp salt

1 tsp cinnamon

⅓ cup brown sugar

2 eggs

brown sugar for sprinkling

Filling

4 cloves, ground

1 tsp cinnamon

2 cups granulated sugar

2 cups freshly grated coconut

2 tbs melted butter

Glaze

¾ cup sugar

Warm the milk with the butter to 115–120°F.

Combine 2 cups flour with the yeast, orange zest, salt, cinnamon and sugar.

Add the milk to the flour mixture and beat in the eggs, using an electric mixer. Add enough extra flour to make a sticky dough.

Turn onto a floured surface and knead in enough of the remaining flour to make a smooth elastic dough. Place in a mixing bowl, cover and let rise until doubled in volume.

Meanwhile, make the coconut filling. Bring ½ cup water to a boil in a medium saucepan. Add the spices then the sugar and stir to dissolve. Add the coconut and cook on medium heat until the mixture begins to bubble and thicken.

Continue cooking, stirring frequently, for about 10–15 minutes until the mixture comes together. Add a small amount of water if necessary to prevent sticking. Remove the coconut when it is cooked and still juicy, do not let the mixture dry out. Leave to cool.

To make the sugar glaze, cook the sugar in ½ cup water until melted and syrupy. Remove from the heat and leave to cool.

Divide the dough in half. Roll each piece into a rectangle 12 by 8 inches. Spread each rectangle with 1 tablespoon melted butter, then spread each half with half of the coconut mixture, leaving a 1-inch margin around each piece of rolled dough.

Roll up each piece jelly-roll style, beginning from a long end. Slice the rolls into 1½-inch thick slices and place the slices in greased muffin cups.

Cover and let rise until doubled in size, about 15–20 minutes.

Preheat the oven to 375°F.

Bake for 20–25 minutes until golden. Glaze with the sugar syrup and sprinkle with brown sugar. Return to the oven and bake for 5 minutes longer.

Makes 24

Cinnamon swirl loaf

2¼ cups milk

2 tbs butter

5½–6 cups all-purpose or bread flour

1 tbs instant yeast

⅓ cup sugar

2 tsp salt

1 egg

Filling

1 tbs ground cinnamon

½ cup brown sugar

4 tbs melted butter

Warm the milk with the butter to 110–115°F.

Place 2 cups flour, the yeast, sugar and salt in the bowl of an electric mixer or food processor and mix well.

Add the milk and egg to the yeast mixture.

Continue to add the balance of the flour and knead to make a pliable dough that is smooth and elastic.

Cover and let rise in a warm place until doubled in size, 45–60 minutes.

Meanwhile, combine the cinnamon with the sugar for the filling.

Punch down the dough and turn onto a lightly floured surface. Shape into two balls and cover. Grease two 8 x 4 x 2-inch loaf pans.

Roll each ball of dough into a rectangle 8 by 12 inches. Brush 2 tablespoons melted butter on each piece of dough, leaving a 1-inch border free from butter. Sprinkle evenly with the cinnamon sugar.

Roll up the dough like a jelly roll, starting from the short end. Seal and place into the prepared loaf pans.

Cover and let rise until doubled in size, about 30–45 minutes.

Preheat the oven to 400°F.

Bake the loaves for about 45 minutes until brown.

Remove from the pans and leave to cool on wire racks.

Makes 2

'When I was growing up and became old enough to prepare my own breakfast, French toast was one of my favourite Saturday morning treats. I still love it today. Make this with home-made bread, it is denser and will hold up better. Good French toast should be golden on the outside, moist on the inside, so you must leave enough time for the bread to soak up all the egg mixture that it can.'

French toast

4 eggs

¾ cup milk

1 tsp vanilla extract

1 tsp cinnamon

6 slices bread, cut about 1 inch thick

¼ cup vegetable oil

Beat the eggs well then add the milk, vanilla and cinnamon.

Dip the bread slices into the milk mixture then place in a shallow bowl. Repeat. Then pour the remaining milk mixture over the bread slices and let sit for about 10 minutes.

Heat the oil in a frying pan and shallow-fry the bread until golden on both sides.

Drain and serve with syrup or honey.

Serves 4-6

Banana-stuffed French toast

2 eggs

1 cup milk

2 tbs sugar

1 tsp vanilla extract

1 banana

a pinch of cinnamon

a pinch of grated nutmeg

1 tbs brown sugar

6-8 slices bread, cut about 2 inches thick

Preheat the oven to 350°F. Grease a shallow casserole dish.

Beat the eggs well with the milk, sugar and vanilla and place in a shallow dish.

Peel and slice the banana and combine with the spices and brown sugar.

Slice each piece of bread through the middle to about three-quarters of the way down; do not cut through.

Stuff the banana slices into the cuts in each piece of bread.

Dip the bread into the egg mixture and place in the prepared dish.

Bake for 15–20 minutes until golden and puffed.

Serve with honey or syrup.

Serves 3-4

Pumpkin bread

½ cup unsalted butter

1½ cups brown sugar

4 eggs

3 cups grated uncooked
    pumpkin

3⅓ cups all-purpose flour

2 tsp baking soda

1 tsp baking powder

1 tsp salt

2 tsp ground cinnamon

1 tsp grated nutmeg

⅔ cup raisins

⅔ cup coarsely chopped nuts
    (optional)

½ cup toasted pumpkin seeds

Preheat the oven to 350°F. Grease the bases only of two 9 x 5 x 3-inch loaf pans.

Beat the butter and sugar in a large mixing bowl until creamy.

Add the eggs one at a time and continue beating until light coloured.

Add the pumpkin and ⅔ cup water and blend.

In a separate bowl mix the flour, baking soda, baking powder, salt and spices. Add to the pumpkin mixture and mix until just combined.

Stir in the raisins, nuts, if using, and half the pumpkin seeds and divide between the prepared pans. Sprinkle with the remaining pumpkin seeds.

Bake until a wooden pick inserted into the centre comes out clean, about 45–50 minutes.

Loosen the sides of the loaves from the pans and leave in the pans to cool slightly.

Remove from the pans and cool completely before slicing.

To store, wrap and refrigerate for up to 10 days or freeze.

Makes 2

Cake doughnuts

These doughnuts have a delightful cakey texture and are a great treat to all!

3¼ cups all-purpose flour

2 tsp baking powder

½ tsp salt

½ tsp cinnamon

¼ tsp grated nutmeg

2 eggs, beaten

¾ cup granulated sugar

1 tsp vanilla extract

⅔ cup milk

¼ cup melted butter

vegetable oil for frying

½ cup granulated sugar combined with ½ tsp cinnamon

Combine the flour, baking powder, salt, cinnamon and nutmeg in a large mixing bowl.

In another mixing bowl combine the eggs, ⅔ cup sugar and vanilla and beat until light and thick.

Combine the milk and butter.

Add the flour mixture and milk mixture alternately to the sugar mixture. Beat after each addition until just blended.

Cover and chill for 2 hours.

Lightly flour the work surface and roll out the doughnut dough to ½ inch thickness. Cut with a floured 2½-inch doughnut cutter.

Heat some oil in a deep pan and fry the doughnuts for about 1 minute per side or until golden, turning once.

Remove and drain on paper towels. Sprinkle with the sugar and cinnamon mixture before serving.

Makes 16

'Freshly grated coconut is used in a myriad of ways in Trinidad and Tobago cuisine. But it's never more delicious than in the dense, moist and spicy coconut pudding called pone.

Pone is a combination of coconut and provisions, sweetened with cane sugar and flavoured with lots of aromatic spices such as cinnamon and clove. It is baked and cut into squares and enjoyed as a snack. Fresh coconut is recommended and you must grate it on a hand grater: food processors tend to grate the coconut too large so that the juices from the coconut are not released.

Pone is indeed a local delicacy that is still enjoyed by many. It cannot be found pre-packaged in supermarkets but it is stocked by many a local bakery and it is still sold by vendors who sell home-made goodies from their baskets on a daily basis.

An intriguing sweet, historically pone was and still is a great way to use up extra provisions; dried coconuts were always on hand. The recipe may seem complex but really it's a simple, stir-together one that once you've attempted it, you'll indeed be making again and again!'

Cassava pone

1 lb cassava, grated
1 dried coconut, grated
4 oz pumpkin, grated
1 cup granulated sugar
2 tbs butter
1 tsp cinnamon
¼ tsp allspice
¼ tsp grated nutmeg
¼ tsp white pepper
1 tsp Angostura bitters

Preheat the oven to 350°F. Grease an 8-inch square baking pan.

Combine the cassava, coconut, pumpkin and sugar in a mixing bowl.

Rub the butter into the mixture until it becomes like breadcrumbs. Add the cinnamon, allspice, nutmeg and white pepper.

Combine the bitters with ¼ cup water and add to the mixture. Stir well, the mixture should be moist.

Spoon the mixture into the pan, pressing down on it to smooth the surface.

Bake for 45–50 minutes until nicely browned and the mixture starts to pull away from the sides of the pan.

Remove from the oven and cool in the pan.

Cut into squares.

Serves 10–12

Sweet potato pone

12 oz sweet potato, grated
4 oz cassava, grated
¼ cup grated pumpkin
1 dried coconut, grated
1¼ cups sugar
2 tbs butter
¼ tsp white pepper
1 tsp cinnamon

Preheat the oven to 350°F. Grease an 8-inch square baking pan.

Combine the sweet potato, cassava, pumpkin, coconut and sugar in a mixing bowl.

Rub the butter into the mixture until it becomes like breadcrumbs. Add the white pepper and cinnamon.

Add ⅓ cup water to the mixture and stir well. The mixture should be moist.

Spoon the mixture into the pan, pressing down on it to smooth the surface.

Bake for 45–50 minutes until nicely browned and the mixture starts to pull away from the sides of the pan.

Remove from the oven and cool in the pan.

Cut into squares.

Serves 10–12

Coconut drops

¼ cup butter

½ cup sugar

1 egg, lightly beaten

½ tsp Angostura bitters

1 tsp vanilla extract

3 cups all-purpose flour

3 tsp baking powder

2 tsp cinnamon

2 cups finely grated coconut

½ cup raisins (optional)

Glaze
   2 tbs sugar
   ¼ cup hot water

Preheat the oven to 350°F.

Cream the butter and sugar until light and creamy. Add the egg and beat well. Stir in the bitters and vanilla.

Combine the flour, baking powder and cinnamon and add to the creamed mixture. Stir in the coconut and raisins, if using, and add a little water if necessary to moisten the batter. The batter should be firm – too soft or runny a batter will result in the drops not holding their shape while baking.

Drop the batter by spoonfuls onto a greased baking sheet and bake for 20–30 minutes until firm and golden.

To make the glaze, combine the sugar and hot water. Brush the drops with the glaze, sprinkle with a little extra sugar and return to the oven for another 3 minutes or so.

Makes about 24

Daisy ring

3½–4 cups all-purpose flour

1 tbs instant yeast

2 tbs sugar

a pinch of salt

¾ cup milk

¼ cup butter

2 eggs

1 quantity powdered sugar frosting (see page 296)

Filling

1 cup assorted dried fruit

2 tbs sugar

1 tsp cinnamon

2 tbs melted butter

Place the flour, yeast, sugar and salt in a bowl and stir to combine.

Warm the milk with the butter to 115–120°F. Add the eggs to the milk and beat.

Add this mixture to the flour mixture and knead to a soft dough.

Turn onto a floured surface and knead for a few minutes more adding more flour only if necessary to give a smooth dough.

Cover and let rise until doubled in volume, 45–60 minutes.

Combine the dried fruit with the sugar and cinnamon. Set aside.

Punch down the dough and roll out to a 14-inch circle.

Place a drinking glass in the centre of the dough circle. With a knife, divide the dough into four cutting only up to the glass. Then divide each quarter into five pieces, again, cutting only up to the glass. You will have 20 pieces.

Brush every other piece of dough with melted butter and sprinkle with the dried fruit mixture.

Rope or twist two pieces of dough together, pinch the ends and coil towards the centre. Continue with the other pieces. You will have 10 coils.

Remove the glass, cut one coil from the circle and place in the centre.

Cover and let rise until doubled in size, about 30–40 minutes.

Preheat the oven to 375°F.

Bake for about 20–25 minutes.

Remove from the oven and let cool.

Drizzle with powdered sugar frosting.

Bellyful

A traditional heavy cake served as an afternoon snack.

¼ cup butter

1 cup brown sugar

1 egg

½ cup browning

⅔ cup warm water

1 tsp vanilla extract

2 cups all-purpose flour

1 tsp baking powder

1 tsp cinnamon

¼ tsp grated nutmeg

Preheat the oven to 350°F. Grease a 9-inch baking pan.

Cream the butter with the sugar until creamy. Add the egg and beat well.

Combine the browning with the water and vanilla then add to the creamed mixture.

Combine the flour, baking powder, cinnamon and nutmeg.

Add to the butter mixture and stir gently.

Pour into the baking pan and bake for 50 minutes,

Cool before serving.

Pancakes

2 cups all-purpose flour

2 tsp baking powder

½ tsp baking soda

1 tsp cinnamon

a pinch of salt

1 tbs brown sugar

2 eggs

1 cup thin yogurt or 1 cup milk combined with 1 tbs lime juice.

⅓ cup vegetable oil

1 tsp vanilla extract

butter or vegetable oil for frying

Combine the flour, baking powder, baking soda, cinnamon, salt and brown sugar in a mixing bowl.

Beat the eggs with the yogurt or milk, oil and vanilla. Add to the flour mixture and stir to just combine.

Heat a little butter or vegetable oil in a griddle or non-stick frying pan on medium heat.

Pour in a small amount of batter and let it spread to a 4- or 5-inch circle.

When bubbles appear on the surface of the pancake, flip and cook until golden on the other side.

Remove from pan and repeat until all the batter is used up. To keep warm, wrap in a towel and place in a warm oven.

Makes 4–6

Banana pancakes

1 cup all-purpose flour

1 tbs brown sugar

1 tsp cinnamon

1 tsp baking powder

½ tsp baking soda

¼ tsp salt

1 egg

½ cup milk

1 tbs vegetable oil

½ tsp vanilla extract

1 cup chopped ripe banana

butter for frying

Combine the flour, sugar, cinnamon, baking powder, baking soda and salt in a mixing bowl.

In a separate bowl beat the egg until light. Add the milk, oil, vanilla and banana.

Add the wet ingredients to the flour mixture and stir until just combined. The batter should be lumpy.

Heat a non-stick frying pan and grease it with a small amount of butter.

Spoon about ⅓ cup of batter onto the hot frying pan and spread gently. When small bubbles appear on the top side of the pancake and the edges look cooked, flip the pancake. Cook for a short while longer and remove to a plate.

Keep the pancakes warm while you are cooking the remainder.

Serve with pancake syrup or maple syrup.

Makes 8

Oatmeal yogurt pancakes

¾ cup plain yogurt

½ cup skimmed milk

½ cup quick-cooking oatmeal

1 egg

1 tsp vanilla extract

1 tbs vegetable oil

1¼ cups all-purpose flour

2 tbs brown sugar

2 tsp baking powder

½ tsp baking soda

a pinch of salt

butter for frying

Combine the yogurt, milk and oatmeal and let stand for about 10 minutes.

Beat the egg and add the vanilla and oil. Stir into the yogurt mixture.

Combine the flour with the brown sugar, baking powder, baking soda and salt. Add the oatmeal mixture to the flour mixture and stir until combined.

Heat a non-stick frying pan; grease with a small amount of butter.

Spoon about ⅓ cup of batter onto the hot frying pan and spread gently.

When small bubbles appear on the top side of the pancake and the edges look cooked, flip the pancake. Cook for a short while longer and remove to a plate.

Keep the pancakes warm while you are cooking the remainder.

Serve with pancake syrup or maple syrup.

Makes 8

Store Bay, Tobago

Sugar cane

Confections, jams and jellies

The saying, 'She/he has a sweet tooth' means that person is addicted to sweets; the popular, traditional sweets of Trinidad and Tobago will create a sweet tooth in you even if you are not guilty of having one!

Sweets play an integral part in our culinary heritage and it's an area of our cuisine that has maintained a high degree of tradition. Many local sweets are now packaged and sold at food stores across the nation, at candy counters in the shopping malls and at the airports.

All our ethnic influences stand together at the candy counter. There are brightly coloured sugar cakes, along with sugar-crusted kurmas, cream-coloured barfi decorated with hundreds and thousands, molasses and coconut toolum balls, green paw paw balls glistening with granulated sugar, and sweet and sour tamarind balls. There are also coconut, peanut, chocolate, guava, raisin and milk-flavoured fudges on sale. All of these confections are still made in our homes.

Long ago, hard candy-making was also widespread. Sweets like halay, peppermint blocks and levanee were popular amongst children and were sold for pennies during school time by vendors.

In Tobago, local candy-making has become an industry, especially at the airport, where many Tobago ladies peddle their goods of bene balls, coins, squares and sticks, multicoloured sugar cakes, tamarind balls and caramelized nut cakes. The entrance to Store Bay beach is populated with vendors selling an array of these sweets, as is Pigeon Point, where ladies walk along the sandy beach with their large trays filled with bene confections and sugar cakes.

Jams and jellies are also popular on our islands and this is reflected by the numerous varieties and brands on grocery shelves. Pineapple and guava jams are the most popular, other local varieties include orange marmalade, sorrel and guava jellies. I love guava jelly or jam spread on a cracker – it's a great teatime treat, and the manufacturers have done themselves proud in capturing the essence of a guava in a bottle. When in season we are also treated to guava cheese, a dense, sticky sweet made from fresh-cooked guavas, sugar and spices. When set it is cut into small squares. The texture is somewhat chewy but full of great guava flavour!

'*When I was growing up, chilli bibi was one of my favourite sweets. It's made from roasted ground corn and granulated sugar. It used to be sold poured into skinny paper cones.*'

chilli bibi

4 cups dried corn in season
about 1½ cups granulated
sugar

Parch the corn in a heavy-bottomed pan or iron pot, stirring continuously until the corn turns a light brown colour.

Remove from the heat and grind the corn, a little at a time, in a mill with some granulated sugar. The mixture should be powdery; be careful not to use too much granulated sugar as it will make the chilli bibi too heavy.

Halay

2 cups granulated sugar
a pinch of cream of tartar
food colouring
icing sugar for dusting

Heat 1 cup water in a heavy saucepan. Add the sugar and cook, stirring, until the sugar has dissolved.

Add the cream of tartar and cook until a candy thermometer registers 258°F.

Stir in enough food colouring to achieve the colour of your choice.

Pour the mixture onto a large porcelain tile or a marble slab and let cool for 5 minutes.

Using a large knife blade, draw in the edges and divide into two.

Dust your hands with icing sugar, to prevent sticking, and knead the mixture.

Pull the candy, making a thick ribbon, and cut into 2-inch lengths. Leave overnight, then wrap in plastic paper. It will be soft and chewy.

Makes 36

Bene balls

4 cups bene (sesame) seeds
4 cups granulated sugar
a pinch of salt

Heat a non-stick frying pan, add the bene seeds and parch until they become a dark golden colour.

Place the sugar in a large heavy saucepan and cook until it melts to a thin consistency. Add the toasted bene seeds and stir well to coat with the sugar. Add the salt.

Remove from the heat and drop by heaped teaspoonfuls onto an oiled baking tray.

Oil your hands and roll each heap into a smooth ball.

Place on an oiled plate until dried then wrap in plastic wrap.

Makes about 48

Bene balls for sale at Store Bay

Toolum

A heady mixture of good strong molasses and coconut, spiced with orange peel, toolum is a chewy and very satisfying candy.

2 cups brown sugar

½ cup molasses

3 cups freshly grated coconut

6-inch piece of dried orange peel, broken into small pieces

1 tbs grated ginger

Heat the sugar in a heavy saucepan until it liquefies and turns an amber colour.

Add the molasses and coconut and stir well.

Add the orange peel and ginger and continue to cook on a low heat for a few minutes more until the mixture pulls away from the sides and bottom of the pan.

Remove from the heat and cool slightly, then drop by tablespoonfuls onto a greased baking sheet. Roll each heap into a ball.

Leave to cool then place in an airtight jar. The longer the toolum is left uncovered the harder it becomes.

Makes 48

Tamarind balls

4 cups shelled tamarind, broken into segments

1 tbs baking soda

1 tbs salt

½ hot pepper, seeded and chopped

½ cup boiling water

about 6 cups granulated sugar

Remove any strings from the tamarind segments. Place in a large non-reactive mixing bowl and sprinkle with the baking soda, salt and hot pepper.

Pour the boiling water over. Stir well. The mixture will become frothy and then thicken.

Add 1 cup sugar and stir well until it is incorporated. Gradually add two more cups of sugar.

Stir well; the mixture will be quite firm at this point. Cover and leave overnight.

The next day add enough sugar to bring the mixture to a firm consistency that can be rolled into balls.

Roll into 1½-inch balls. Roll the balls in sugar and set aside on a tray to dry a little before wrapping in plastic.

Store in a glass jar.

Makes about 72

Unshelled tamarind

Paw paw balls

1 green paw paw, about 3 lb

1 tsp lime zest

juice of 1 lime

2 cups granulated sugar

2 drops green food colouring

1 drop yellow food colouring

Wash and peel the paw paw. Remove the seeds and grate the flesh. Squeeze out excess juice from the flesh. You should have about 2 cups pulp.

Place the pulp in a heavy medium saucepan and add the lime zest, lime juice and sugar. Cook, stirring, for about 15 minutes. The mixture should begin to gel.

Add the food colouring and stir well.

Remove from the heat. Let cool, then roll into 2-inch balls.

Roll the balls in granulated sugar. Store in a glass jar.

Makes about 20

Nut cakes

2 cups granulated sugar

3 cups roasted salted peanuts, skins removed

1 tbs butter

Place the sugar and ⅓ cup water in a heavy saucepan. Cook until the sugar has dissolved and the mixture turns amber in colour.

Spread the peanuts on a greased baking tray.

Stir the butter into the sugar syrup and pour onto the peanuts, covering them generously.

Let set then break into pieces or cut into squares.

Local candies (*clockwise from top left*): fudge, sugar cake, paw paw balls, toolum, tamarind balls, nut cake

White sugar cake

4 cups granulated sugar

½ tsp cream of tartar

4 cups grated fresh coconut (peel the coconut before grating)

2 cloves

½ tsp almond extract

Boil the sugar with the cream of tartar and 1 cup water until the syrup spins a thread when lifted with a fork or bubbles the size of large pearls appear on the surface.

Add the grated coconut and cloves to the mixture and stir constantly.

Boil until the mixture leaves the bottom and sides of the pan easily. It should still contain some syrup.

Remove from the heat and add the almond extract. Beat with a spoon until the mixture becomes thick.

Either drop by spoonfuls onto a greased cookie tray and let harden or place the mixture into a 9-inch square greased baking tray and cut into squares when cool.

Note

For coloured sugar cake, add colouring to colour as you desire.

For chip chip sugar cake, cut the coconut into small chips instead of grating.

For brown sugar cake, use brown sugar instead of granulated and grate the coconut with the brown skin. Omit the almond extract and add a piece of cinnamon stick.

Chocolate fudge

3 cups granulated sugar

2 heaped tbs cocoa powder, sifted

2 tins sweetened condensed milk

1 tsp vanilla extract

2 tbs butter

Combine the sugar with the sifted cocoa powder. Place in a saucepan and stir in the condensed milk.

Cook on a moderate heat until the sugar dissolves. Do not allow the mixture to boil until the sugar has completely dissolved.

Bring to a boil and boil for about 45 minutes, until the candy gets to the soft-ball stage (see below). Stir in the vanilla and butter.

Remove from the heat and beat well until the mixture thickens and leaves the side of the pan. Pour into a greased tin.

When cool, cut into squares (before the fudge hardens too much).

Makes 18–24

Note

The soft-ball stage is when a little of the mixture dropped into a glass of water forms a soft ball or when the mixture registers 238°F on a candy thermometer.

Milk fudge

2 cups sugar

1 tin evaporated milk

2 tbs butter

1 tsp vanilla extract

Heat the sugar in the milk until it has dissolved.

Boil the mixture, stirring all the time, until it comes to the soft-ball stage (see opposite page).

Stir in the butter and vanilla.

Remove from the heat and beat well until the mixture thickens and leaves the side of the pan. Pour into a greased tin.

When cool, cut into squares (before the fudge hardens too much).

Makes about 12

Note
For peanut fudge, add ¼ cup finely chopped peanuts to the fudge mixture when the mixture begins to thicken.

Coconut fudge

grated flesh of 1 coconut

½ cup hot water

1⅔ cups evaporated milk

2 cups granulated sugar

2 tbs butter

Combine half the grated coconut with the hot water. Let it steep for 10 minutes then strain the mixture through a thin tea towel, squeezing out the coconut. Retain the milk (there should be ½ cup), discard the coconut husk.

Add the coconut milk to a saucepan with the evaporated milk. Stir in the sugar.

Heat until the sugar dissolves then boil until the soft-ball stage is reached (see opposite page).

Add the butter and beat for about 8 minutes.

Add the remaining grated coconut. Stir well then pour into a greased tin.

When cool, cut into squares (before the fudge hardens too much).

Makes about 24

Indian candies (*from left to right*): kurma, barfi, sugared goolab jamoon, jelabi

Kurma

4 cups all-purpose flour
1 tsp powdered ginger
1 tsp cinnamon
½ cup butter
4 tbs condensed milk
vegetable oil for deep-frying

Place the flour and spices in a bowl. Add the butter and rub into the flour.

Add the condensed milk and bring the mixture together, adding enough water to knead to a firm dough.

Divide into two. Roll out the dough to desired thickness and cut into strips or squares.

Heat the oil in a deep pot or wok and deep-fry the kurma until golden brown.

Drain and drench with sugar syrup, turning to coat until the sugar crystallizes.

Sugar syrup

2 cups granulated sugar

Boil the sugar in 1 cup water until thick and bubbling vigorously. Once the sugar spins a thread boil for another 2 minutes, then pour, while still hot and bubbling, onto kurma and goolab jamoon.

'Kurma, goolab jamoon and barfi are the three most popular East Indian sweets and can be found at any food store.'

sugared goolab jamoon

4 cups all-purpose flour
1 tsp cinnamon
1 tsp ground cardamom
1 cup butter
½ cup evaporated milk
14-oz tin condensed milk
vegetable oil for deep-frying

Place the flour and spices in a bowl. Add the butter and rub into the flour.

Add both milks and knead to a smooth stiff dough.

Pinch off 2-inch pieces of dough and roll each into a ball, tapering the ends until you have an oblong shape, then roll the ends further, almost to a point.

Heat the oil in a deep pot or wok and carefully deep-fry until dark golden brown. Keep the heat moderate or the dough will burn.

Drain and pour sugar syrup over (see opposite page), turning to coat until the sugar crystallizes.

Makes 36

Barfi (East Indian fudge)

2 cups granulated sugar
1 tbs grated ginger
1 lb full-cream milk powder
1 cup thick or heavy cream
hundreds and thousands for decoration

Grease a 9-inch square glass dish.

Combine the sugar, ginger and ¾ cup water in a small saucepan.

Boil for about 10 minutes, just until the sugar spins a thread.

Combine the powdered milk with the cream and mix thoroughly. Pass the mixture through a sieve.

Pour the sugar syrup into the sieved milk mixture and mix well.

Press the mixture into the prepared dish using the back of a spoon. Decorate with hundreds and thousands.

When cool, cut into squares.

Makes about 24

Easy rasgullah

1 cup all-purpose flour

½ cup full-cream milk powder

¼ cup ground almonds

1 tsp baking powder

⅛ tsp baking soda

½ tsp ground cardamom

2 tbs butter

¼ cup plain yogurt

vegetable oil for deep-frying

Syrup

2 cups sugar

6 cardamom pods, bruised

1 tsp rose water

Place all the dry ingredients in a bowl. Add the butter and rub in to fine crumb stage.

Stir in the yogurt. Add 2–3 tablespoons water and knead to a soft dough.

Form the dough into 20 small balls.

Heat the oil over a moderate heat and deep-fry the rasgullahs until golden. Take care not to overheat the oil.

Remove from the pan and drain.

To make the syrup, combine the sugar with 1 cup water in a saucepan. Add the cardamom and boil until the sugar has dissolved, about 5 minutes.

Add the rose water then pour over the rasgullahs. Let sit at room temperature until ready to serve.

Serves 10

Jelabi

2 cups all-purpose flour

1–2 cups warm water

oil for deep-frying

Syrup

2 cups granulated sugar

1 cup water

1 tsp grated orange zest

Combine the flour with just enough warm water to make a thick but pourable batter. Cover and set aside for about 2 days. This allows the batter to take on an almost sourdough flavour.

Combine the syrup ingredients in a saucepan. Boil for 5 minutes and then let cool.

Heat the oil in a deep-fryer. Pour the batter from a funnel or jug in a thin stream into the hot oil to form a pattern of overlapping swirls, about 4 inches in diameter.

Fry until golden, turn, and finish frying on the other side.

Drain on paper towels then place in the sugar syrup.

Makes 8 large jelabi

Kheer (Indian sweet rice)

½ cup short-grain or arborio rice

7½ cups milk

2 cardamom pods

¾ cup sugar

1 tbs toasted almonds, coarsely chopped

⅓ cup raisins

Soak the rice in ⅔ cup water for 30 minutes. Then boil the rice in the water until all the water dries up. Remove the pot from the heat.

Add the milk and cardamom pods to the rice and stir well. Simmer on a low heat for 1½ hours, stirring occasionally to ensure the rice does not stick to the bottom and sides of the pan. At this point the rice will be of a creamy consistency.

Now add the sugar, stirring constantly over a low heat until the sugar is dissolved and the rice is creamy.

Remove from the heat and take out the cardamom pods. Serve in individual bowls, decorated with toasted almonds and raisins.

Serves 8

'Kheer, sewine and halwah are traditionally served on the Muslim festival of Eid ul-Fitr.'

Sewine

2 tbs unsalted butter

4 oz vermicelli (sewine)

½ cup sugar

1 cinnamon stick

1½ cups evaporated milk

½ cup condensed milk

1 cup milk

1 tsp cinnamon

½ tsp crushed cardamom pods

raisins and toasted almonds to
    decorate

Melt the butter in a large frying pan. Break the vermicelli into pieces and add to the pan. Turn frequently until the vermicelli is quite brown. Remove.

Bring 2 cups water to a boil in a saucepan. Add the sugar, cinnamon stick and browned vermicelli and cook until soft, about 5–7 minutes.

Meanwhile, pour the three types of milk into a heavy saucepan. Add the spices and bring to a boil.

Combine the sewine with the milk and serve decorated with almonds and raisins.

Serves 6–8

Halwah

2 cups sugar

2 cups unsalted butter

4 cups all-purpose flour, sifted

½ cup raisins

⅓ cup mixed glacé cherries and
    almonds, chopped

1 tbs cinnamon

½ tbs cardamom seeds

a pinch of salt

Boil the sugar in 2 cups water for about 10 minutes until dissolved. Keep on simmer.

Melt the butter in a large sauté pan. When it has melted, stir in the flour and cook on medium heat until it becomes a rich brown colour.

Add the sugar syrup and stir. Turn off the heat and keep stirring until the mixture becomes fluffy and soft in texture.

Add the fruits, nuts, spices and salt.

Pour into a serving dish and leave until cool.

Serves 10

Chunky orange marmalade

3 lb oranges
juice of 2 lemons
8 cups sugar

Remove any stems from the oranges. Scrub thoroughly.

Peel the zest (coloured portion) off the orange with a potato peeler or sharp knife, leaving the white pith behind. Cut the zest into ¼-inch strips.

Cut the oranges in half and squeeze out all the juice.

Save the seeds, cut away the white pith and separate from the pulp.

Tie the pith and seeds in a fine cloth.

Cut the pulp coarsely and place in a large pan together with the strips of zest and the pith and seeds in the cloth.

Add the orange juice, lemon juice and 8 cups water.

Boil over a low heat for about 2 hours until reduced by half. Remove the cloth with the seeds. Add the sugar and stir well until it has dissolved.

Turn up the heat and let the marmalade boil vigorously for about 20–30 minutes until it reaches 220°F.

Leave to cool for about 20 minutes, remove any scum from the surface, and pour into sterilized jars.

Makes seven 12-oz jars

Pineapple jam

1 large pineapple, 4–5 lb
1 lime
granulated sugar

Peel the pineapple and grate or chop in a food processor.

Place in a large pan and cover with water. Cut the lime in half and add to the pan. Bring the mixture to a boil and cook for 5 minutes.

Remove from the heat and measure the mixture: for every cup of pineapple mixture add ¾ cup granulated sugar.

Return the pineapple and sugar mixture to the pan, bring to a boil then simmer for about 20 minutes until the mixture is thick.

Spoon into sterilized jars.

Makes about two 14-oz jars

Guava cheese

2–3 lb very ripe guavas
2 cups granulated sugar
1-inch piece cinnamon stick

Slice the guavas and pass through a sieve to extract the pulp.

Cook the guava pulp with the sugar until the mixture becomes thick and bubbling. Stir well to prevent sticking.

Cook until it reaches the soft-ball stage (see page 324) and the mixture leaves the sides and bottom of the pan.

Pour into a greased glass dish.

Leave to cool then cut into squares.

Guava jam

25 ripe guavas
granulated sugar
1 piece cinnamon stick
1 tsp lime juice

The day before, place the guavas whole in a large heavy saucepan. Cover well with water and boil until the guavas are very soft, about 50 minutes. Cover and leave overnight.

The next day strain the guavas, keeping the juice. Push the guavas through a sieve to extract the pulp.

Combine the guava pulp with the juice and add ¾ cup granulated sugar for every cup of guava mixture.

Pour into a saucepan, add the spice and lime juice and boil for about 20–30 minutes until the mixture has thickened.

Spoon into sterilized jars.

Makes about four 14-oz jars

Guava jam and guava cheese

Five fingers (carambola)

Drinks

Both fruit-based and milk-based drinks are enjoyed on our islands, and the flavours will take you to opposite ends of the scale, from the sweet smooth tastes of our milky punches to the bitterness of mauby and the sourness of sorrel. We enjoy milk punches made from just about any non-citrus fruit coupled with a nut or seed added for extra nourishment. Punch vendors can be found at strategic locations around the country, and they will blend your favourite flavour on the spot. Varieties include peanut, sour sop, barbadine, linseed, fig, carrot and pumpkin – to name just a few. Sea moss, a seaweed-based drink, is another popular punch packed with vitamins. The jelly can be purchased at our grocers or you can prepare your own from the dried seaweed. Most of these punches boast aphrodisiac and healing powers!

Coconut water, cool and refreshing, straight from the nut is available round the clock. Mauby is a beverage brewed from the bark of a tree, sweetened, and spiced up with star anise, cinnamon, clove and bay leaves. It's light, refreshing and bitter to the very end. Nothing beats an ice-cold glass of home-made mauby on a blistering hot day.

Sorrel, rich, smooth with a slight sour flavour; ginger beer, full-bodied with a bite to the back of your throat; and ponche de crème, creamy and intoxicating, are our signature Christmas drinks. Sorrel vendors can be seen as early as November, and on into February, selling fresh sorrel from their loaded tray vans.

Citrus fruits are made into delightful fresh juices when in season, and passion fruit and guava are also popular flavours.

Then there are our rum-based drinks. Nothing beats a Trini rum punch, sweet with cane sugar syrup, refreshing with fresh lime juice, mysterious with Trini golden rum – an enticing and intoxicating blend that will have you weak at the knees!

sea moss drink

1 lb sea moss
juice of 1 lime
evaporated milk and sugar to taste
Angostura bitters

Soak the sea moss with the lime juice overnight.

Wash thoroughly and cook in a pressure cooker for 20–30 minutes until the texture of the sea moss resembles a mass of jelly.

Leave to cool.

For each serving, blend about ½ cup with evaporated milk and sweeten with sugar to taste. Add a few drops of bitters.

Makes 3 cups

Note
The cooked sea moss can be bottled and refrigerated.

You may add 1 tablespoon linseed to this punch for extra nourishment.

Mauby drink

4 pieces mauby bark
1 bay leaf
2 cloves
2-inch piece cinnamon stick
4 star anise
sugar syrup (see page 341)

Place the mauby and spices in a large saucepan. Add 2 cups water, bring to a boil and remove from the heat.

Leave to cool.

Strain and sweeten to taste with basic sugar syrup.

Makes 2 cups unsweetened mauby

From left: sea moss, mauby, sorrel drinks

Peanut punch

4 tbs peanut butter
¾ cup milk
1 tbs brown sugar

Blend all the ingredients together and serve over cracked ice.

Serves 1

Sour sop punch

1 ripe sour sop
1 cup condensed milk
3 cups milk
Angostura bitters

Peel the sour sop, cut into pieces and crush with a little water in a bowl.

Extract the pulp and juice by pushing through a food mill or sieve, using the back of a spoon.

Mix the sour sop pulp with both milks and add a few dashes of bitters.

Chill and serve over ice.

Serves 6

Note
For barbadine punch, follow this method using a barbadine instead of a sour sop.

Pineapple passion with lime

2 cups pineapple juice
¼ cup passion fruit juice
2 tbs fresh lime juice
⅓ cup sugar syrup
fresh fruit to decorate

Blend the juices and sugar syrup together, pour over crushed ice and decorate.

Serves 4–6

Basic sugar syrup

2 cups granulated sugar

Combine the sugar with 1 cup water in a small saucepan.
Cook over medium heat until the sugar has dissolved. Boil for 10 minutes.
Cool, bottle and refrigerate until ready for use.

Passion fruit syrup

This is a great way to use up excess passion fruit for use in fruit punch and other drinks.

4 cups sugar
pulp from 8 passion fruit

Combine the sugar and 4 cups water in a large non-reactive saucepan and heat until boiling.

Add the passion fruit pulp and boil for a further 20 minutes until the mixture begins to thicken.

Remove from the heat, cool and bottle.

Refrigerate and use in place of regular sugar syrup in fruit juices or punches.

Pineappleade

1 large ripe pineapple
⅓ cup fresh lime juice
1½ cups sugar
8 cups filtered water

Peel and grate the pineapple. Place into a large glass jug or bowl. Add the lime juice.

Boil the sugar with 2 cups filtered water.

Pour the hot syrup onto the pineapple. Add the rest of the water, stir and cover. Let stand for 1–2 hours.

Strain to remove the pulp.

Refrigerate until ready to use.

Makes about 10 cups

Mango papaya orange slush

A splash of rum is great in this drink.

2 cups cubed mango
2 cups cubed papaya
1 cup orange juice
ice
mango wedges to decorate

Place the fruits and juice into a blender.

Add ice and process to a slushy consistency.

Pour into glasses, decorate with mango wedges and serve immediately.

Serves 4

Ponche de crème

6 eggs
1 tsp minced lime zest
3 x 14-oz tins evaporated milk
1½ tins condensed milk (14 oz)
2 cups dark rum
½ tsp grated nutmeg
1 tsp Angostura bitters
lime slices to decorate

Process the eggs with the lime zest in a blender until light coloured and fluffy.

Add the evaporated and condensed milks and process to blend well.

Add the rum, nutmeg and bitters. Mix well, taste and adjust flavourings to suit.

Serve over crushed ice and decorate with lime slices.

Makes about 10 cups

Ginger beer

1 lb green ginger
1 lime
2 cloves
sugar syrup (see page 341)

Wash, peel and grate the ginger.

Peel and juice the lime. Keep the peel (green part only).

Mix the ginger with 10 cups water, the cloves, lime juice and lime peel.

Pour this mixture into clean bottles and leave to ferment for about 1 day, preferably in the sun.

Strain the ginger beer and sweeten to taste with basic sugar syrup.

Refrigerate until ready to use.

Makes 10 cups

Note
An alternative method is to boil the water then add the grated ginger, cloves and a piece of cinnamon stick. Cover and let steep for about 2 days, strain and sweeten.

Sorrel

To make sorrel drink, clean the sorrel by removing the seeds and put the sepals into a large non-reactive pot. Add some cloves and cinnamon bark according to taste – the precise quantities don't matter. Add enough boiling water to barely cover the sorrel, cover tightly and steep overnight.

Sweeten to taste with basic sugar syrup (see page 341). Chill and serve over crushed ice or with club soda for a refreshing sorrel cooler!

Sorrel vendor

Trini rum punch

2 cups granulated sugar

3 cups Trinidad dark rum

1 cup freshly squeezed lime juice

1 tsp Angostura bitters

1 tsp freshly grated nutmeg (more or less, to taste)

maraschino cherries to decorate

Place the sugar with 4 cups water in a small saucepan over a low heat. Stir to dissolve then boil for about 6–8 minutes. Leave to cool.

Combine the cooled syrup with the rum, lime juice and bitters. Stir in the nutmeg.

Refrigerate in a glass jug or bottles until ready for use.

To serve, pour over glasses filled with cracked ice.

Decorate with cherries and more grated nutmeg if needed.

Makes about 10 cups

Rum punch for sale

'*Trinidad cocoa is a blend of cocoa and spices, available in block form. This was the hot beverage served for breakfast in many homes around the country. It is rich, chocolaty, spicy and satisfying.*'

Cocoa tea

2 blocks local cocoa
about 1½ cups full-cream milk
sugar

Grate the cocoa blocks and combine in a saucepan with the milk.
Bring to a boil then strain.
Sweeten to taste.

Serves 2

Cocoa on the tree

Chutneys and pepper sauces

Pepper sauce, chutney and kutchela are all fiery condiments used widely to brighten and excite our taste buds, whether we are enjoying a plate of Creole or Indian foods, a light snack or an Indian delicacy. Although our cuisine would still be exciting and delicious without these condiments, when they are added to our foods the resulting flavours just push the total taste experience to higher levels!

Everyone has their own version of pepper sauce. There is a hot and tasty virgin pepper sauce, made with ground peppers, garlic, vinegar and salt. Then there is a mustard-based pepper sauce, in which carrot and pickles are added for different flavours.

East Indian condiments include the spicy kutchelas made with shredded green mango or pommecythyres, hot peppers, garlic and masala powder. Our chutneys – usually slathered onto hot Indian delicacies – are made with grated green mango or tamarind. All these condiments are so popular that local manufacturers bottle many versions.

Green mango chutney

2 large green mangoes, peeled and grated

1 tsp minced garlic

¼ cup chadon beni (cilantro)

salt and freshly ground black pepper

1 tsp pepper sauce (more or less, to taste)

about 1 tsp sugar

Place all the ingredients except the sugar in a blender and blend to a fine consistency.

Add just enough sugar to balance the sourness of the mangoes. Adjust salt to taste.

This will keep for 2 weeks in a glass bottle in the refrigerator.

Makes about 1 cup

Pommecythere chutney

Pommecytheres are also called golden apples.

4 large pommecytheres

1 tsp minced garlic

1 tsp ground hot pepper

⅓ cup chopped chadon beni (cilantro)

1 tsp salt

about 1 tsp sugar

Place all the ingredients except the sugar in a blender and blend to a fine consistency.

Add just enough sugar to balance the sourness of the pommecytheres. Adjust salt to taste.

This will keep for 2 weeks in a glass bottle in the refrigerator.

Makes about 1 cup

Four leaves of Spanish thyme (podina) may be chopped and added to these recipes

Mangoes (*top*)
Pommecytheres (*bottom*)

Tamarind chutney

2 cups peeled, ripe tamarind pods

2 tbs salt

2 cups granulated sugar

2 tbs freshly ground, roasted geera (cumin)

½ hot pepper, seeded and minced (more or less, to taste)

6 garlic cloves, minced

Put the tamarind pods in a small saucepan and barely cover with boiling water. Let steep for 30 minutes.

Remove the seeds from the tamarind and discard (a potato crusher works well to separate the seeds from the pulp).

Return the tamarind pulp to the pan and add the salt, sugar, geera, pepper and garlic. Stir to mix. Bring the mixture to a boil then remove from the heat.

Leave to cool. Taste and adjust seasonings. The chutney should be slightly sour-sweet in flavour.

Stored in covered glass jars this will keep in the refrigerator for up to 2 months.

Makes 3 cups

Coconut chutney

1 coconut, cracked and meat removed in large pieces

1 hot pepper, seeded

4 garlic cloves

1 small onion

2 blades chadon beni (cilantro)

Wash and dry the coconut meat. Roast over an open flame until browned all over.

Place the roasted coconut in a blender with the pepper, garlic, onion and chadon beni and blend.

Add salt to taste and serve.

Refrigerate for up to 1 day only.

Makes 1 cup

Chadon beni mayo

½ cup low-fat mayonnaise

1 tbs finely chopped chadon beni (cilantro)

1 garlic clove, minced

½ tsp pepper sauce

Combine all the ingredients. Cover and refrigerate until ready for use.

Makes ½ cup

Chilli pineapple dip

1 cup low-fat mayonnaise

2 tbs fresh lime juice

½ cup chopped fresh pineapple

1 tsp chilli powder

1 garlic clove, minced

salt

¼ cup chopped chadon beni (cilantro)

Combine all the ingredients except the chadon beni. Stir in the chadon beni and serve with fritters.

Makes about 1 cup

Note
It's easy to double up the ingredients to make a larger quantity, if desired.

Barbecue sauce

2 tbs vegetable oil

1 onion, grated or minced

1 cup tomato ketchup

¼ cup brown sugar

2 tbs yellow mustard

2 tbs Worcestershire sauce

1 tsp hot pepper sauce

3 garlic cloves, minced

Heat the oil in a small saucepan. Add the onion and sauté until fragrant.
Add all the other ingredients and cook until the mixture begins to boil.
Remove from the heat and cool.

Makes about 3 cups

Paramin Hills

Trini fresh herb seasoning paste

4 large bunches of seasoning (chives, parsley, thyme, celery)

1 cup garlic cloves

⅓ cup white vinegar

Clean the seasonings, wash and chop.

Combine the chopped seasonings with the garlic and vinegar in a blender or food processor to make a thick purée or paste.

Transfer to a covered glass jar.

This will keep in the refrigerator for about 2 weeks.

Makes about 1 cup

Virgin pepper sauce

15 scotch bonnet or habanero peppers

6 garlic cloves

⅓ cup white vinegar

2 tsp salt

Wash the peppers and remove the stems.

Place the peppers in a food processor or blender and add the garlic, vinegar and salt. Blend to a thick purée, or leave chunky if preferred.

Pour into a clean glass jar and place in a sunny position in the kitchen for about 2 weeks.

Store in the refrigerator for up to 2 months.

Makes one 8-oz jar

Mustard-based pepper sauce

To the above recipe add ¼ cup peeled, diced green paw paw, ¼ cup diced carrot and 2 teaspoons mustard powder.

Clockwise from top right: virgin pepper sauce, green mango chutney, chunky lime pepper sauce, mango kutchela

Chunky lime pepper sauce

2 limes

20 scotch bonnet or habanero peppers

10 garlic cloves

¼ cup thinly cut mori or white radish

¼ cup diced green paw paw

¼ cup thinly cut carailli

⅔ cup white vinegar

3 tsp salt

Cut the limes into ½-inch pieces, place in a small saucepan and add ½ cup water. Bring to a boil and remove from the heat.

Slice the peppers and chop the garlic finely.

Combine the peppers, garlic and chopped vegetables. Add the vinegar, salt and boiled limes with their liquid. Stir everything together.

Store in glass jars in the refrigerator for up to 2 months.

Makes two 10-oz jars

Mango kutchela

10 green mangoes

20 garlic cloves, peeled

4 hot peppers, scotch bonnet or Congo

1 small packet amchar masala

about 1 cup mustard oil

Peel the mangoes and grate. Squeeze out the liquid from the grated mangoes and lay flat on a large tray. Dry, by placing either in the sun or in a 200°F oven for a few hours.

Place the dried mangoes in a bowl. Mince the garlic and peppers and add to the mangoes, then stir in the amchar masala.

Pour on the mustard oil and stir just until it coats the mango. You may not need all the oil. Adjust seasonings to taste.

Store in jars in the refrigerator for up to 1 year.

Makes about four 8-oz jars

Conversion tables

Weights

1 ounce	30 grams
8 ounces or ½ pound	250 grams or ¼ kilogram
16 ounces or 1 pound	500 grams or ½ kilogram

Volumes

1 teaspoon	5 ml
1 tablespoon	15 ml
1 cup	250 ml or 8 fluid ounces

1 cup flour = 125 g/4 oz
1 cup granulated sugar = 250 g/8 oz
1 cup icing sugar = 125 g/4 oz
1 cup butter = 250 g/8 oz
1 cup rice = 200 g/6 oz
1 cup dried beans = 200 g/6 oz

Oven temperatures

250°F = 120°C
300°F = 150°C
350°F = 180°C
400°F = 200°C
450°F = 230°C
500°F = 260°C

Index